Lecture Notes in Computer Science   12724

More information about this subseries at http://www.springer.com/series/7408

Daniela Fogli · Daniel Tetteroo ·
Barbara Rita Barricelli ·
Simone Borsci · Panos Markopoulos ·
George A. Papadopoulos (Eds.)

End-User Development

8th International Symposium, IS-EUD 2021
Virtual Event, July 6–8, 2021
Proceedings

 Springer

Editors
Daniela Fogli
Ingegneria dell'Informazione
Univ degli Studi di Brescia
Brescia, Italy

Barbara Rita Barricelli
University of Brescia
Brescia, Italy

Panos Markopoulos
Department of Industrial Design
Eindhoven University of Technology
Eindhoven, The Netherlands

Daniel Tetteroo
Eindhoven University of Technology
Eindhoven, The Netherlands

Simone Borsci
University of Twente
Enschede, The Netherlands

George A. Papadopoulos
University of Cyprus
Nicosia, Cyprus

ISSN 0302-9743   ISSN 1611-3349 (electronic)
Lecture Notes in Computer Science
ISBN 978-3-030-79839-0   ISBN 978-3-030-79840-6 (eBook)
https://doi.org/10.1007/978-3-030-79840-6

LNCS Sublibrary: SL2 – Programming and Software Engineering

This Springer imprint is published by the registered company Springer Nature Switzerland AG
The registered company address is: Gewerbestrasse 11, 6330 Cham, Switzerland

Preface

Welcome to the proceedings of the 8th International Symposium on End-User Development (IS-EUD 2021), organized by the University of Cyprus and held virtually during July 6–8, 2021. End-user development (EUD) aims at empowering end users to develop and adapt systems at a level of complexity that is adequate to their expertise, practices, and skills. EUD may occur along the entire software lifecycle, with the purpose of making users able to participate in artifact development, not only during the design phase but also during actual use. Originally, EUD was conceived as a more general instance of end-user programming; thus, scholars proposed methods, techniques, and tools that allowed end users to modify or extend software artifacts, such as spreadsheets, web applications, video games, and mobile applications. In the so-called Internet of Things era, end-user development moved on to address the problem of defining and modifying the behavior of smart environments, including smart objects, pervasive displays, smart homes, smart cities, and so on. Therefore, the term 'end-user development' has acquired a broader meaning, covering approaches, frameworks, and socio-technical environments that allow end users to express themselves in crafting digital artifacts that encompass both software and hardware technology. Recent research and technological trends like Artificial Intelligence (AI), big data, cyber-security, robotics, and Industry 4.0, have contributed to a renewed vision of end-user development, by providing tools and platforms that allow end users to harness the power of AI to create solutions involving computer vision, image processing, and conversational user interfaces, as well as solutions for smart environments. Such developments lower the threshold for creating AI solutions, and expand the programmer base for such solutions, by extending AI application both for professional and discretionary use.

IS-EUD is a bi-annual event for researchers and practitioners with an interdisciplinary approach to EUD, including Human-Computer Interaction, Software Engineering, Computer Supported Cooperative Work, Human-Work Interaction Design, and related areas.

The 2021 edition of IS-EUD focused on "Democratizing AI Development", namely on EUD for AI-based systems, where end users are called on to become end-user developers of intelligent agents, digital twins, collaborative systems, and social robots. Theoretical and empirical work analyzing pros and cons of this new EUD wave, identifying requirements for end-user development of AI, and acceptance of related solutions were invited. In this edition, we discussed the adoption of EUD in new fields, the proposal of novel EUD paradigms, and the impact of AI-based EUD in terms of user acceptability and appropriation. Software infrastructures and eco-systems supporting the re-use of solutions and the emergence of meta-design practices were of particular interest, linking the challenges relating AI to topics central to the IS-EUD community.

IS-EUD 2021 collected research contributions as full papers, short papers, work-in-progress and doctoral consortium papers that presented

- New, simple, and efficient environments for end-user development
- New processes, methods, and techniques for empowering users to create, modify, and tailor digital artifacts
- Case studies and design implications on challenges and practices of end-user development
- Theoretical concepts and foundations for the field of end-user development
- Methods and techniques for end-user development of AI-based devices
- Approaches to end-user development based on conversational interfaces
- Methods and tools to deal with cybersecurity through end-user development

The paper track received 26 submissions of full and short papers, of which we accepted 11 full papers and 4 short papers after a rigorous double-blind review process.

The program was opened by the keynote speaker Gerhard Fischer, Professor Emeritus of Computer Science at the University of Colorado Boulder, USA, who explored the relationship between specific AI approaches, meta-design, and cultures of participation, to illustrate different design strategies that will advance EUD not only as a technology but also as a cultural transformation.

Due to the COVID-19 pandemic, this edition of IS-EUD 2021 was held online, thus limiting the interaction opportunities that have always characterized the past editions of this symposium. This is one more reason to thank all the authors and reviewers for their commitment and contribution to make the symposium a successful event!

May 2021

Daniela Fogli
Daniel Tetteroo
Barbara Rita Barricelli
Simone Borsci
Panos Markopoulos
George A. Papadopoulos

Organization

General Chairs

George A. Papadopoulos   University of Cyprus, Cyprus
Panos Markopoulos   Eindhoven University of Technology, the Netherlands

Program Chairs

Daniela Fogli   University of Brescia, Italy
Daniel Tetteroo   Eindhoven University of Technology, the Netherlands

Short Paper Chairs

Barbara Rita Barricelli   University of Brescia, Italy
Simone Borsci   University of Twente, the Netherlands

Work in Progress Chairs

Carmen Santoro   ISTI-CNR, Italy
Jelle Van Dijk   University of Twente, the Netherlands

Demo Chair

Stefano Valtolina   University of Milan, Italy

Workshop Chairs

Styliani Kleanthous   Open University, Cyprus
Simone Stumpf   City, University of London, UK

Doctoral Consortium Chairs

Monica Maceli   Pratt Institute, USA
Antonio Piccinno   University of Bari Aldo Moro, Italy

Steering Committee

Carmelo Ardito   Politecnico di Bari, Italy
Simone Barbosa   Pontifical Catholic University of Rio de Janeiro, Brazil
Alexander Boden   University of Bonn-Rhein-Sieg, Germany
Boris De Ruyter   Philips Research, the Netherlands
Gerhard Fischer   University of Colorado Boulder, USA

Daniela Fogli	University of Brescia, Italy
Alessio Malizia	University of Pisa, Italy
Panos Markopoulos	Eindhoven University of Technology, the Netherlands
Anders Morch	University of Oslo, Norway
Fabio Paterno	CNR-ISTI, Italy
Antonio Piccinno	University of Bari Aldo Moro, Italy
Volkmar Pipek	University of Siegen, Germany
Simone Stumpf	City, University of London, UK
Stefano Valtolina	University of Milan, Italy

Program Committee

Carmelo Ardito	Politecnico di Bari, Italy
Barbara Rita Barricelli	University of Brescia, Italy
Andrea Bellucci	Universidad Carlos III de Madrid, Spain
Alexander Boden	University of Bonn-Rhein-Sieg, Germany
Simone Borsci	University of Twente, the Netherlands
Paolo Bottoni	Sapienza University of Rome, Italy
Paolo Buono	University of Bari Aldo Moro, Italy
Federico Cabitza	University of Milano-Bicocca, Italy
Silvio Carta	University of Hertfordshire, UK
Luigi De Russis	Politecnico di Torino, Italy
Boris De Ruyter	Philips Research, the Netherlands
Giuseppe Desolda	University of Bari Aldo Moro, Italy
Jelle van Dijk	University of Twente, the Netherands
Sergio Firmenich	Universidad de La Plata, Argentina
Daniela Fogli	University of Brescia, Italy
Rosella Gennari	Free University of Bozen-Bolzano, Italy
Thomas Herrmann	University of Bochum, Germany
Catherine Letondal	ENAC, France
Angela Locoro	Carlo Cattaneo University, Italy
Thomas Ludwig	University of Siegen, Germany
Monica Maceli	Pratt Institute, USA
Alessio Malizia	University of Pisa, Italy
Marco Manca	CNR-ISTI, Italy
Panos Markopoulos	Eindhoven University of Technology, the Netherlands
Maristella Matera	Politecnico di Milano, Italy
Alessandra Melonio	Free University of Bozen-Bolzano, Italy
Alberto Monge Roffarello	Politecnico di Torino, Italy
Anders Morch	University of Oslo, Norway
Teresa Onorati	Universidad Carlos III de Madrid, Spain
Fabio Paternò	CNR-ISTI, Italy
Antonio Piccinno	University of Bari Aldo Moro, Italy
Fabio Pittarello	Università Ca' Foscari Venezia, Italy
Carmen Santoro	CNR-ISTI, Italy
Lucio Davide Spano	University of Cagliari, Italy

Simone Stumpf   City, University of London, UK
Daniel Tetteroo   Eindhoven University of Technology, the Netherlands
David Tree   University of Hertfordshire, UK
Tommaso Turchi   University of Hertfordshire, UK
Stefano Valtolina   University of Milan, Italy
Marco Winckler   University of Nice Sophia Antipolis, France

Contents

Short Papers

Work-in-Progress Papers

Doctoral Consortium

Invited Talk

End-User Development: Empowering Stakeholders with Artificial Intelligence, Meta-Design, and Cultures of Participation

Gerhard Fischer[✉]

Center for LifeLong Learning & Design (L3D), Department of Computer Science
and Institute of Cognitive Science, University of Colorado, Boulder, USA
gerhard@colorado.edu

Abstract. End-User Development (EUD) represents the objective to empower all stakeholders (designers, users, workers, learners, teachers) to actively participate and to make their voices heard in personally meaningful problems. Artificial Intelligence (AI) is currently being considered world-wide as a "deus ex machina"—despite lacking a generally accepted definition, it is credited with miraculous abilities to solve all problems.

The presentation will explore and differentiate how AI approaches can support or inhibit different stakeholders to cope with wicked problems in a changing world for which EUD is essential.

The relationship between specific AI approaches and meta-design and cultures of participation (being promising frameworks to support EUD) will be explored and critically assessed and prototypical system developments will be described to illustrate different design strategies that will advance EUD not only as a technology, but as a cultural transformation.

Keywords: End-User Development (EUD) · Artificial Intelligence (AI) ·
Artificial General Intelligence (AGI) · Human-Centered AI (HCAI) · AI for
Specific Purposes (AISP) · Meta-design · Cultures of participation · Cultural
transformations

1 Introduction

In a world that is not predictable and in which change is the only constant, improvisation, evolution, and innovation are more than luxuries: they are necessities. The challenge of design is not a matter of getting rid of the emergent, but rather of including it and making it an opportunity for more creative and more adequate solutions to problems. *End-user development (EUD)* provides the enabling conditions for empowering stakeholders by defining the technical and social conditions for broad participation in design and decision making activities.

Artificial Intelligence (AI) is currently being considered world-wide as a "deus ex machina" and is promoted by politicians and scientists having miraculous abilities to solve all problems.

© Springer Nature Switzerland AG 2021
D. Fogli et al. (Eds.): IS-EUD 2021, LNCS 12724, pp. 3–16, 2021.
https://doi.org/10.1007/978-3-030-79840-6_1

Both EUD and AI are *"suitcase words"* [1]: words carrying many meanings so researchers and practitioners can talk about complex issues in shorthand. Suitcase words contain multiple and expanding meanings across very different contexts and can lead to misunderstandings when we assume that everyone attributes the same meaning to them. To identify research themes surrounding EUD (Fig. 1) and AI (Fig. 2) represent an attempt to unpack EUD and AI as suitcase words by exploring specific aspects of them.

The paper characterizes EUD and AI in the first two sections and explores in the following sections (1) the relationship between them, (2) their roles and contributions to democratizing the design, use, and evolution of socio-technical environments in specific domains, and (4) challenges for future developments. The analysis of themes, concepts, principles, differentiations, and prototypes attempts to envision a future of EUD by exploiting promises and avoiding pitfalls of different AI approaches towards the empowerment of all stakeholders.

2 End-User Development (EUD)

EUD [2] is instrumental for the ability to reformulate knowledge, to express oneself creatively and appropriately, and to produce and generate information rather than simply to comprehend it. It supports diverse audiences in designing and building their own artifacts by situating computation in new contexts, by generating content, and by developing tools that democratize design, innovation, and knowledge creation. EUD is necessary for coping with *wicked problems* [3] for which the framing of problems is incomplete at design time and continues throughout the whole life cycle of a system in order to respond to the ongoing changes of a living world.

An early inspiration for the desirability and necessity for EUD was articulated by Ivan Illich with *convivial systems* envisioned to *"give each person who uses them the greatest opportunity to enrich the environment with the fruits of his or her vision"* [4]. This objective distributes control among all stakeholders (e.g.: system designers and end-users) and it grants autonomy for end-users to modify computational artifacts to their needs.

Different aspects of EUD have been pursued in numerous domains addressing a variety of challenges and objectives. Figure 1 provides a selection of these domains as an attempt for unpacking EUD as a suitcase word into more specific objectives. The variety of the domains transcends currently existing narrow views of EUD (e.g. seeing it only as a technical challenge to support new ways of end-user programming). It represents a *vision for the future of EUD* as a fundamental research area to increase the quality of life for all humans by democratizing the design and use of social policies and computational artifacts and by increasing the collective creativity to respond to wicked problems. The current world-wide struggle to cope with the disruption and upheaval caused by Covid-19 provides an important examples illustrating these arguments.

The domains mentioned in Fig. 1 can be briefly described as follows:

- *End-User Programming (EUP)* [5] empowers and supports end-users to program and *End-User Software Engineering (EUSE)* adds to EUP the support for systematic and disciplined activities for the whole software lifecycle;

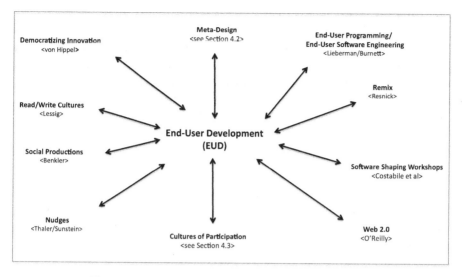

Fig. 1. Different Domains of End-User Development (EUD)

- *Remix* [6] supports a core design principle and computational practice that any-one can remix another user's project and add their own ideas (successfully employed in Scratch);
- *Software Shaping Workshops* [7] allows end users to carry out their activities and adapt environments and tools without the burden of using traditional programming languages by using high-level visual languages tailored to their needs;
- *Web 2.0 technologies* [8] support websites that allow mass participation by end-users (as practiced in Wikipedia and Open Source);
- *Democratizing Innovation* [9] provides argumentation that active end-users can develop what they want, rather than relying on professional designers and manu-facturers to act as their agents;
- *Read/Write Cultures* [10] explores intellectual property issues allowing all stakehold-ers to share their creative contributions transcending the limits of Read/Only cultures in which people are restricted to consumption;
- *Social production* [11] analyzes frameworks and examples for effective, large-scale cooperative efforts of peer production;
- *Nudges* [12] provide examples of major social policies issues in which choice archi-tects try to motivate people to engage in certain actions and behavior, but simultane-ously provide them with EUD opportunities to have complete choice over their own actions by supporting a methodology characterized as "libertarian paternalism" [12].

The contributions of *meta-design* and *cultures of participation* will be discussed in more detail in Sects. 4.2 and 4.3.

3 Artificial Intelligence (AI)

There is no generally accepted definition for AI and there is no defined boundary to separate "AI systems" from "non-AI systems". Despite this shortcoming AI is currently being considered world-wide as a "deus ex machina" and it is credited with miraculous abilities to solve all problems and exploit all opportunities of the digital age.

Figure 2 makes an attempt (analogous to Fig. 1 for EUD) to unpack the "suit-case word" AI into more specific research areas (most of them still being only vaguely defined). The overview differentiates between.

- *Artificial General Intelligence (AGI)* [13] is the envisioned objective to create intelligent agents that will match human capabilities for understanding and learning any intellectual task that a human being can. While some researchers consider AGI as the ultimate goal of AI, for others AGI remains speculative as no such system has been demonstrated yet. Opinions vary both on whether and when AGI will arrive, if at all.
- *AI for Specific Purposes (AISP)* [14] is an engineering discipline that explores specific well-defined problems for which AI systems performs better than human beings. Many successful contributions have occurred in achieving these objectives providing the basis for the current hype surrounding AI. Human involvement is not a relevant design criteria in these approaches.
- *Human-Centered AI (HCAI)* [15, 16] (closely related to *intelligence augmentation* [17, 18]) is focused on improving the quality of life of humans by creating AI systems that amplify, augment, and enhance human performance in ways that make systems reliable, safe, and trustworthy.

AISP is focused on "tame" problems whereas HCAI is addressing "wicked" problems [3] for which framing a problem is as important as solving a problem and for which no correct solutions and no boundaries exist. This article is focused on the mutual dependencies between EUD and HCAI in which all human stakeholders play a critical role and the algorithms are glass boxes instead of black boxes capable of explaining how they reach decisions.

The current views and the goals and objectives of future developments of AI can be differentiated into three major categories (the edited book by [19] contains over one hundred short opinion pieces of prominent AI researchers and critics that address these different perspectives):

- *AI Utopians (or Euphoriker)* [13] believe that AGI is a realistic and desirable goal for the not too distant future and advocating trans-humanism and singularity are desirable and inevitable objective*s*;
- *AI Pessimists (or Apokalyptiker)* [20] argue that AI has failed and the objectives of AGI are dangerous for the future of the human race;
- *AI Realists* assert that there is on one hand substantial progress in pursuing and incorporating AI approaches addressing fundamental societal problems and on the other hand there are just as many unsolved problems for which human intelligence will be far superior to artificial ones for decades to come. They address the reluctance in many segments of society to allow computers to take over tasks that simple models perform

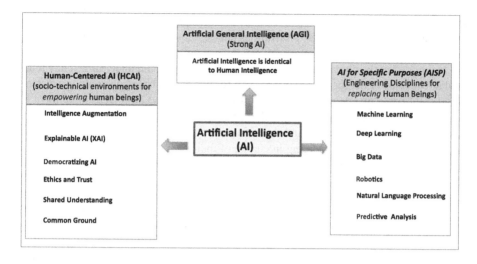

Fig. 2. Differentiating AI Approaches

demonstrably better than humans. Their efforts are focused not on AGI but on the improvement of tools in the AISP domains and using HCAI for creating supportive socio-technical environments.

The argumentation of this paper is grounded in the basic assumption that in order to advance the EUD agenda the objectives of the "AI Realists" are the most promising way to pursue.

4 Integrating EUD and AI

Democracy distributes the power to process information and make decisions among many stakeholders (meta-designers and end-users, choice architects, and citizens) acting at different times (e.g.: design time and use time). Democratizing the development, evolution, and use of socio-technical environments is the essence of EUD and provides the intellectual glue between the different domains mentioned in Fig. 1.

The core theme of IS-EUD 2021 is whether AI will further enhance or hinder the possibilities and support for EUD. The differentiations of EUD and AI by unpacking them as suitcase words provide a basis to assess this question in specific contexts.

EUD is required and most valuable in coping with wicked problems in a changing world. AI has been most successful in providing solutions for specific problems (right column in Fig. 2). The efficiency of the algorithms based on their increasing complexity will shift more and more authority from humans to AISP systems. The usefulness and strengths of AISP systems (e.g.: relying on Google's search algorithm for finding relevant and trustworthy information, navigating in physical space with GPS systems, accepting the suggestion of recommender systems for movies to see, articles and books to read, partners to meet, etc.) is evident from their wide spread use. Their negative impacts can be seen that we as individuals and societies increasingly depend on AI algorithms we do not understand because their motivations and intentions shaping their workings, are hidden from us.

In contrast to the objectives of EUD, AI developments could undermine many practical advantages of democracy, and they may further concentrate power among a small elite [21]. People may be forced (or may give up voluntarily) an increasing amount of authority, control, and autonomy over their lives because they will trust the algorithms more than their own judgment and decision making. They will become dependent on high-tech scribes rather than being in charge of their own destiny. These dangers exist specifically for AISP approaches exploiting nonhuman abilities. For example: "Big Data" approaches [22] base their results primarily on *correlations* (not knowing *why* but only *what*). It is important to note that correlations do not imply causations. It may well be that for many everyday needs, knowing what is good enough. But human reasoning and EUD is dominated by causality: therefore HCAI approaches augmenting human intelligence require knowledge about causal relationships for shared understanding and common ground and true understanding. The fact that correlations do not imply causalities (even many in the press and some researchers often imply otherwise) is nicely illustrated by Khan in his episode "Eating Breakfast May Beat Obesity" [23].

The *design trade-offs* [24] between AI and EUD (situated and analyzed in specific contexts) need to be further explored grounded in an initial understanding that position them as opposites on a spectrum of autonomy and control (AI being low in control and autonomy and EUD being high in control and autonomy). Additional important objectives should be pursued such as (1) exploring further synergistic opportunities (as we have attempted in our research effort [25] by using AI components for supporting EUD activities (thereby lowering the bar for people to engage in EUD and to suggest opportunities for EUD), and (2) strengthening and operationalizing HCAI by supporting EUD.

4.1 Explainable AI (XAI)

Explainable AI (XAI) [26] refers to methods and techniques that enable humans to understand, trust, and modify the reasoning and results of AI programs. AISP systems learn to solve problems such as classifying inputs (e.g., is this a picture of a cat or dog?) or making decisions (e.g., what treatment should be given to a patient with particular symptoms?) by automatically generalizing from a large set of examples [22]. The inner workings of such systems are a "black box": given a question, systems provide an answer, but they cannot explain how or why they reached the answer. Lacking the ability to explain itself, systems cannot be trusted particularly in high-stakes applications.

As an example: imagine someone is using her favorite GPS system to find her way in an unfamiliar area, and the GPS directs her to turn left at an intersection, which strikes her as wrong. If the navigation was coming from a friend in the passenger seat reading a map, she may ask, "Are you sure?". However, users do not have any way to query their GPS system. Most current GPS systems are not capable of meaningful explanations, they cannot describe their intentions in a way users would understand, and they cannot convey confidence in the route they have selected.

XAI is an important step toward helping AI systems and people work together in a synergistic fashion. Humans trust and assist other humans based on common ground and shared understanding. We trust others if we understand how others think, so that we have common ground to resolve ambiguities. We trust them if they have the integrity to admit mistakes and accept blame. We trust them if we have shared values [27].

Shneiderman developed a model for HCAI [28] focused on three major objectives: trust, reliability, and safety. His extensive framework for these objectives (supported by numerous examples) represents important foundations for developing XAI systems.

4.2 Meta-Design

Design (being another suitcase word) is focused on how things ought to be in order to attain desired functions and meanings [29]. *Meta-design* ('design for designers') [30, 31] is a theoretical framework to conceptualize and to cope in unique ways with design problems. It is focused on open-ended co-design processes in which all the involved actors actively participate in different ways [32]. It is grounded in the fundamental assumption that design is not a matter of getting rid of the emergent, but rather of including it and making it an opportunity for more creative and more adequate solutions to problems. Many design approaches force all the design intelligence to the earliest part of the design process, when everyone knows the least about what is really needed. The understanding of a problem cannot be complete at any time due to the situated, tacit, and evolving nature of knowledge work [33].

Meta-design provides the enabling conditions for putting users in charge who act until they experience a breakdown that may lead them to reflection and learning new relevant topics on demand. These breakdowns are experienced by end-users at use time and not by system builders at design time [31]. End users need the ability to evolve and refine their problem framing and problem solving attempts. Meta-designers use their own creativity to produce socio-technical environments in which other people can be creative. They define the *technical* and *social* conditions for broad participation in design activities.

Making systems modifiable has to be a design objective for the original system. Adding system components to allow for end-user modifiability in a system constructed without this goal in mind is a nearly impossible task. Meta-Design can be supported with the *Seeding, Evolutionary Growth, and Reseeding (SER) Model* [34]. The SER model is a descriptive and prescriptive model for creating systems that best fit an emerging and evolving context. Instead of attempting to build complete systems, the SER model advocates building *seeds* that can evolve over time. It postulates that systems that evolve over a sustained time span must continually alternate between (1) periods of planned activity and unplanned evolution, and (2) periods of deliberate (re)structuring and enhancement. A seed is something that has the potential to change and grow. In socio-technical environments, seeds need to be designed and created for the technical as well as the social component of the environment.

Meta-design will benefit from the following developments that can be effectively supported by HCAI: (1) offer *task-specific languages* supporting human problem-domain interaction [35]; (2) provide *programming environments* (such as Scratch [6]) that protect users from low-level computational drudgery; (3) support *customization, reuse, and redesign* effectively [36]; (4) tailor *software applications* at use time with component-based approaches [37]; and (5) advance construction kits to *domain-oriented design environments* with intelligent support systems [38].

4.3 Cultures of Participation

Cultures of participation [39] have emerged as the result of the shift from consumer cultures (in which people are confined to passive recipients of artifacts and systems) to cultures in which users are actively involved in the development and evolution of solutions to their problems.

Professional programmers and domain professionals define the endpoints of a continuum of computer users. The former like computers because they can program, and the latter because they get their work done. The goal of supporting domain professionals to develop and modify systems does not imply transferring the responsibility of good system design to the end-user [5]. Normal users will in general not build tools of the quality a professional designer would. However, if a tool does not satisfy the needs or the tastes of the end-users (who know best what these requirements are), then EUD and HCAI support should assist stakeholders to adapt and evolve their systems.

A fundamental challenge for cultures of participation is to conceptualize, create, and evolve socio-technical environments that not only enable and support users' participation, but also successfully *encourage* it. Participation is often determined by an individual's assessment of value/effort. The effort can be reduced by providing the right kind of tools with meta-design, and the value can be increased by contributing to framing and solving a personally meaningful problem and sharing the results with others.

5 Socio-Technical Environments Exploring EUD and AI Perspectives

To assess the viability and applicability of the concepts and components of the framework described in the previous sections, we have developed prototypes in a variety of different domains. Some of these approaches will be briefly described.

5.1 Adaptive and Adaptable Systems

In socio-technical environments modeling changing worlds, the shared knowledge between users and systems should not be static, but should increase and change over time. There are two major ways that this can be achieved: making systems *adaptive* and/or *adaptable*. Table 1 provides a summary of different characteristics associated with the two types of systems. Adaptive systems rely primarily on AI system components whereas adaptable systems exploit different aspects of EUD.

A successful combination for the integration of adaptive and adaptable components can be illustrated using the *"Auto Correct" feature of Microsoft Word* as a simple example. This feature automatically detects and corrects misspelled words, e.g.: "hte" is transformed into "the" and (2) "EHR" into "HER". Changes will not necessarily be noticed by users. While the first transformation is wanted, the second one is not wanted in specific contexts. For example: we sent a letter to a National Science Foundation department called "Education and Human Resources" addressing them with "HER" rather than "EHR" (probably not creating a favorable impression at an agency that was funding our research). In another context (the medical domain) "EHR" may mean "Electronic Patient Record". The designers of "AutoCorrect" recognized the limitations of determining the context in the abstract, and they provided an adaptable EUD tool allowing for users to overwrite the system's feature with specific situated needs of users that include the deletion and addition of specific rewrites and/or the option to turn off the feature altogether. This simple example shows that AI and EUD components can successfully be combined.

Table 1. A comparison between adaptive and adaptable systems

	Adaptive (AI Focus)	Adaptable (EUD Focus)
Definition	Dynamic adaptation by the system itself to current task and current user	Users change the functionality of the system
Knowledge	Contained in the system; projected in different ways	Knowledge is extended by users
Strengths	Little (or no) effort by users; no special user knowledge is required	Users are in control; users know their tasks best
Weaknesses	Users often have difficulties developing a coherent model of the system; loss of control	Users must do substantial work and need to learn adaptation components
Mechanisms	Models of users, tasks, and dialogs; incremental update of models	Support for end-user modi-fiability and development
[1] Applications	Active help systems, critiquing systems, recommender systems	Construction kits, macros, specification components

5.2 Domain-Oriented Design Environments (DODEs)

Domain-oriented systems (as an alternative to general purpose programming language) put end-users in charge by supporting human problem-domain interaction. This section briefly describes the steps (emphasizing EUD and AI aspects) leading towards our long-term vision of *domain-oriented design environments (DODEs)* [40].

Domain-oriented *construction kits* reduce the demands for users by providing high-level building blocks for reuse, redesign, and remixing. They intentionally sacrifice generality for more elaborate support of domain semantics. But construction kits by themselves provide insufficient support for creating interesting, high quality artifacts, because they do not support shortcomings of the artifact under construction.

DODEs enrich constructions kits with a variety of HCAI systems, including: (1) *specification components* allowing users to communicate specific aspects of problems to DODEs to increase the shared understanding; (2) *critics* analyzing an artifact under development by using design principles to detect and critique suboptimal solutions and inform users that the current design violates standard rules; and (3) *catalogs* of previous developed solutions supporting design by modification rather than starting from scratch.

Support for EUD is critical for DODEs. They need to evolve to capture the evolution of artifacts meeting the demands of a changing world. We have explored and implemented principles for EUD in our prototypes [25] including the design of (1) new design objects, (2) new critiquing rules, and (3) additional requirements derived from the needs of disabled persons. All of these components rely and can and should be further enhanced with HCAI techniques.

5.3 Context-Aware Systems

Context-aware systems [41] are grounded in the basic assumption that the scarce resource for many people in today's world is not information but human attention creating the challenge not to deliver more information "to anyone, at anytime, and from anywhere," but to provide *"the 'right' information, at the 'right' time, in the 'right' place, in the 'right' way, to the 'right' person."*

Context-aware systems rely on models of tasks and users. *Personalization* represent a prominent technique that has been widely used to escape global group identities and replace them with much more detailed predictions for each individual.

The further development of context-aware systems raises numerous issues for EUD and HCAI research activities such as: (1) how to *identify and infer user goals* from low-level interactions?; (2) how to *integrate different modeling techniques* (e.g., adaptive and adaptable components? see Table 1); (3) how to capture the *larger and unarticulated context* for understanding what users are doing and the associated costs for providing design rationale, tagging and rating an artifact, curation of large information repositories; and (4) how to identify the *pitfalls* associated with context-aware systems such as filter bubbles and "group think" as consequences of personalization and privacy protection.

6 Challenges for the Future

To create a synergy between EUD and HCAI, research activities have to identify the social abilities, technical skills, and cultural competencies needed by people to participate in these activities. The scope of human-centered design needs to be broadened from the usability of systems to providing resources, incentives, and information to encourage and sustain participation. A deeper understanding will be required to differentiate domains in which EUD and HCAI will flourish and be successful from the domains for which they are not suited. A few of these global challenges will be briefly elaborated.

6.1 EUD Objectives for Democratizing AI

EUD objectives for democratizing AI are more relevant and more applicable in the "open" domains of HCAI (left column in Fig. 2), then in the "closed" AISP systems (right column in Fig. 2). But aligning AI capabilities with EUD objectives, it should not be overlooked that these approaches present a number of important design trade-offs that require careful attention and further exploration including:

- *establishing different discourses:* to deeply understand the potential transformation of human lives enriched rather than limited by HCAI technologies, discourses and investigations must not only be focused around technological issues but explore motivation, control, ownership, autonomy, and quality;
- *deskilling and overreliance:* using hand-held calculators, spelling correctors, navigation systems, and automatic translators, will humans loose important cognitive capabilities and how can an overreliance on external tools be avoided?;
- *participation overload:* in the context of cultures of participation will the support for active engagement lead to participation overload (particularly in personally irrelevant activities)?
- *learning demands:* how to cope with extensive learning demands required by tools that allow humans to exploit the benefits of complex HCAI technologies in distributed cognition approaches?

6.2   Participation Overload in the Context of Personally Irrelevant Problems

Our research in meta-design and cultures of participation has identified a fundamental design trade-off between developments that should be avoided: (1) in *personally meaningful activities* someone wants to be a designer but is forced to be a consumer versus (2) in *personally irrelevant activities* someone wants to be a consumer but is forced to be a designer.

The second development leads to *participation overload in* "Do-It-Yourself (DIY)" societies. Currently, AI techniques are employed in numerous contexts that allow or force people such as (1) to check out their own groceries or check in by themselves at airports; (2) make their own travel arrangements (including relying on aggregator systems such as Kayak or prediction systems such as FareCast); (3) take care of their banking needs; (4) write and typeset their papers, and (5) constantly provide feedback about services (e.g.: for hotels, flights, repair shops, support provided via the Internet).

Participation overload will become a burden in complex, unfamiliar, and personally irrelevant domains where freedom of choice becomes a burden rather than a benefit and people would prefer not spending time on a problem or activity at all. The problem can be illustrated and analyzed with the concept of *"libertarian paternalism"* [12], a design-trade-off discussed in behavioral economics and public policy. The approach explores middle ground as the choice between paternalism (being prescriptive) and libertarian (being permissive) by distributing control with nudges between choice architects (e.g.: policy makers in governments, designers, teachers, meta-designers) and users (e.g.: citizens, learners, end-users). A reasonable amount of paternalism (e.g. by establishing sensible defaults) will reduce the burden on users and simultaneously the libertarian components will respect the autonomy of users.

6.3   Cultural Transformations

The context for human development is always a culture, never an isolated technology. EUD and HCAI are *society-changing inventions* with the potential making it easier to deal with the world's complexity and wicked problems.

Providing all citizens with the means to become co-creators of new ideas, knowledge, and products and giving them more control to evolve systems in personally meaningful activities presents one of the most exciting innovations and transformations with profound implications in the years to come. This objective characterizes the vision behind EUD as a *cultural transformation*. To make this vision a reality, the EUD research community needs to establish new discourses and shared languages about concepts, assumptions, values, stories, metaphors, design approaches, and learning theories.

EUD developments will erode monopoly positions held by professions, educational institutions, experts, and high-tech scribes. They will empower all stakeholders to design, build, and evolve their own artifacts supported by meta-designers and choice architects who create environments to foster cultures of participation. These objectives will situate computation in new cultural and material contexts. HCAI developments will make a contribution to these objectives when they are focused on *enhancing* quality of life, not ignoring or diminish it.

For analyzing the promises and the pitfalls associated with different approaches *there are no decontextualized sweet spots* but the investigations must be situated and explored in specific contexts. The objectives "self-driving cars" and "mobility for all" can illustrate the distinction between technological objectives and cultural transformation. Ten years ago, self-driving cars (focused on technological advances) seemed to be more a topic for science fiction than a near-term reality, but rapid progress is now made at the technological level towards this goal. While self-driving cars are an important component of "mobility for all" (conceptualized as a cultural transformation), they are only *one component* in a complex network of interrelated topics. By considering "mobility for all" as another wicked problem with no boundaries, the following objectives and design trade-offs need to be taken into account: (1) reduce the need for it (e.g.: by facilitating working from home) versus supporting it; (2) improve mass transportation instead of focusing on individual car traffic; (3) limit the environmental damage with electric cars; (4) explore different models of ownership of automobiles (including car sharing); (5) support the independence of people unable to drive, and (6) reduce the number of accidents and traffic deaths.

7   Conclusions

To deeply understand the potential transformation of human lives enriched rather than limited by EUD and HCAI technologies, discourses and investigations must not only be focused around technological issues but explore motivation, control, ownership, autonomy, quality of life, and cultural transformation. Changes in complex environments are not primarily dictated by technology but they are the result of a shift in human behavior and social organization. The design of socio-technical environments requires the co-design of social and technical systems.

While the growth of technologies such as EUD and AI is certain, the inevitability of any particular future is not. In a world facing wicked problems the aim is not to find truth, but to improve the quality of life for all humans. A mutually beneficial relationship between EUD and AI will not happen by itself but will require a serious commitment to the objective to initiate cultural transformations that will empower all stakeholders.

Acknowledgements. The author wishes to thank Daniela Fogli, Anders Morch, Antonio Piccinno, Ben Shneiderman, Daniel Tetteroo, and the three reviewers who provided insightful comments that greatly improved earlier versions of this article.

References

1. Minsky, M.: The Emotion Machine. Simon & Schuster (2007)
2. Lieberman, H., Paterno, F., Wulf, V. (eds.) End User Development. Kluwer Publishers: Dordrecht, The Netherlands (2006)
3. Rittel, H., Webber, M.M.: Planning problems are wicked problems. In: Cross, N. (eds.) Developments in Design Methodology, 1984. John Wiley & Sons, New York, pp. 135–144 (1984)
4. Illich, I.: Tools for Conviviality. Harper and Row, New York (1973)
5. Burnett, M.M., Scaffidi, C.: End-user development. In: Soegaard, M., Dam, R.F. (eds.) The Encyclopedia of Human-Computer Interaction, 2nd edn. The Interaction Design Foundation: Aarhus, Denmark (2013)
6. Resnick, M.: Lifelong Kindergarten — Cultivating Creativity through Projects, Passion, Peers, and Play: Cambridge. MIT Press, MA (2017)
7. Costabile, M.F., et al.: End user development: the software shaping workshop approach. In: Lieberman, H., Paternò, F., Wulf, V. (eds.) End User Development 2006, pp. 183–205. Springer, Dordrecht (2006). https://doi.org/10.1007/1-4020-5386-X_9
8. O'Reilly, T.: What Is Web 2.0 - Design Patterns and Business Models for the Next Generation of Software (2005). http://www.oreillynet.com/pub/a/oreilly/tim/news/2005/09/30/what-is-web-20.html
9. von Hippel, E.: Democratizing Innovation. MIT Press, Cambridge (2005)
10. Lessig, L.: Remix: Making Art and Commerce thrive in the Hybrid Economy. Penguin Press, New York (2008)
11. Benkler, Y.: The Wealth of Networks: How Social Production Transforms Markets and Freedom. Yale University Press, New Haven (2006)
12. Thaler, R.H., Sunstein, C.R.: Nudge — Improving Decisions about Health, Wealth, and Happiness. Penguin Books, London (2009)
13. Kurzweil, R.: The Singularity is Near. Penguin Books (2006)
14. Brynjolfsson, E., McAfee, A.: The Second Machine Age: Work, Progress, and Prosperity in a Time of Brilliant Technologies. W. W. Norton & Company (2014)
15. Shneiderman, B.: Bridging the gap between ethics and practice: guidelines for reliable, safe, and trustworthy Human-Centered AI systems. ACM Trans. Interact. Intell. Syst. (TiiS) **10**(4), 1–31 (2020)
16. Hai, S.: Stanford University Human-Centered Artificial Intelligence (2021). https://hai.stanford.edu
17. Engelbart, D.C.: Toward augmenting the human intellect and boosting our collective IQ. Commun. ACM **38**(8), 30–33 (1995)
18. Markoff, J.: Machines of Loving Grace (The Quest for Common Ground Between Humans and Robots) (2016). Harpercollins
19. Brockman, J., (ed.) What to Think About Machines That Think: Today's Leading Thinkers on the Age of Machine Intelligence (2015). Harper Perennial.
20. Hawking, S., et al.: Transcendence looks at the implications of artificial intelligence - but are we taking AI seriously enough? Independent, 23 October 2017
21. Harari, Y.N.: Why Technology Favors Tyranny. Atlantic, October 2018

22. Mayer-Schönberger, V., Cukier, K., Data, B.: New York. Houghton Mifflin Harcourt, NY (2013)
23. Khan, S.: Correlation and Causality (2021). https://www.khanacademy.org/math/statistics-probability/designing-studies/sampling-and-surveys/v/correlation-and-causality
24. Fischer, G.: Design Trade-Offs for Quality of Life ACM. Interactions **25**(1), 26–33 (2018)
25. Fischer, G., Girgensohn, A.: End-user modifiability in design environments. In: Human Factors in Computing Systems, (CHI'90) (Seattle, WA), pp. 183–191. ACM, New York (1990)
26. Turek, M.: Explainable AI (XAI), DARPA. (2018). https://www.darpa.mil/program/explainable-artificial-intelligence
27. Clark, H.H., Brennan, S.E.: Grounding in Communication. In: Resnick, L.B., Levine, J.M., Teasley, S.D. (eds.) Perspectives on Socially Shared Cognition, pp. 127–149. American Psychological Association (1991)
28. Shneiderman, B.: Human-Centered AI (forthcoming). Oxford University Press (2022)
29. Simon, H.A.: The Sciences of the Artificial, 3rd edn. The MIT Press, Cambridge (1996)
30. Fischer, G., Fogli, D., Piccinno, A.: Revisiting and broadening the meta-design framework for end-user development. In: Paternò, F., Wulf, V. (eds.) New Perspectives in End-User Development, pp. 61–97. Springer, Cham (2017). https://doi.org/10.1007/978-3-319-60291-2_4
31. Binder, T., Things, D., et al.: Cambridge. MIT Press, MA (2011)
32. Manzini, E.: Design, When Everybody Designs — An Introduction to Design for Social Innovation. The MIT Press, Cambridge (2015)
33. Winograd, T., Flores, F.: Understanding Computers and Cognition: A New Foundation for Design. Ablex Publishing Corporation, Norwood (1986)
34. Fischer, G., et al.: Seeding, evolutionary growth and reseeding: the incremental development of collaborative design environments. In: Olson, G.M., Malone, T.W., Smith, J.B. (eds.) Coordination Theory and Collaboration Technology, pp. 447–472. Lawrence Erlbaum Associates, Mahwah, NJ (2001)
35. National-Research-Council, Beyond Productivity: Information Technology, Innovation, and Creativity. Washington, DC: National Academy Press (2003)
36. Morch, A.: Three levels of end-user tailoring: customization, integration, and extension. In: Kyng, M., Mathiassen, L. (eds.) Computers and Design in Context, pp. 51–76. MIT Press, Cambridge, MA (1997)
37. Wulf, V., Pipek, V., Won, M.: Component-based tailorability: enabling highly flexible software applications. Int. J. Hum Comput Stud. **66**, 1–22 (2008)
38. Fischer, G., et al.: Embedding critics in design environments. In: Maybury, M.T., Wahlster, W. (eds.) Readings in Intelligent User Interfaces, pp. 537–559. Morgan Kaufmann, San Francisco (1998)
39. Fischer, G.: Understanding, Fostering, and Supporting Cultures of Participation. ACM Interactions 2011. **XVIII.3**: pp. 42–53 (2011)
40. Fischer, G.: Domain-oriented design environments. Autom. Softw. Eng. **1**(2), 177–203 (1994)
41. Fischer, G.: Context-aware systems: the 'right' information, at the 'right' time, in the 'right' place, in the 'right' way, to the 'right' person. In: Tortora, G. (eds.) Proceedings of the Conference on Advanced Visual Interfaces (AVI), 2012, Capri, Italy, May, pp. 287–294. ACM (2012)

Full Papers

Reconsidering End-User Development Definitions

Nikolaos Batalas[1]([✉]), Ioanna Lykourentzou[2], Vassilis-Javed Khan[3],
and Panos Markopoulos[1]

[1] Eindhoven University of Technology, Eindhoven, The Netherlands
p.markopoulos@tue.nl
[2] Utrecht University, Utrecht, The Netherlands
i.lykourentzou@uu.nl
[3] Sappi Europe, Watermael-Boitsfort, Belgium
Javed.Khan@sappi.com

Abstract. We consider definitions that End-User Development and related fields offer for end-user developers, and identify the persistence of viewing end-user development as antithetical to professional development across the years, even as focus has shifted from the identity and then to the role of the developer, and later to the intent of the development effort. We trace the origins of this antithesis to the days of End-User Computing in organizational settings, and argue that modern software development resides in a different paradigm, where end-user Development is part and parcel of any programming endeavour, in professional or other settings. We propose that current development practice, both for those traditionally regarded as end-user and as professional developers, can be better served by EUD as a field, if the focus is shifted to the nature of the task itself, and how technical it needs to be, by way of the platforms that development takes place on.

Keywords: End-user development · Technical development · Definitions

1 Introduction

End-User Development (EUD) is a field of academic research dedicated to the making of software. Related fields such as End-User Programming (EUP) or End-User Software Engineering (EUSE) also address specific aspects of software creation/maintenance. The terms are distinct; EUP can be considered as being about program creation itself, whereas EUSE addresses concerns around reliability, reuse and maintainability. EUD claims to address the wider range of practices that are involved in software development, including design practices. As such, EUD can be considered to be the more encompassing term, inclusive

© Springer Nature Switzerland AG 2021
D. Fogli et al. (Eds.): IS-EUD 2021, LNCS 12724, pp. 19–35, 2021.
https://doi.org/10.1007/978-3-030-79840-6_2

of EUP and EUSE[1]. In this text, the term end-user development will be the umbrella term for all aspects of practice with regard to the end-user production of software, unless referencing specific cases, and EUD will denote the wider field of research, inclusive of topics researched by EUP and EUSE.

EUD's objectives for software construction differ from the traditional academic disciplines dedicated to the task. Such disciplines as Computer Science (CS), Electrical Engineering (EE) or Software Engineering (SE) emphasize specialized knowledge that relates to the construction of software, on areas that include the following:

- the construction of computing machinery on a physical substrate, and the ways these can be controlled and composed into more complex systems that are able to execute programs (which can generally be seen as sets of instructions that operate on data, or produce signals for adjacent systems).
- the ways in which computational problems can be classified, and the finding of efficient solutions for solving classes of problems, in terms of execution time and memory use, as well as studying the properties of relevant data structures.
- the methods via which the development and maintenance of software can be practiced systematically and with discipline, so that reliable results can be reached with predicable use of resources.

EUD on the other hand, aims to make easier the construction of computer programs, or the modification of existing software to alter or extend its functions, but without demanding that the developers should have to employ the depth of knowledge and expertise that it takes to develop software on the technical level that the traditional disciplines are concerned with, regardless of how familiar they are with them.

This paper raises the issue that consideration needs to be placed towards the ways with which academic communities regard End-User Development and its place within the wider landscape of software production. It is motivated by a contradiction observed when applying prevailing definitions of end-user developers to a specific case of software development in clinical psychology, and which arises from the tendency to define end-user developers by juxtaposing them against professional developers. The paper traces the origins of the term end-user developer, and the evolution of software development practices, to show that on one hand, conceptions of end-user developers are rooted in organizational settings of the past that do not necessarily persist any more, and on the other hand, that an

---

[1] It is interesting to note here the observation by Barricelli et al. [2], that the choice of field to which authors will ascribe their work tends to be a matter of academic culture. European authors will file their work under EUD because of its namesake European Commission initiative, the European Network of Excellence on End-User Development (EUD-Net) which created a network of researchers and relevant conferences. American authors, on the other hand, will prefer the term EUP, which did originate in the United States, and a small subset of those, the community of US universities that participated in the EUSES Consortium pursue work under EUSE.

important quest of software development has been to render itself into an EUD endeavour, with successes along the way. Finally, it invites researchers to reconsider the scope of EUD, from addressing specific types of expertise or intent, to encompassing the whole range of software development. ·

2   A Cause to Reconsider Commonly Used Definitions

Over time, various definitions of EUD have been offered with regard to who the end-user developer is or what they do. Although the end-user developer tends to be defined in some way as an opposite of the professional developer, attempts at definitions have varied, mostly in service of illustrating a particular point that the author is making. With regard to the workplace, some authors have seen end-user programmers as those who have non-programming jobs to perform, or do not care about computers, but still have to program [14,41]. In researching more accessible ways to produce software, authors have regarded end-user developers as novices to computer programming or less skilled at it [31,46]. Yet others have argued that skill and expertise is irrelevant [29].

In more detail, considering someone as an end-user developer due to aspects of personal identity (e.g., by being a novice [14] or not caring about computers [41]) excludes potential categories of end-user developers, such as system administrators or research scientists, labelled as professional end-user developers [51], who possess or acquire the technical knowledge to develop software in order to further their professional goals. To overcome such issues, Lieberman et al. [32] cast the end-user developer as *a role*, in which someone *acts as* (rather than *is*) a non-professional, and offer a definition for the field of research, rather than the end-user developer or their activities. They define EUD as "a set of methods, techniques, and tools that allow users of software systems, who are acting as non-professional software developers, at some point to create, modify or extend a software artefact". The antithesis to the professional developer, found in earlier definitions, remains, but a definition for the end-user developer is missing.

In a later definition, Ko et al. [29] acknowledge the problems of considering end-user programmer characteristics as a matter of personal identity. They propose that the characterization of one as being end-user vs. professional developer is a matter of intent, and as such, expertise and skill in programming are irrelevant. End-user and professional developer are two endpoints of a spectrum, and one's place on it is determined by the number of users they are building the software for. If they are serving their own needs, they are end-user developers. If they are serving a large population of users of their software, they are a professional developer. The authors here offer a way to discern between end-user development and professional development, since the number of users functions as an indicator of whether the software is intended for personal or wider user, and therefore a measure of how important it is for the software to be reliable, and therefore might require professional software engineering practices. According to this view, end-user development is development for one's own self, irrespectively of how experienced the programmer is, whereas developing for others, is a characteristic of professional development.

Ambulatory Assessment is a research method predominantly used within clinical psychology, with the purpose of capturing bio-psycho-social processes in the context of daily life [12], gathering self-reports and sensor measurements from groups of people, by sampling them repeatedly over time. Researchers who use it, deploy sampling instruments to a population of participants in their natural settings, and use the collected data to discover ways in which the constructs under investigation relate to each other. Oftentimes, they also seek to offer personalized interventions to each participant, based on data collected. Data collection happens increasingly via mobile platforms such as smartphones and wearables, and considerable effort goes into the making of tools to enable clinical psychologists to define what data these platforms collect and how [3, 22, 49]. With these tools, psychologists do not merely produce parameters for the configuration of pre-built software, but effectively write programs consisting of function calls, which perform such actions as instantiating user-interfaces or invoking the sampling of hardware sensors, which are either executed sequentially or as a result of conditional branching according to the evaluation of logical statements (if-then-else), which involve variables representing user or system states.

Researchers who employ these methods, distribute their programs to potentially hundreds of users, who participate in their studies, to use for recording data. They might also share them with other members of their research community, who wish to reuse them. We would traditionally (in terms of identity or role) reason about these psychologists as end-user programmers, given the fact that their formal training or work practices do not usually include elements of CS, EE or SE that would justify viewing them as professional programmers, and the fact that the tools that allow them to create these programs are tailored to their own professional domain. Yet in producing and distributing their programs, they do not singly intend them for themselves or for others, but for both. They aim both to collect longitudinal data for their own research purposes, but also to produce programs that their participants can use to supply this data. Depending on what view of their intent we espouse, we could use the criteria proposed by Ko et al. [29] to classify the same activity as either end-user programming, or professional programming, but definitions of end-user programming or development consider these notions to be opposites. This contradiction motivates us to wonder about the discriminatory power these definitions, which define end-user development as opposite to professional development, have across various modern development configurations.

For this reason we will try to better understand the two aspects that these definitions address, that of the end-user and that of the professional developer. In the rest of this paper we will discuss these concepts in more detail, and argue that modern software-development practices in professional settings are rife with EUD success stories. Given our motivating contradiction, we will suggest that it is less fruitful to regard EUD-research as applicable only to non-professional instances and it is worth to pursue a definition of end-user development driven by platform and outcome instead.

3   End-User Development Is an Evolving Concept

The term *end user* is arguably an invention of IBM in the 1950s [34]. It was used to point to people, such as corporate executives, who would be the budget holders responsible for commissioning the purchase of computing technology [42]. They were considered to be separate from *intermediate users*, usually experts who would operate the machines [45], working in units known as data processing departments, and tasked with performing computations in answer to questions posed to them by management.

In the 1960s and 1970s, solid state transistors and the microchip brought speed and power to mainframes, and gave rise to minicomputers. Computing became dramatically cheaper and thus more accessible to members of organizations working outside of data processing centers. The end users were now people with access to machines, and computing departments started dealing with the strategies for organizations to provide their members with access to applications of the enterprise, as well as manage their workload.

As the trend continued in the late 1970s and 1980s, employees were able to procure their own personal microcomputers [4] independently of a dedicated department. End users were now the users of application software which they did their own data processing with. The field of End-User Computing (EUC) came more prominently into being, specifically concerned with enabling and supporting computing performed by employees within organizational settings. Growing demand for software solutions led EUC research to consider how to enable these end users to become developers of their own programs [36], and practice End-User Programming (EUP).

For the purpose of studying the use of computers in organizational settings, several taxonomies of users were proposed [11,13,36,48], examining what sort of use was made of Information Systems and for what purposes. Classifications of this sort make sure to set apart data-processing professionals, who are employed to write code for others. Workers of the organization, who are trained in other domains but write code, are classified as amateurs [36] and are considered to only write code for themselves [56], evidently so because they are not employed to write code for others in the first place. It should be noted that data-processing professionals are designated thus by decree of the organization. Demand for such workers was too great to fulfill by sourcing them from specific educational backgrounds or certifications, as is the case with members of a traditional professional class, and in order for employees to qualify for the computing-related departments, organizations would oftentimes have to provide specialized training [50].

Therefore, each role of programmer is essentially fixed to the department's mission, with employees of the data processing department considered to be the professional ones. As a result, EUP is not concerned with programming professionals because it is not concerned with the data-processing department, and not necessarily because the professionals do not carry out similar tasks or do not need to be supported in similar ways, e.g. by making the understanding or modification of code more accessible for those just-starting professionals who do not yet have vast experience. This organizational distinction is perhaps the reason why end-user developers are juxtaposed against professional developers, to this day.

During this time and into the 1990s, the Graphical User Interface (GUI) was popularized, and desktops became more user-friendly, and were adopted even more widely. As one of the main reasons to purchase desktop computers for offices, the electronic spreadsheet became one of the most popular applications for data processing by end users. It offered an easy to understand and visually manipulate data, and allowed users to perform bulk operations on it in ways more intuitive than the type definitions, loops and memory management of typical programming. It became one of the most prominent success stories in literature for EUP [8].

Gradually, EUC in organizations became less concerned with application software and EUP. Data processing departments evolved into Information Technology (IT) departments, managing the technology infrastructure which allowed an organization to run, i.e. hardware, networks, software licences and data storage, and supporting end-users in accessing it. Availability, scalability and security became the more central issues.

EUP moved into the domain of Human Computer Interaction (HCI) [40], where research was invested in understanding and supporting programming tasks, both as a general issue, and also within specific application domains. As computing became a staple of daily life in various forms, discussions on EUP also became disentangled from organizational settings. More recently, in the 2000s, research programs in the European Union and in the United States brought about EUD as defined by Lieberman et al. [32] and EUSE as discussed by Ko et al. [29], and which we discussed in Sect. 2. In both research programs, the contrast of end-users against professional programmers from the EUC days of large organizational settings has been carried over into the modern wider landscape of software development.

Regardless, it is easy to identify parallels between concerns that EUD pursues, and advances in software development practice. In Table 1 we list such counterparts to EUD pursuits surveyed by Patterno [44]. In the following section we will argue that many of the advances that are considered part of modern professional programming, are essentially EUD advances.

4   Software Development Is an Evolving End-User Development Practice

It can be argued that programmers have always tried to build platforms that would allow them to function as end-user developers on. That is, as people who want to get their work done and should not have to care about (some aspects of) the computer, as in Nardi [41]. We maintain that the evolution of computer programming and its related tools is very much an EUD success story.

Historically, many advances in computer programming have come in the form of layers of abstraction, whereby two things are achieved; the creator of the abstraction is able to suppress details of the underlying layers, which are irrelevant

Table 1. EUD pursuits and corresponding advances in software development practice

End-User Development (EUD) pursuits	EUD examples from development practice
A main goal in EUD is to reduce the learning effort that might be required to produce non-simple/complex functionality	Programming languages share similar goals. Features such as garbage collection and dynamic typing make for simpler languages, and less bureaucratic code that is easier to modify. IDE[a]-features like predictive text are helpful too
Some EUD approaches aim to enable users to compose and customize sets of available basic elements, which other programmers have developed	A lot of software libraries are produced in service of such goals, e.g., by packaging complex processes into simple purpose-specific function calls with accessible names and simpler argument lists[b]. Many examples can be found across systems of libraries specializing in GUI, audio, graphics, I/O, numerical methods, etc.
EUD investigates collaboration processes and environments, bur the diversity of the backgrounds of people involved might raise special concerns	Yet many software projects employ very different roles, requiring not only software design and coding, but also the facilitation of design processes, the production of sketching and prototyping materials, or documentation. Online collaboration tools support many of these tasks, using intuitive interfaces when GUIs are involved, or accessible syntax of text[c], for producing and sharing materials
A central issue of EUD is the discovery and utilization of intuitions, metaphors, and concepts familiar to the domain of interest so that designs can be explored and specifications for software can be produced	UX design methods, requirements elicitation, and agile practices aim to understand the domain in which a piece of software is meant to function, and derive the specifications, according to which it can be built so that it is effective and intuitively usable

[a] Integrated Development Environments (IDEs) are classes of applications that automate much of the work that goes into software development, e.g., maintaining code libraries and versioning, compilation, linking. They often include helper applications for writing code visually, e.g., UI editors where drag and dropping interface elements on a canvas generates blocks of code.

[b] An exemplar of this is jQuery, a JavaScript library for Web-browsers, mainly for manipulation of the Document Object Model (DOM), which is the data structure web browsers use to represent an HTML document programmatically. jQuery was ubiquitous in web development in the late 2000s and early 2010s. It provides a uniform Application Programming Interface (API) across all browsers, which at the time still had significant differences in their implementation of the DOM, offered higher level helper functions (e.g., click() on top of addEventListener()), which could also operate on aggregate objects and which are chainable, making for terse and easy to read programs.

[c] Markdown is an example of this, which is a now ubiquitous plain-text formatting language that keeps the original text readable, but also contains formatting instructions for parsers to produce rich documents e.g., in HTML.

to the programming task, and also to invent and express the model of a machine which is more relevant to the task, and perhaps even already familiar to the user of that abstraction [33].

In more detail, after initial innovations in performing binary operations with relays and switches [52] and the first electronic computers in the 40s, the 50s saw the rise of the stored program and the programmable computer, where the hardware does not need to be re-wired per program. Adams [1] discusses how subroutines, accessible as symbols of abbreviated words make it possible for the increasing number of computer users to produce usable programs of numerical analysis. His focus lies on allowing entry level programmers to achieve results, and envisions that a verbal statement of the problem will be sufficient for the computer of the future.

In subsequent years, a host of programming languages and compilers were invented by people who wished to program computers in terms closer to their level of expertise or to their application domain. Many of the innovations we regard today as arcane programming tools, were driven by the personal needs of their inventors to get their job done. For example, FORTRAN, offering a way to define algebraic expressions, was heralded as a "revolution", one that would "have engineers, scientists, and other people actually programming their own problems without the intermediary of a professional programmer" [18]. UNIX came into being because of the desire of its makers to have their own time-sharing system [47]. Programming languages at levels higher than Assembly, such as C, offer programmers the model of an abstracted computer, and allow them to (largely) not care about the particulars of the hardware itself. Fischer [20] acknowledges the promise of these innovations for making systems more "convivial" [26] a term which designates technologies that foster creative connections amongst people and their environments, combative to the alienation suffered on account of industrialization [10], being treated as mere consumers.

Innovations with regard to making code reusable, rendered so by programming-language constructs such as classes, objects, encapsulation, and distributing as code libraries, is a way of making these software artifacts end-user programmable. Notably, programmers in their daily practice set intermediate personal goals to structure their code in such ways as to build abstractions and interfaces and hide its complexity, so as to later render themselves end-users of it, and make it easier for themselves to get their job done by using it as a functional unit.

Furthermore, software development is not a single domain, and does not imply a uniform technical profile of a practitioner [15]. Different developers hone their craft on vastly different technical or creative problems, have domain knowledge on different levels of abstraction within the software-hardware stack, many of which have their own elaborate theoretical backgrounds (e.g. graphics programming vs database programming) and are end-users of various tools and platforms in order to carry out their work. Illustrative of this are job listings seeking programmers, which advertise not only for a particular application domain (e.g. front-end development) or a specific programming language (e.g. JavaScript) but for familiarity with specific code libraries and APIs (e.g. Angular vs React). It can very well be the case that the pro in one field is naive in another.

There's also a large selection of software tools in support of communities. Those involved in a project or making use of it can share their issues and seek support on how to solve problems in knowledge markets like StackOverflow. They can report bugs and propose desired features in issue trackers. They pull ready to use components from package managers which manage their updates automatically. They can put up for discussion and run programs in code sandboxes so that others do not have to replicate their development environment in order to view them. Such tools provide rich avenues for facilitating cultures of participation, which is also a vision for EUD [19].

5   Professional Software Development

In the previous sections we have seen that so-called professional computer-programming and software-development domains are regarded as separate from end-user development, to a large extent due to legacy organizational points of view for each practice. We have also pointed out that in many respects, as evidenced by directions in which computer programming practice has evolved, professionals pursue methods and tools that lessen the effort of their practice and increase the reliability of their outcomes, in directions parallel to those that EUD does. In this section we will examine various implications of the term *professional* as is applied to software development, and why it is not the best way to, by negation, define end-user development.

5.1   Connotations of Professionalism

The definition of the professional is a complex subject of sociology, and several approaches exist in establishing criteria by which to identify professionals, and the processes through which occupations become professions. Visiting the main trends through which sociology discusses professions and professionals, will give us some indication of the rich and complex landscape against which these discussions take place.

Trait-based views [23] derive sets of characteristics that distinguish a profession from an occupation, such as having an organized body of knowledge from which the provision of services flows, and having autonomy from employing organizations and authority over the recipients of their services (i.e., having clients, not customers). This authority is sanctioned by the community at large, imparted through accreditation by controlled training centers, and regulated through a formally established code of ethics. The distinction that such traits provide is considered to be quantitative, not qualitative [23], therefore occupations that are not professional will be found to also possess them, but to a lesser degree. This places any given occupation on a spectrum of professionalization, where at one end the traditional professions can be found (e.g., physician, attorney, scientist) and at the other those that completely lack these traits.

Various views examine how occupations become professions. The functionalist view regards the ways in which professions function for the benefit of the larger societal context, and examines interactions between professions, society and structures of authority such as the state or military. Professions provide services based on knowledge that is that is both of great importance, and that could be harmful if abused. They ideally support social responsibility and contribute to the avoidance of authoritarianism and anarchy [16, page 17].

On the other hand, the conflict approach examines the process of professionalization, as motivated by the endemic self-interests of the professionals. Traits such as certification and licensing, regulated by professional associations, are seen as devices for occupational control, restricting the supply of labour and enhancing the status and earnings of the professional. To sustain such control, professional associations must also attend to the quality of their services [16, page 18].

Evidently, professions and the professionals are created through complex dynamic societal processes, and can have different expressions in different locales, e.g., they are often purposefully shaped by state policies. Therefore, professionalism cannot be reduced to mere technical expertise (as is the case with EUC), which is the focal point in organizational settings [17, page 100]. To do so, would be to exclude from consideration influential demands on the shape of both the professionals' modes of performing work, but also the realms of their responsibility. Many skilled labourers call themselves professionals, but they do so, as many others who perform skilled labour, within and in reference to the complexities and their manner of developing their knowledge, practicing their vocation and offering their services along their career path. Used in daily life, the term *professionalism* conveys the colloquial sense, and can be considered the opposite of amateur, associated with performing the work for payment, or not botching the job, concepts which aren't necessarily mutually exclusive.

5.2 Software Development Does Not Have a Singular Model of Labour

Developers of software in particular take up the occupation through a variety of paths, not all of which originate from academic education [54]. Indicatively, McConnell [35], summarising published demographics [24,53,55], notes how in the USA, there are 50,000 new developers each year, but only 35,000 software-related degrees are awarded each year. Muffatto [38, page 50] presents the findings of several studies on the demographics of open source developers, according to which, in terms of education 20% have just a high school degree, and in terms of professional background, 20% are students in academia. Paterno [44] states that "more and more applications are being written not by professional developers, but people with expertise in other domains". Developers can arrive from academic education, to training on the job, to self-study. The roles that participate in the making of software have expanded and diversified as computers acquire more capabilities and form factors. For example, whereas before the era of multimedia, in the 1980s, it was enough to have the skills of a computer programmer, in the era of the World Wide Web it became crucial to employ the skills of a graphic designer. Nowadays the development of many types of software is increasingly an interdisciplinary effort, populated both by professionals in the more traditional sense, with education and certification in their own fields, and knowledge workers of more recent fields of expertise that take part in software development. For example, user-facing pieces of software have contributions from User Experience (UX) designers or psychologists (such as workplace psychologists) who pay attention to requirements, or projects with frequent update cycles employ experts in tools for Continuous Integration/Continuous Deployment (CI/CD).

As software permeates ever more aspects of daily life, its misfunctions, which happen by unintended design [21], can effect loss of income[2], amplify inequality[3] or even cost lives[4]. There is therefore very active discussion within software development communities but also in legal, governmental circles, and society at large, with regard to the greater responsibility that needs to be taken up by software developers, providers, and the regulation of their services. However, software development as such, still lacks the training, qualifications, and modes of regulation that are associated with the traditional professions [39]. There is yet no standard of care that software development professionals can be expected to uphold when cases are tried in legal courtrooms [9]. Potentially, a trajectory could be charted where future legislators will require certain types of software development to be carried out in the more traditionally professional sense, while others not.

To illustrate the different modes in which software can be produced, the diversity of roles that may take up its production, as well as how ubiquitous it is becoming in modern societies, it may be useful to draw analogies to the production, preparation and use/distribution/consumption of food in various settings, and the diversity of configurations in which this activity can be encountered[5]. Food is produced, processed, prepared, and consumed at various levels of preparation, and engages a wide range of workers with equally varying expertise, from highly trained, expert chefs who explore novel gastronomic horizons, to teenagers assembling hamburgers out of industrially manufactured compo-

---

[2] The cost of poor quality software in the US in 2018 was estimated to be approximately $2.84 trillion dollars, the largest component of which (37.46%) were losses from software failures, at $1.064 trillion [30].

[3] opaque algorithms assessing the risk of an offender repeating a crime, heavily used in the judicial system of the USA, have been suspect of encoding societal and racial biases [25], resulting in harsher punishments [43].

[4] The two fatal accidents of the Boeing 737 MAX aircraft in 2018 and 2019 have been attributed to Boeing's introduction of a software component, called the Maneuvering Characteristics Augmentation System (MCAS), which was working against the pilot's maneuvers. MCAS was unique to that aircraft, and its existence had largely been kept quiet [27].

[5] The choice of analogy is not unfamiliar. Algorithms are often compared to food recipes [28], and there is an abundance of programming "Cookbooks" for various frameworks and Software Development Kits (SDKs) or problem domains. One important exception is that to a certain extent, food production is more regulated than software.

nents, and of course also in non-professional environments, e.g., at home, for own consumption. They ways in which all handlers of food oversee the supply of materials, create recipes, and execute them, do have aspects that are specific to the person's particular position (e.g., freedom for initiative, or supply of special materials and tools), but also many other aspects (tools, methods and raw or processed materials) are shared widely across all configurations, irrespectively of whether they function as professionals or not.

Such is the diversity of configurations that can found in the production of software as well, e.g., having highly tailored solutions created for unique clients by highly specialized experts, or maintaining legacy systems from past eras of computing, or customizing the same blueprint for different customers. There is of course art, craft, and science in many stages of software development, and a growing, detailed body of knowledge with regard to good practices for producing software [7]. However, not all the components that make up a software product are developed in the same way. For example, even while inventing novel solutions for a particular problem, a developer will be the end user of packaged components that encapsulate often complex functionality. There is therefore no way to exclude particular methods or tools from the arsenal of anything that might for any number of reasons be considered professional practice.

If EUD's goal to facilitate design exploration, specification and implementation of software artifacts, and produce methods and systems that make problem solving through programming more accessible for people who would not be expected to develop software without its interventions, then it can provide similar benefits, such as easier implementation of complex functionality and greater accessibility to unfamiliar systems and to people who do develop software. Moreover, the methods and tools that EUD produces can certainly constitute means, with which software services that bear professional characteristics can be built.

As history has shown, (professional) developers will take up this challenge to empower themselves anyway. Taking these into account, given how software development has changed since the first investigations of EUP, and the multiple connotations of professionalism, it might now be opportune to explore other directions for defining end-user development, than continuing to use the professional/non-professional dichotomy. Table 2 shows how end-user development can be a concern orthogonal to professionalism, not opposite to it.

Table 2. Disentangling end-user development from professionalism allows more nuance in classifying development activities. Here, four broad-spectrum examples of domain and platform are mentioned, but further nuance can be afforded as one looks at different sub-problems and how they are solved.

	End-user development	Technical development
Amateur	Excel macros with Visual Basic For Applications	Home automation with Raspberry Pi
Professional	Interactive UI prototyping with inVision	Game development with the Unreal Engine

6   Replacing Professional Development with Technical Development

If professionalism is a concern independent from end-user development, then we propose that the term *technical development* take its place as the notion that is opposite to end-user development. In his Theoretical Introduction to Programming, Mills [37] devotes a section to the notion of Technical Programming:

> Technical programming is about defining a specific problem as clearly as possible, and obtaining a clear solution.[...] It has much in common with the technical (rather than bureaucratic) aspects of all engineering disciplines.[...] Precise sub-problems are identified.[...] What is or is not technical, depends on the techniques available.

The term *technical* translates only to the characteristics of the development task itself, not the person performing it, and denotes the kind of engagement with problem-solving that demands good grounding in methodology, and the ability to identify sub-problems and to give structure to the problem domain [37]. For example, where end-user programming would consist of, e.g., using function calls on a platform/abstraction, Technical Programming would be building the platform/abstraction in the first place, and exposing the functions that subsequently end-user programmers can call.

Software is developed on some sort of platform, or if viewed in greater detail, various components of a larger piece of software are developed on several complementary platforms. A Platform is a framework (be it hardware or software) that supports other programs. Platform studies [5] offer the theoretical framework both for conducting a discourse on platforms and when and whether it is useful to view a given system as such [6], not only from a technical, but also from a cultural perspective. We can regard as platform the hardware of a computer, an operating system, an API (e.g. OpenGL), a toolkit (such as Qt), or an application such as the Web-browser. Platforms that enable software development, expose concepts to the user in which certain types of problems and solutions can be directly expressed. For example, a programming language like C enables one to write loops, so when iterating over a set of instructions is the issue, there is a concept available directly related to that. Likewise, Matlab offers a function for computing the Discrete Fourier Transform (DFT) of a signal, so a solution that can be expressed in terms of a DFT can be supported by that platform.

A platform then enables end-user development for a given task, to the extent that it offers readily accessible functionality, that allows the task to be accomplished in more or less straightforward ways (e.g., a certain function call), rather than requiring the implementation of deeper-layered functionality in order to later enable it. On the other hand, technical development occurs to the extent that the concepts that are related to a particular solution also need to be developed, in order then to be used.

7 Resolution of the Contradiction

We propose that a platform-driven lens can be developed to help determine the nature of one's software development task at a specific point in time, as being end-user development or technical development, and to what degree. In adopting a platform-driven view, one would have to acknowledge that end-user development is part and parcel of any creative programming endeavour, and practiced routinely alongside technical development in professional or other settings, since making use of the abstractions a platform offers, is to perform end-user development on it. As these abstractions are used in the service of solving more technical problems, so does the development task become of a technical nature, possibly leading to a new layer of abstraction, and the cycle repeats.

A platform-driven view can help avoid the contradiction that comes up in our motivating case of clinical psychologists writing Ambulatory Assessment (AA) programs, where the twofold intent these researchers pursue in writing and distributing their data-collection programs can have their work classified as either opposite, i.e., end-user development or professional development. In a platform-drive view, when the encode tasks of their own problem domain as programs, expressed in familiar terms by way of purposely-built tools, or software components, the perform end-user development, but in cases when deeper layers of system functionality needs to be accessed to implement constructs of the higher-level domain, development becomes more technical in nature.

For example, Batalas et al. [3] offer a set of components written in HTML5, which render user interfaces for data input when invoked. These components constitute a layer built on top of the syntactic structural elements of a web-page as defined by the W3C standard (e.g., div, span, p), and provide a way to write a web-application for data collection using terminology of the researcher's domain instead. By using these components, the researchers perform end-user programming, but they would have to do more technical work if they wanted to produce new interfaces at the same semantic level, since they would have to have knowledge of the underlying layer, which is the web-browser with its Document Object Model, Document Flow, Cascading Style Sheets and JavaScript APIs.

8 Conclusion

The roles of the end-user and the developer are largely inventions of the platform being used each time. In other words, it is not only the case that users, who put requirements forward, and developers, who design and write the code, shape software platforms. It also happens that through the conventions they employ, abstractions that they put forward and types of work they allow, software platforms also in effect bring into being the substance of what their end-users or those who develop on them do. As the platforms evolve through history, so does our understanding of who the end-user developers are and what they do, and so do the definitions of end-user development that researchers consider representative.

In this work however, we have avoided stating any particular wording for another definition of end-user development, and we regard this to be out of the scope of the discussion presented here. Rather, we consider it more productive to submit the points made here to the consideration of the researchers in the field and hopefully enrich relevant discourse. These points include the legacy origins of viewing end-user development as opposite to professional development, the extent to which this view is representative of modern software-development configurations, and the possibility to instead account not for the identity or role of the developer, nor for their intent in developing a piece of software, but for the nature of the task (i.e. how technical it is) when performed on a given platform.

Increasingly, software development takes place on such multiple layers of abstraction, with platforms and tools for the construction of software already delivered to the developers, that an end-user development aspect is always involved. For this reason, we propose that a platform-driven view of end-user development, inclusive of all types of developers as beneficiaries of EUD's findings, could better reflect this state of things and, in this manner, better anticipate the future.

References

1. Adams, C.W.: Small problems on large computers. In: Proceedings of the 1952 ACM National Meeting (Pittsburgh), pp. 99–102 (1952)
2. Barricelli, B.R., Cassano, F., Fogli, D., Piccinno, A.: End-user development, end-user programming and end-user software engineering: a systematic mapping study. J. Syst. Softw. **149**, 101–137 (2019)
3. Batalas, N., Khan, V.J., Franzen, M., Markopoulos, P., aan het Rot, M.: Formal representation of ambulatory assessment protocols in html5 for human readability and computer execution. Behav. Res. Methods **51**(6), 2761–2776 (2019). https://doi.org/10.3758/s13428-018-1148-y
4. Benson, D.H.: A field study of end user computing: findings and issues. Mis Quarterly, pp. 35–45 (1983)
5. Bogost, I., Montfort, N.: New media as material constraint: an introduction to platform studies. In: Electronic Techtonics: Thinking at the Interface. Proceedings of the First International HASTAC Conference, pp. 176–193 (2007)
6. Bogost, I., Montfort, N.: Platform studies: frequently questioned answers. Digital Arts Culture **2009** (2009)
7. Bourque, P., Fairley, R.E. (eds.): SWEBOK: Guide to the Software Engineering Body of Knowledge. IEEE Computer Society, Los Alamitos, CA, version 3.0 edn. (2014). http://www.swebok.org/
8. Burnett, M., Cook, C., Rothermel, G.: End-user software engineering. Commun. ACM **47**(9), 53–58 (2004). https://doi.org/10.1145/1015864.1015889
9. Choi, B.H.: Software as a profession. Harvard J. Law Technol. **33** (2020)
10. Clearver, H.: Industrialism or capitalism? conviviality or self-valorization? (1987). https://la.utexas.edu/users/hcleaver/hmconillich.html
11. Committee, C.E.U.F., et al.: Codasyl end user facilities committee status report (1979)
12. Conner, T.S., Mehl, M.R.: Ambulatory assessment: Methods for studying everyday life. Emerging Trends in the Social and Behavioral Sciences: An Interdisciplinary, Searchable, and Linkable Resource (2015)

13. Cotterman, W.W., Kumar, K.: User cube: a taxonomy of end users. Commun. ACM **32**(11), 1313–1320 (1989)
14. Cypher, A., Halbert, D.C.: Watch What I Do: Programming by Demonstration. MIT Press, Cambridge (1993)
15. Denning, P.J.: Computing the profession. In: Computer Science Education in the 21st Century, pp. 27–46. Springer (2000)
16. Dent, M., Bourgeault, I.L., Denis, J.L., Kuhlmann, E.: The Routledge Companion to the Professions and Professionalism. Routledge (2016)
17. Elliott, P.R.C.: The sociology of the professions. Macmillan International Higher Education (1972)
18. Ensmenger, N.L.: The Computer Boys Take Over: Computers, Programmers, and the Politics of Technical Expertise. MIT Press, Cambridge (2012)
19. Fischer, G.: End-user development and meta-design: foundations for cultures of participation. In: Pipek, V., Rosson, M.B., de Ruyter, B., Wulf, V. (eds.) IS-EUD 2009. LNCS, vol. 5435, pp. 3–14. Springer, Heidelberg (2009). https://doi.org/10.1007/978-3-642-00427-8_1
20. Fischer, G., Girgensohn, A.: End-user modifiability in design environments. In: Proceedings of the SIGCHI Conference on Human Factors in Computing Systems, pp. 183–192 (1990)
21. Floridi, L., Fresco, N., Primiero, G.: On malfunctioning software. Synthese **192**(4), 1199–1220 (2015)
22. Froehlich, J., Chen, M.Y., Consolvo, S., Harrison, B., Landay, J.A.: MyExperience: a system for in situ tracing and capturing of user feedback on mobile phones. In: MobiSys'07: Proceedings of the 5th International Conference on Mobile Systems, Applications and Services, pp. 57–70. ACM (2007). https://doi.org/10.1145/1247660.1247670
23. Greenwood, E.: Attributes of a profession. Social work, pp. 45–55 (1957)
24. Hecker, D.E.: Occupational employment projections to 2012. Monthly Lab. Rev. **127**, 80 (2004)
25. Huq, A.Z.: Racial equity in algorithmic criminal justice. Duke LJ **68**, 1043 (2018)
26. Illich, I., Lang, A.: Tools for conviviality (1973)
27. Johnston, P., Harris, R.: The boeing 737 max saga: lessons for software organizations. Softw. Quality Prof. **21**(3), 4–12 (2019)
28. Knuth, D.E.: The Art of Computer Programming, vol. 1. Addison-Wesley, Massachusetts (1973)
29. Ko, A.J., et al.: The state of the art in end-user software engineering. ACM Comput. Surv. **43**(3), 1–44 (2011). https://doi.org/10.1145/1922649.1922658. http://portal.acm.org/citation.cfm?doid=1922649.1922658
30. Krasner, H.: The cost of poor quality software in the us: A 2018 report. Consortium for IT Software Quality, Tech. Rep 10 (2018)
31. Lieberman, H.: Your Wish is my Command: Programming by Example. Morgan Kaufmann, San Francisco (2001)
32. Lieberman, H., Paternò, F., Klann, M., Wulf, V.: End-user development: an emerging paradigm. In: Lieberman, H., et al. (eds.) End User Development, pp. 1–8. Springer, Dordrecht (2006). https://doi.org/10.1007/1-4020-5386-X_1
33. Liskov, B., Zilles, S.: Programming with abstract data types. ACM Sigplan Notices **9**(4), 50–59 (1974)
34. Mackay, W.E.: Users and customizable software: a co-adaptive phenomenon. Ph.D. thesis, Citeseer (1990)
35. McConnell, S.: Code Complete, 2nd edn. Microsoft Press (2004). http://portal.acm.org/citation.cfm?id=1096143

36. McLean, E.R.: End users as application developers. MIS quarterly, pp. 37–46 (1979)
37. Mills, B.I.: Theoretical Introduction to Programming. Springer Science & Business Media, New York (2005)
38. Muffatto, M.: Open source: a multidisciplinary approach, vol. 10. World Scientific (2006)
39. Muzio, D., Ackroyd, S., Chanlat, J.-F.: Introduction: lawyers, doctors and business consultants. In: Muzio, D., Ackroyd, S., Chanlat, J.-F. (eds.) Redirections in the Study of Expert Labour, pp. 1–28. Palgrave Macmillan UK, London (2008). https://doi.org/10.1057/9780230592827_1
40. Myers, B.A., Ko, A.J., Burnett, M.M.: Invited research overview: end-user programming. In: CHI'06 Extended Abstracts on Human Factors in Computing Systems, pp. 75–80 (2006)
41. Nardi, B.A.: A Small Matter of Programming: Perspectives on End User Programming. The MIT Press, Cambridge (1993)
42. Noyes, J., Baber, C.: User-Centred Design of Systems. Springer Science & Business Media, New York (1999)
43. Pasquale, F.: Secret algorithms threaten the rule of law (2018)
44. Paternò, F.: End user development: survey of an emerging field for empowering people. ISRN Softw. Eng. **2013**, 11 (2013)
45. Plusch, S.P.: The evolution from data processing to information resource management. Technical report, ARMY WAR COLL CARLISLE BARRACKS PA (1984)
46. Repenning, A., Ioannidou, A.: What makes end-user development tick? 13 design guidelines. In: Lieberman H., et al. (eds.) End User Development. Human-Computer Interaction Series, vol. 9, pp. 51–85. Springer, Dordrecht (2006)
47. Ritchie, D.M., Thompson, K.: The unix time-sharing system. Bell Syst. Tech. J. **57**(6), 1905–1929 (1978)
48. Rockart, J.F., Flannery, L.S.: The management of end user computing. Commun. ACM **26**(10), 776–784 (1983)
49. Rough, D., Quigley, A.: Jeeves-a visual programming environment for mobile experience sampling. In: 2015 IEEE Symposium on Visual Languages and Human-Centric Computing (VL/HCC), pp. 121–129. IEEE (2015)
50. Ruiz Ben, E.: Defining expertise in software development while doing gender. Gender, Work Organ. **14**(4), 312–332 (2007)
51. Segal, J.: Professional end user developers and software development knowledge. Department of Computing, Open University, Milton Keynes, MK7 6AA, UK, Tech. Rep (2004)
52. Shannon, C.E.: A symbolic analysis of relay and switching circuits. Electr. Eng. **57**(12), 713–723 (1938)
53. Snyder, T.D., Tucker, P., Stone, A.: Digest of education statistics. National Center for Education Statistics (2002)
54. Thayer, K., Ko, A.J.: Barriers faced by coding bootcamp students. In: Proceedings of the 2017 ACM Conference on International Computing Education Research, pp. 245–253 (2017)
55. US Bureau of Labor Statistics: Occupational Outlook Handbook 2004–05 edition. Bureau of Labor Statistics (2004)
56. Weinberg, G.M.: The psychology of computer programming; 1971. von Nostrand Reinhold, New York (1998)

An End-User Development Approach to Secure Smart Environments

Bernardo Breve[1], Giuseppe Desolda[2(✉)], Vincenzo Deufemia[1], Francesco Greco[2], and Maristella Matera[3]

[1] Computer Science Department, University of Salerno, Fisciano, Italy
{bbreve,deufemia}@unisa.it
[2] Computer Science Department, University of Bari Aldo Moro, Bari, Italy
{giuseppe.desolda,francesco.greco}@uniba.it
[3] Department of Electronics, Information and Bioengineering,
Politecnico di Milano, Milan, Italy
maristella.matera@polimi.it

Abstract. Given the spread of the Internet of Things (IoT) technology, in several contexts there is a growing need for laypeople to configure their smart devices. Task Automation Systems (TASs) have emerged as tools to simplify the definition of rules for personalizing the behavior of such devices. However, one aspect often neglected by current TASs, which is instead typical of IoT technologies, relates to the security and privacy threats exposed by the "connected" devices. This paper tries to address this problem and illustrates a user-centered design that eventually led to identify a visual paradigm that facilitates the end users in understanding and controlling security and privacy threats.

Keywords: End-user development · Internet of Things · Cyber security

1 Introduction

Many environments we live in include multiple connected devices. The Internet of Things (IoT) has indeed favored the development of the so-called *smart objects*, which are digital devices embedding sensors and/or actuators. Since they are also able to connect to the Internet, the peculiarity of such devices is that they can communicate to create ecosystems of heterogeneous and distributed services [5]. Let us think to smart homes where people can install IP cameras, smart vacuum cleaners, smart appliances (e.g., washing machine, drying machine) and synchronize them to facilitate and optimize their tasks (e.g., surveillance, energy optimization, house cleaning).

Given the spread of such technology also in contexts where lay people need to configure their devices, in the last years, Task Automation Systems (TASs) have emerged as tools to support non-technical users in defining the personalized behavior of smart objects. By exploiting proper visual mechanisms, TASs facilitate the definition of Event-Condition-Action (ECA) rules, a programming paradigm commonly adopted for specifying a smart object's behavior. For example, IFTTT is a popular tool that enables

© Springer Nature Switzerland AG 2021
D. Fogli et al. (Eds.): IS-EUD 2021, LNCS 12724, pp. 36–52, 2021.
https://doi.org/10.1007/978-3-030-79840-6_3

customizing smart devices through the visual definition of ECA rules in the form: "IF a smart object detects an event, THEN the same or a different smart object executes an action". With TASs the users can therefore take advantage of their smart objects by creating synchronizations that accommodate their everyday needs.

One aspect often neglected by current TASs, which is instead typical of IoT, is that "connected" smart objects are vulnerable in terms of security. These devices are an attractive target for external malicious attackers since they provide entry points to user's online services and physical devices [33, 39]. Also, data can be arbitrarily manipulated by attackers and cause damage. This problem is amplified when end users, not fully aware of these risks, put in communication devices by using TASs. In many situations, end users do not have sufficient skills in security and privacy, in particular when they deal with IoT devices [24]. In addition, they under-evaluate the importance of these aspects in defending their smart environments, thus they neglect countermeasures that might protect the security of their smart devices [1, 25].

This paper tries to address this problem and proposes a visual paradigm that supports users, even those who do not possess technical skills in IoT and security, in securing their smart environments. The paper's contributions refer to different aspects. After discussing some related works (Sect. 2), the paper introduces a new smart object, called *Intrusion Defender*, that can monitor and detect attacks against smart devices (Sect. 3). It then illustrates a design process carried out to identify abstractions that in TASs can support users in customizing the Intrusion Defender behavior (Sect. 4). Finally, it reports on a user study focusing on the usability of the proposed abstraction mechanisms (Sect. 5). The paper ends by discussing the main results of the evaluation study (Sect. 6) and outlining the future work (Sect. 7).

2 Background and Related Work

In the Internet of Things (IoT), different connected objects interact with each other, with human beings and with the environment to exchange data, reacting to real-world events, triggering actions and activating services [5]. This technological landscape provides great opportunities, new capabilities, but also risks and new problems. Indeed, the users' interaction with such objects can be monitored by unauthorized parties, their inappropriate use can generate undesired and unexpected effects and can activate a function of intelligent services that do not match the actual needs of the end users.

One research line that has gained momentum in the last years refers to the design of tools that allow the end users to control and customize the behavior of IoT devices installed in smart environments where they work or live. Several works highlight the benefits of combining IoT devices, i.e., sensors and actuators, and other software services by means of personalization techniques [31]. However, the strong heterogeneity of smart objects poses important challenges for the definition of methodologies and tools that can empower the end users to make sense of this promising technology [41]. End-User Development fits very well this problem [27] as it focuses on the design of tools that can allow the end users to compose the applications they use or to create brand new ones and to support work practices [12].

In relation to the EUD of IoT systems, event-driven, rule-based approaches have received interest, since end users can easily reason about contextual events and the corresponding behavior of their applications [43]. Different Web tools have revisited the trigger-action rule paradigm to address the problem of Task Automation (TA). In particular, Task Automation Systems (TASs) are software tools deployed as websites or mobile apps, that support non-technical users to configure the behavior of smart objects installed in a smart environment. Typically, the configuration occurs by a) graphically sketching the interaction among the objects (e.g., drawing graphs that represent how events and data parameters propagate among the different objects to achieve their synchronization), or b) visually defining Event-Condition-Action (ECA) rules, for example through wizard-like interfaces that guide the users through different steps of rule definition. TASs like Node-RED or Microsoft Flow provide graph-based notations that support a high degree of freedom in terms of customized behavior but do not match the mental model of most end users, especially those without technical skills [29]. On the other hand, tools like IFTTT, Zapier, and Atooma propose an easy-to-use visual paradigm for ECA rule definition, which can be easily mastered by most users; however, the notation has low expressive power and does not address complex requirements for smart object synchronization. Therefore, even if the paradigm ease of use offers several opportunities for the EUD of smart environments, the restricted expressive power limits the effectiveness of such tools. In particular, addressing security and privacy aspects is almost impossible, and this creates tension with the need to address the vulnerability of smart objects [28].

A smart environment can have different security and privacy issues. For example, data exchanged among smart objects can be intercepted by malicious attackers for fraudulent purposes [28]. Usually, smart objects are equipped with limited hardware given their small size and this limits the adoption of high-level security protocols or defensive systems inside the smart devices. Finally, smart objects are also exposed to physical tampering, wardriving, malicious software and side-channel attacks. It is therefore of paramount importance to provide TASs with mechanisms that can guide users while controlling the security of their smart environments.

According to [47], IoT environments should improve users' technology threat models, which enable the conscious management of privacy and security risks, and communicate best practices suitable for the smart spaces. Transferred into the EUD context, this recommendation implies that EUD environments should support users during the creation of rules, guiding possible privacy or security violations and ad-hoc elements in the rule definition language that can facilitate the definition and deployment of rules addressing these issues. Along this line of action, [39] defined security lattices to understand how the flow of statements within IFTTT recipes could lead to the generation of potential security risks. This is an interesting work, which suggests ways to extend TASs with debugging capabilities, but that, however, does not sufficiently empower the end users to configure the security of their smart environments. This is instead the goal of our work, which focuses on proper paradigms for the end users to become aware of possible security threats and be enabled to control them.

The EUD environment should also support end users in the management of access control and authentication to the smart objects. In this context, [22] suggested using a capability-centric model to fit the access control and authentication mechanisms to the variety of smart objects and features they can perform. For example, rather than allowing the users to have complete access to a smart object, a more adequate solution would be to configure the access schemes only on certain capabilities, such as turning on/off the device, update the software, and so on. This would also reduce the complexity of system configurations addressing security and privacy problems. In line with this recommendation, our work concentrated on identifying categories of attacks and related countermeasures that could make sense for the end users who have not sufficient knowledge in security aspects.

3 Intrusion Defender: A Smart Object to Secure Smart Environments

In order to extend TASs with security management capabilities, we built a smart object, called Intrusion Defender (ID), that monitors the network traffic of a private area network (PAN) to detect anomalous events. The events occurring on a PAN might originate from cyberattacks that a malicious individual could launch against a smart environment, e.g., a smart home, with the intent of stealing sensitive data acquired by smart objects or deactivating intrusion detection systems controlling the smart environment.

ID has been developed on top of Snort, a software monitoring and identifying network threats. It is an Open-Source Network Intrusion Detection System that monitors the packets of the network traffic, which travel to and from all smart objects in the smart environment. A network packet can carry data related to an exchange of information that takes place between a smart device and the Internet. Some features of this network traffic, e.g., the number of packets sent in a given time frame or the type of packets received and sent, provide important clues for identifying cyberattacks. By monitoring these features, which are called *signatures*, Snort can identify the intrusions by performing a fast comparison with the signatures contained within a database of pairs (attack, signature). Once an attack is identified, Snort generates an event reporting the main information about the attack. All the generated events are stored into a database.

To effectively defend a smart environment from external cyberattacks, Snort has to be configured to monitor the network locally, i.e., within the PAN. Indeed, it is not possible to remotely monitor the exchange of packets between smart devices of a PAN from outside the network. The individual smart devices communicate with the outside through the router, which masks the information generated by the smart objects. Thus, ID has been implemented as a smart object that acts as an intermediary in the communication between the smart devices and the router, by intercepting and analyzing the network traffic for possible network intrusions. This solution is also the safest from the data management point of view. In fact, a different solution would allow the smart devices to share their information externally so that the ID could retrieve this information remotely. However, this type of solution would expose the smart environment to an even higher risk since the communication could be intercepted by an external malicious attacker. Performing the network analysis locally avoids sharing more information than the one required by the smart devices to behave as they are designed to.

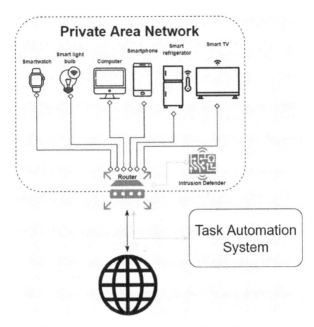

Fig. 1. Reference architecture for the secured smart home environment.

The ID has been installed on a Raspberry Pi, a particularly inexpensive single-board computer, small in size and low in energy consumption [9]. On the Rasberry Pi, therefore, the Snort software has been installed, the launch of which depends on the execution of some scripts, which contain the commands and parameters necessary for Snort to know the type of monitoring that must be carried out. The board also contains databases storing both the signature repository that Snort uses for analysis and the archive of all the events associated with cyberattacks that Snort can detect. The database is then made available to the other components of the smart environment.

Figure 1 summarizes the architecture of the smart environment after the installation of the Intrusion Defender. The previously established connections between the various smart objects and the router are preserved from the introduction of the ID within the PAN. Indeed, the ID behaves like any smart object connected to the smart home environment. Once connected, it analyzes the network packets by interacting with the router; when a cyberattack is detected, it sends the information about the identified event directly to the TAS.

Besides managing the detection of attacks at runtime, the TAS also provides the environment for configuring the rules defining countermeasures for security attacks. In our research, we adopted the EFESTO-5W platform, which offers a visual paradigm for ECA rule definition that has proved to be effective for different application domains [2–4, 7, 14]. In the following sections, we will illustrate the design process that eventually led to extending EFESTO-5W to support the definition of ECA rules covering ID events.

4 Design of Abstraction Mechanisms to Customize Smart Environments Security Through ECA Rules

The configuration of the ID device requires IT and cybersecurity expertise. For example, it reports the detected cyberattacks in a log file or in a dashboard, in both cases targeted to experts. However, countermeasures to defend the PAN devices must be taken by the user, who has to be aware of the meaning and level of risk of cyberattacks. Also, countermeasures like switching off the attacked devices must be configured by developing, for example, scripts in programming languages such as JavaScript or Python. Therefore, users with no expertise in IT and cybersecurity, who are the majority of the actual users of smart environments, would be excluded from the effective use of the ID, or in general, from the use of similar technical devices for cyber defense.

To solve these problems, this article proposes a solution to configure the behavior of the ID by using Task Automation Systems, and in particular EFESTO-5W. The final goal is to make possible the creation of Event-Condition-Action (ECA) rules that can be triggered when an attack is detected by the ID, for example, by defining a rule like *"IF the ID detects the attack X then switch off the attacked device"*. This research goal poses two main challenges. First, the ID is able to detect several attacks (35 in the current implementation), and this high number can overload the users with too much information. Second, the detected attacks refer to cybersecurity concepts (e.g., DDoS, man in the middle, etc.), which are too technical and complex for lay users.

To address the first challenge, a card sorting session was carried out with 11 IT and cybersecurity experts, to reduce the number of ID-detected attacks to be exposed to the users. All the possible attacks have been grouped based on their meaning and consequences on the attacked devices. For the identified groups, the event descriptions that the users can select when creating ECA rules have been designed by adopting the Communication-Human Information Processing (C-HIP) model [46]. C-HIP frames the most important activities and entities involved in the communication of a warning, and sets the foundation for structuring warning messages. Lastly, to make the description text clearer, we iteratively refined the descriptions of the events by using metrics for the evaluation of text comprehension, readability and sentiment. In the following, these activities are illustrated in detail.

4.1 A Card-Sorting Study to Reduce Information Overload

The definition of ECA rules by using TASs is the ground of the proposed solution. An example of ECA rules in smart homes might be "IF the motion sensor detects a person THEN switch on the smart lamp". Regardless of the visual metaphor implemented by a TAS, the definition of an ECA rule like this does not require technical IT knowledge but only knowing the smart objects' functionalities. However, when dealing with devices like the ID, the creation of an ECA rule could be more complex. Indeed, the events detected are exposed in the technical language (see the ID events reported in the Appendix), thus an ECA rule would be, for example, something like *"IF the ID detects an unusual client port connection on the device X THEN switch off device X"*. The number of all the possible events can be high and sometimes the differences between different events are related to technical nuances which might not be meaningful for non-technical users. In other words, a simplification of the ID events is required, in relation to both their multiplicity and technical description. For this purpose, as a first step, we conducted a card sorting session to identify groups of events to be represented by a unique name. Card sorting is a low-tech approach used to generate a dendrogram (category tree) or folksonomy [38]. It is widely used during the design of interactive systems to optimize the information architecture, menu item organization, or navigation paths. HCI expert identifies key concepts and reports them on cards (e.g., Post-it notes). A group of users, individually, are required to arrange the cards according to their preferences and following the study goal (e.g., structuring menu items). Typically, a number of 10/15 users is sufficient to obtain reliable results [34].

We recruited 11 IT and cybersecurity experts as study participants; two HCI experts then managed the study. Given the COVID-19 pandemic, the study was carried out remotely by using the *kardSort* platform [6]. Since the original ID events are often too short and meaningless, all of them were converted into a clearer description, so that participants can better understand their meaning and consequences of the detected attacks. For example, the original event "malware-cnc" was replaced with the description "Detected infected device sending system information to other infected devices"[1].

The final 35 descriptions were registered as cards in the kardSort platform and the study was set up as "open", meaning that no predefined categories were defined but the users were completely free to arrange the cards. In addition, an introductory text was added in kardSort to instruct participants they had to create groups containing cards reporting similar attacks (e.g., DoS and DDoS) and/or having the same consequences (e.g., that tries to collapse a device). The study lasted 2 days and each participant spent around 20 min.

Table 1. List of the final 6 groups and their original labels.

	Class	Labels
1	DOS	System-call-detect; denial-of-service; successful-dos; attempted-dos; misc-attack
2	Malware	Malware-cnc; shellcode-detect; inappropriate-content; trojan-activity; file-format; suspicious-filename-detect;
3	Privilege escalation	Attempted-user; unsuccessful-user; default-login-attempt; suspicious-login; successful-admin; successful-user; attempted-admin
4	Data exfiltration	sdf; web-application-attack; successful-recon-limited; successful-recon-largescale; attempted-recon
5	Suspicious connection	Misc-activity; tcp-connection; non-standard-protocol
6	Suspicious traffic	Protocol-command-decode; bad-unknown; client-side-exploit; web-application-activity; string-detect; unknown; network-scan; icmp-event; unusual-client-port-connection

[1] The complete list of the 35 original ID events and their extended descriptions (expressed in Italian) is reported in the Appendix at this link https://tinyurl.com/Q-EFESTO-ID.

The results have been analyzed by using Casolysis [40]. This tool implements two methods for the analysis of open tests, namely Hierarchical Clustering (Single Link, Average Link, Complete Link) and Section Label Analysis (SLA). For our analysis, we used the Average Link since it typically performs better than other solutions [37]. Finally, a threshold for the similarity of the clustering algorithm was set to 0.68/1 to obtain a low number of categories that include attacks that can reasonably stay in the same group. In the end, we obtained 6 groups of events, as reported in Table 1. The final groups represent the basis for the design of the final messages, as reported in the next section.

4.2 Design of the Event Description for the ID Smart Object

Reducing the 35 ID events in 6 groups solved the problem of the information overload that users might have if using the original ID events. However, this phase did not solve the problem of the technical skills required to understand the ID events. Therefore, we designed, for each group, a short title, and an event description that explains the attack and its consequences. Since the ID event can be seen as a warning event that users adopt in the ECA rule definition, as the ground of this design phase we used the Communication-Human Information Processing (C-HIP) model, which defines the critical route and sets the foundation for structuring warning messages [46].

The C-HIP model summarizes the most important activities and entities involved in the communication of a warning. The model starts with a source delivering a warning through a channel to a receiver, who then takes it along with other stimuli (environmental or internal) that subject the message to a lot of distractions or distortions. It then identifies a set of steps between the delivery of a warning and the user's final behavior or response, which is usually based on the effect of the various processes such warnings had undergone. In [46] the authors also define a set of design guidelines related to the C-HIP model and present rules for descriptive text: i) Briefly describe the risk and consequences of not complying with advice; ii) Illustrate clearly how to avoid the risk; iii) Be transparent and avoid technical jargon where possible; iv) Be as brief as possible.

- Based on prescriptions and guidelines of the C-HIP model, we designed the descriptions for the 6 ID events, generating them following a template purposely defined:

Title + Hazard Identification + Effects of a successful attack

The generation of these messages was carried out iteratively, considering metrics that perform static evaluations of the readability and sentiment of the event messages. Indeed, conveying the hazard messages to all users is not simple, as reported in [16, 23]. Readability metrics measure the degree to which a person can read, easily understand, and find interesting that text [13]. Among the most popular metrics, we used the Flesch Reading Ease formula, the Flesch-Kincaid Grade Level, and the SMOG formula [15, 18, 32]. The Flesch–Kincaid Reading indicates how difficult a text can be understood and it is measured in an interval between 1 and 100 [19]. The higher this score, the easier for a particular text to be read by the majority of people [15]. The Flesch–Kincaid Grade Level Test [18, 19] reflects the US education system needed to understand a text. It ranges from o to 18, where 0 indicates a basic level (learning to read a book) while 18 indicates an advanced level (an academic paper); the lower the easier it to read. The SMOG (Simple Measure of Gobbledygook) estimates the years of education a person needs to be able to comprehend a passage [36]. These three readability measures have been calculated by using the platform readable [35]. Regarding sentiment analysis, texts convey emotions which are key components to effectively communicate messages and to understand reactions to messages [42]. For warning messages, a negative valence is preferred to alert users about potential dangers. The text sentiment analysis was carried out by using the IBM Watson platform [45].

Table 2. Event messages and related readability and sentiment scores.

	Event message (title + description)	Flesch-kincaid	Flesch reading	SMOG index	Sent.
1	Someone is trying to collapse a smart device down!	5.0	75.5	8.8	– 0.74
	Someone is attacking one of your smart devices. This has the goal to make the device collapse	5.1	73.8	10.1	0.00
2	Virus threat in a smart device!	2.5	87.9	3.1	– 0.83
	A virus has infected one of your smart devices. This virus can compromise your device and your privacy (e.g., steal your files and passwords)	6.8	67.8	11.2	– 0.81
3	A hacker is breaking in a smart device!	3.8	82.4	3.1	0.62
	A non-authorized user has accessed one of your devices (or is trying to). If not stopped, this user may damage your device and steal your private data	5.9	77.8	8.8	0.00

(continued)

Table 2. (*continued*)

	Event message (title + description)	Flesch-kincaid	Flesch reading	SMOG index	Sent.
4	There's a danger of data theft from a smart device	3.7	86.7	3.1	− 0.50
	Someone is trying to steal your private data on one of your smart devices. This can threaten your privacy (e.g., pictures/video stolen)	6.9	66.4	10.1	− 0.92
5	A suspicious event has occurred in your network	6.7	61.2	8.8	0.00
	Someone is looking for vulnerabilities in your network. This event might reveal an incoming attack	9.4	41.3	8.8	− 0.85
6	Threats coming from outside your network	4.5	73.8	3.1	− 0.69
	Suspicious activity is going on against your network. Someone could be trying to attack and access your network	6.9	61.4	8.8	− 0.87

The resulting messages for the 6 ID events, as well as their final readability and sentiment scores, are reported in Table 2. The ID device and its events have been integrated into the EFESTO-5W platform. Figure 2 reports the visual representation in EFESTO-5W of an ECA rule to switch off a smart device (Hallway Camera in the example) when ID detects a virus threat in the smart device itself. A video illustrating the creation of ECA rules for the ID in EFESTO-5W is available at https://tinyurl.com/EFESTO-ID. The reported ECA rules refer to the six tasks administered in the evaluation study detailed in the next section.

5 Evaluation

To verify if end users, even without technical skills in IT and cybersecurity, are able to defend their smart environments by defining ECA rules based on the ID device, we conducted a controlled experiment. More formally, the study aims to answer the following research questions:

RQ1. "*Do the designed events enable the users to define ECA rules to protect a smart environment?*

Fig. 2. ECA rule created in EFESTO: it is triggered when a virus threat is detected in a smart device (Hallway Camera) and, in this case, executes the switch off of the attacked camera.

RQ2. "Are there differences between expert and non-expert users in defining ECA rules based on the Intrusion Defender device to protect a smart environment?".

5.1 Study Design and Participants

To answer the two research questions, we adopted a between-subject design, with users' skills as the independent variable. The two between-subject conditions are experts and non-experts. A total of 20 volunteers (6 females) were recruited. 9 of them were non-experts in IT and cybersecurity, while the remaining were mild experts (expertise assessed in a pre-test questionnaire). Their mean age was 27 years (SD = 7.04).

5.2 Procedure

Given the COVID-19 pandemic, the study was performed remotely. To facilitate the remote execution, a tool for remote user testing, eGLU-Box PA, was used [17]. Three evaluators (HCI experts) were involved. A total of 30 candidates among students, friends, family members and colleagues were contacted 5 days before the study by emails, SMS, and phone calls. Candidates were asked to fill in an online form providing demographic data, contact information and answer two questions on a self-evaluation of IT and cybersecurity skills. 20 candidates agreed and were recruited as participants. The evaluators sent an email to all the participants with a link to start the test in eGLU-Box PA, the description of the technical requirements (PC, webcam, microphone, a browser like Chrome, Firefox, or Edge and a stable internet connection), and information on the test duration (around 20 min) so that participants could freely decide when to perform the tests without interruptions and disturbances.

After opening eGLU-Box PA, participants were asked to sign a digital consent form and, if they agreed, eGLU-Box PA checked the functioning of all the peripherals devices needed for data collection (microphone, webcam and screen recording). If no technical problems were detected, eGLU-Box PA showed a video, which asks participants to complete a set of tasks according to a scenario in which a person who lives in a smart home needs to configure the security of some devices. Then, eGLU-Box PA randomly administered six tasks one at a time. For each task, all the participants had a maximum of 5 min. Each task is designed to cover each of the 6 events. Table 3 reports the tasks and the associated ID event. After the task execution, eGLU-Box PA administered the SUS (System Usability Scale) and NASA-TLX questionnaires.

Table 3. List of tasks and the related ID event.

Task instructions	ID event
T1. If a hacker is trying to switch off the lights in the house entrance and it's evening (between 7 pm and 4 am), then turn on the emergency lights outside and send a notification to your smartphone	1
T2. If a virus has infected your vacuum cleaner robot, then stop this robot	2
T3. If a hacker is trying to access your garage camera without your permission, then request to change your garage camera credentials by sending a notification to your email address	3
T4. If a hacker is trying to steal private data from your vacuum cleaner robot, then turn off this robot	4
T5. If a hacker is monitoring your network to try to identify vulnerabilities, then send a notification to your smartwatch	5
T6. If a hacker is attacking your network, then send a notification on your smartwatch	6

5.3 Data Collection and Analysis

To answer the two research questions, for each participant different quantitative and qualitative data were collected. Regarding the quantitative data, we gathered task completion time, task success (success, partial success and failure), SUS score for measuring perceived usability, and NASA-TLX index to assess the perceived workload [20, 21]. For SUS we also analyzed its sub-dimensions - Usability and Learnability [10, 26]. Regarding the qualitative data, significant comments made by the participants were annotated by reviewing the audio/video recordings.

Independent t-test was used to analyze task completion times, SUS scores and NASA-TLX index (they did not violate the normal distribution, the assessment has been performed by using Shapiro–Wilk's test). Pearson Chi-Square was used to analyze success results (nominal values). An alpha level of .05 was used for all statistical tests.

5.4 Results

Performance. The participants' performance was evaluated by measuring the task time and the task success. Regarding the task time, participants spent an average of 112 s to complete a task (only successful or partially successful tasks were computed). In particular, each task required the following time: T1 = 219 s, T2 = 69 s, T3 = 143 s, T4 = 66 s, T5 = 85 s, and T6 = 88 s. The t-test revealed that no differences exist between experts and non-experts in performing all 6 tasks (p = 0.60). A detailed analysis revealed that no differences persist for T1 (p = 0.886), T3 (p = 0.55), T4 (p = 0.224), T5 (p = 0.106) and T6 (p = 0.181) while for T2 a significant difference emerged (p = 0.039).

The analysis of the success rates revealed an overall positive performance of all the participants. The 6 tasks resulted in a 71% of success rate: T1 = 62.5%, T2 = 75%, T3 = 77.5%, T4 = 67.5%, T5 = 80%, and T6 = 67.5%. Pearson Chi-Square revealed that no differences exists between experts and non-experts ($\chi(1) = 2.209$, p = .331). No differences also emerged comparing task success of experts and non-experts for each task (T1: $\chi(1) = 2.229$, p = .317; T2: $\chi(1) = 3.300$, p = .069; T3: $\chi(1) = 2.424$, p = .298; T4: $\chi(1) = 2.181$, p = .336; T5: $\chi(1) = 0.202$, p = .904; T6: $\chi(1) = 1.694$, p = .429).

Perceived Usability. The perceived usability was assessed by analyzing the results of the SUS and NASA-TLX questionnaires. The SUS scores highlighted that, in general, a good usability level in creating ECA rules with ID (SUS Score: $\overline{x} = 83.9$, SD = 11.3; SUS Usability: $\overline{x} = 84.11$, SD = 11.4; SUS Learnability: $\overline{x} = 83.8$, SD = 20.7). No differences emerged in the SUS scores even in comparing experts and non-experts (SUS Score: p = .852; SUS Usability: p = .87, SUS Learnability: p = .394).

The analysis of the NASA-TLX results shows that participants' workload was quite low ($\overline{x} = 24.91$, SD = 12.34). No differences emerged in the workload of experts and non-experts (SUS Score: p = .852; SUS Usability: p = .87, SUS Learnability: p = .307).

6 Discussion

Concerning RQ1, interesting and promising results emerged. Indeed, the overall task success rate is 71%, which can be considered as a positive result. T1 was the most complex since it required to set two actions in the rule. It resulted in the lowest rate (62.5%); however, the analysis of media recording revealed that only one user selected the wrong ID event while 6 users selected one or two wrong actions. The other tasks obtained a higher success rate but some users selected the wrong events: three users for T5, four users for T2, T3, T6, and six users for T4. Focusin on T2, T3, T4 and T6 it emerges that users selected the wrong event more frequently, and a deeper investigation is needed to clarify the users' difficulties in identifying the right ID event. The analysis of video recordings and further reflections on the event descriptions led us to hypothesize that some descriptions can appear too similar to users who do not have a profound knowledge of possible malicious attacks; therefore, they are in trouble guessing which is the right one. This would imply a revision of the event taxonomy.

Even results on task time can be considered positive. Participants spent around 112 s creating the right ECA rule to defend the smart home. Only T1 required an average of 219 s; the analysis of the recorder media confirmed that the complexity of the task caused this higher time since two actions and temporal constraints had to be defined. These good performances have been confirmed by the perceived usability. Indeed, SUS scores (SUS Score: $\overline{x} = 83.9$, SD = 11.3; SUS Usability: $\overline{x} = 84.11$, SD = 11.4; SUS Learnability: $\overline{x} = 83.8$, SD = 20.7) highlighted an excellent usability: with respect to of one thousand studies reported in Bangor et al., SUS score above 68 are considered above the mean and scores above an 80.3 are in the top 10% of scores [8]. Similarly, NASA-TLX revealed that a low workload ($\overline{x} = 24.91$) was required to accomplish the 6 tasks.

With respect to RQ2, the results demonstrated that, in general, there are no differences between experts and non-experts. This result is very important since, typically, tools for advanced configurations are designed for professionals. This limitation is common, for example, for TASs that are created to suit the skills and mental models of technical users [44]. We can safely assume that, thanks to the abstraction mechanisms designed for the ID events, non-experts perform like experts. Of course, the study results are important because both users' performances and usability obtained positive results. The only emerged difference regards the task time spent for T2 since non-experts were slower. The analysis of the recorded media revealed that two users spent more time since they fixed the rule during their creation, in both cases because they selected the wrong action, i.e., switch off instead of stop.

Finally, an interesting behavior has been observed three times in T6. Two non-experts and one expert created the rule by adding two alternative events, i.e., the ones titled "A suspicious event has occurred in your network" and "Threats coming from outside your network". Even if the right event is the second one, this task was considered as a partial success since the created rule produces the expected behavior. However, this aspect deserves more attention since it might be the symptoms that the two events confuse users. For example, the aggregation of the two events into a new one could be a possible solution. Indeed, the two events (5 = A suspicious event has occurred in your network; 6 = Threats coming from outside your network) might appear quite similar and their distinction can easily confuse the users.

7   Conclusion and Future Work

This paper has illustrated a user-centered design that has focused on identifying how to make security and privacy threats easy to understand and control by laypeople. The resulting paradigm for the definition of ECA rules hides technical complexity by exposing to the users a reduced number of categories of threats grouping similar vulnerability problems, and by providing textual descriptions purposely enhanced to comply with text comprehension measures. In order to assess their validity, these mechanisms have been integrated into EFESTO-5W, a TAS that offers a visual, wizard-based paradigm for the definition of ECA rules. This integration has allowed us to conduct a comparative study that showed that non-expert users are enabled to define rules addressing security and privacy, with a performance comparable to one of the expert users. Although the study focused on the EFESTO-5W visual paradigm, we are confident that the general principles that guided the threat categorization and the definition of event descriptions are of general validity, and can be adopted to extend other TAS supporting the definition of ECA rules, e.g., IFTTT. Our future activities will be devoted to systematically assess the suitability of the approach also in other TASs.

Our future work will also focus on extending the visual environment for ECA rule definition to support rule debugging, following for example solutions such as the ones reported in [11, 30]. As also highlighted by [39], debugging will help alert the users in case single rules or flows of multiple rules might generate potential security risks.

Capitalizing on the emphasis posed on the textual descriptions of security events, additional future work will be devoted to improve the paradigm for ECA rule definition by means of conversational technologies supporting voice-based interaction.

Acknowledgment. This work is partially supported by the Italian Ministry of University and Research (MIUR) under grant PRIN 2017 "EMPATHY: EMpowering People in deAling with internet of THings ecosYstems". We also acknowledge the financial support of MIUR through the PON project TALIsMAn - Tecnologie di Assistenza personALizzata per il Miglioramento della quAlità della vitA (Grant No. ARS01_ 01116).

References

1. Alqhatani, A., Lipford, H.R.: There is nothing that i need to keep secret: sharing practices and concerns of wearable fitness data. In: Proceedings of the Conference on Usable Privacy and Security (USENIX 2019), pp. 421–434. USENIX Association (2019)
2. Ardito, C., Buono, P., Desolda, G., Matera, M.: From smart objects to smart experiences: an end-user development approach. Int. J. Hum. Comput. Stud. **114**, 51–68 (2017)
3. Ardito, C., Desolda, G., Lanzilotti, R., Malizia, A., Matera, M.: Analysing trade-offs in frameworks for the design of smart environments. Behav. Inf. Technol. **39**(1), 47–71 (2019)
4. Ardito, C., et al.: User-defined semantics for the design of IoT systems enabling smart interactive experiences. Pers. Ubiquit. Comput. **24**(6), 781–796 (2020). https://doi.org/10.1007/s00779-020-01457-5
5. Atzori, L., Iera, A., Morabito, G.: The internet of things: a survey. Int. J. Comput. Comput. Netw. **54**(15), 2787–2805 (2010)
6. Balachandran, K.: kardSort. Retrieved from https://kardsort.com/ Accessed 14 Mar 2021
7. Balducci, F., Buono, P., Desolda, G., Impedovo, D., Piccinno, A.: Improving smart interactive experiences in cultural heritage through pattern recognition techniques. Pattern Recogn. Lett. **131**, 142–149 (2020)
8. Bangor, A., Kortum, P., Miller, J.: The system usability scale (SUS): an empirical evaluation. Int. J. Hum.-Comput. Interact. **24**(6), 574–594 (2008)
9. Breve, B., Deufemia, V.: Empowering end-users in the specification of security rules. In: Proceedings of the 1st International Workshop on Empowering People in Dealing with Internet of Things Ecosystems - co-located with International Conference on Advanced Visual Interfaces (AVI 2020) (EMPATHY 2020). CEUR-WS (2020)
10. Brooke, J.: SUS-A quick and dirty usability scale. Usability Eval. Ind. **189**(194), 4–7 (1996)
11. Corno, F., Russis, L.D., Roffarello, A.M.: Empowering end users in debugging trigger-action rules. In: Proceedings of the Conference on Human Factors in Computing Systems (CHI 2019), p. 388. Association for Computing Machinery (2019)
12. Costabile, M.F., Fogli, D., Lanzilotti, R., Mussio, P., Piccinno, A.: Supporting work practice through end-user development environments. J. Organ. End User Comput. **18**(4), 43–65 (2006)
13. Dale, E., Chall, J.S.: The concept of readability. Elementary Engl. **26**(1), 19–26 (1949)
14. Desolda, G., Ardito, C., Matera, M.: Empowering end users to customize their smart environments: model, composition paradigms and domain-specific tools. ACM Trans. Comput.-Hum. Interact. **24**(2), 1–52 (2017)
15. DuBay, W.H.: The Principles of Readability. Online Submission (2004)
16. Fagan, M., Khan, M.M.H.: Why do they do what they do?: A study of what motivates users to (not) follow computer security advice. In: Proceedings of the Symposium on Usable Privacy and Security (SOUPS 2016), pp. 59–75 (2016)
17. Federici, S., et al.: UTASSISTANT: a new semi-automatic usability evaluation tool for Italian public administrations. In: Proceedings of the International Conference on Advanced Visual Interfaces - ECONA Workshop (AVI 2018), pp. 1–3 (2018)
18. Flesch, R.: A new readability yardstick. J. Appl. Psychol. **32**(3), 221 (1948)
19. Flesch, R.: Flesch-Kincaid readability test. Retrieved October **26**(2007), 3 (2007)

20. Hart, S.G.: Nasa-task load index (NASA-TLX); 20 years later. Hum. Factors Ergon. Soc. Annu. Meet. **50**(9), 904–908 (2006)
21. Hart, S.G., Staveland, L.E.: Development of NASA-TLX (Task Load Index): results of empirical and theoretical research. Adv. Psychol. **52**, 139–183 (1988)
22. He, W., et al.: Rethinking access control and authentication for the home internet of things (IoT). In: Proceedings of the Conference on Security Symposium (USENIX 2018), pp. 255–272. USENIX Association (2018)
23. Herzberg, A.: Why Johnny can't surf (safely)? Attacks and defenses for web users. Comput. Secur. **28**(1–2), 63–71 (2009)
24. Ion, I., Reeder, R., Consolvo, S.: No one can hack my mind: comparing expert and non-expert security practices. In: Proceedings of the Conference on Usable Privacy and Security (USENIX 2015), pp. 327–346. USENIX Association (2015)
25. Knieriem, B., Zhang, X., Levine, P., Breitinger, F., Baggili, I.: An Overview of the Usage of Default Passwords. In: Matoušek, P., Schmiedecker, M. (eds.) Digital Forensics and Cyber Crime. LNICSSITE, vol. 216, pp. 195–203. Springer, Cham (2018). https://doi.org/10.1007/978-3-319-73697-6_15
26. Lewis, J.R., Sauro, J.: The factor structure of the system usability scale. In: Kurosu, M. (ed.) Human Centered Design. LNCS, vol. 5619, pp. 94–103. Springer, Heidelberg (2009). https://doi.org/10.1007/978-3-642-02806-9_12
27. Lieberman, H., Paternò, F., Klann, M., Wulf, V.: End-user development: an emerging paradigm. In: Lieberman, H., Paternò, F., Wulf, V. (eds.) End User Development. Human-Computer Interaction Series, vol. 9. Springer, Dordrecht (2006). https://doi.org/10.1007/1-4020-5386-X_1
28. Ling, Z., Liu, K., Xu, Y., Jin, Y., Fu, X.: An end-to-end view of IoT security and privacy. In: Proceedings of the IEEE Global Communications Conference (GLOBECOM 2017), pp. 1–7 (2017)
29. Loop11. Loop11 User Testing. Retrieved from https://www.loop11.com/ Accessed 14 Sept 2020
30. Manca, M., Fabio, P., Santoro, C., Corcella, L.: Supporting end-user debugging of trigger-action rules for IoT applications. Int. J. Hum. Comput. Stud. **123**, 56–69 (2019)
31. Markopoulos, P., Nichols, J., Paternò, F., Pipek, V.: Editorial: end-user development for the internet of things. ACM Trans. Comput.-Hum. Interact. **24**(2), 1–3 (2017)
32. McLaughlin, G.H.: SMOG grading-a new readability formula. J. Read. **12**(8), 639–646 (1969)
33. Neshenko, N., Bou-Harb, E., Crichigno, J., Kaddoum, G., Ghani, N.: Demystifying IoT security: an exhaustive survey on IoT vulnerabilities and a first empirical look on internet-scale IoT exploitations. IEEE Commun. Surv. Tutorials **21**(3), 2702–2733 (2019)
34. Nielsen, J.: Card Sorting: How Many Users to Test. Retrieved from https://www.nngroup.com/articles/card-sorting-how-many-users-to-test/ Accessed 14 Mar 2021
35. Readable. readable app. Retrieved from https://app.readable.com/text/ Accessed 14 Mar 2021
36. Scranton, M.A.: SMOG grading: a readability formula by G. Harry McLaughlin Kansas State University (1970)
37. Shinde, P.: Application of existing k-means algorithms for the evaluation of card sorting experiments (2017)
38. Spencer, D.: Card Sorting: Designing Usable Categories. Rosenfeld Media (2009)
39. Surbatovich, M., Aljuraidan, J., Bauer, L., Das, A., Jia, L.: Some recipes can do more than spoil your appetite: analyzing the security and privacy risks of IFTTT Recipes. In: Proceedings of the International Conference on World Wide Web (WWW 2017), pp. 1501–1510. International World Wide Web Conferences Steering Committee (2017)
40. Szwillus, G., Hülsmann, A., Mexin, Y., Wawilow, A.: Casolysis 2.0 - Flexible Auswertung von Card Sorting Experimenten. In: Proceedings of the Usability Professionals (Casolysis 2.0 - Flexible Auswertung von Card Sorting Experimenten) (2015)

41. Tetteroo, D., Soute, I., Markopoulos, P.: Five key challenges in end-user development for tangible and embodied interaction. In: Proceedings of the ACM International conference on multimodal interaction (ICMI 2013), 247–254. ACM, New York (2013)
42. Thelwall, M.: The heart and soul of the web? Sentiment strength detection in the social web with SentiStrength. In: Hołyst, J.A. (ed.) Cyberemotions. UCS, pp. 119–134. Springer, Cham (2017). https://doi.org/10.1007/978-3-319-43639-5_7
43. Ur, B., McManus, E., Ho, M.P.Y., Littman, M.L.: Practical trigger-action programming in the smart home. In: Proceedings of the SIGCHI Conference on Human Factors in Computing Systems (CHI 2014), pp. 803–812. ACM, New York (2014)
44. Wajid, U., Namoun, A., Mehandjiev, N.: Alternative representations for end user composition of service-based systems. In: Costabile, M.F., Dittrich, Y., Fischer, G., Piccinno, A. (eds.) End-User Development. LNCS, vol. 6654, pp. 53–66. Springer, Heidelberg (2011). https://doi.org/10.1007/978-3-642-21530-8_6
45. Watson, I.: Natural Language Understanding. Retrieved from https://natural-language-understanding-demo.ng.bluemix.net/ Accessed 14 Mar 2021
46. Wogalter, M.S., DeJoy, D., Laughery, K.R.: Warnings and Risk Communication. CRC Press (1999)
47. Zeng, E., Mare, S., Roesner, F.: End user security & privacy concerns with smart homes. In: Proceedings of the Conference on Usable Privacy and Security (USENIX 2017), pp. 65–80. USENIX Association (2017)

Comparative Analysis of Composition Paradigms for Personalization Rules in IoT Settings

Simone Gallo, Marco Manca, Andrea Mattioli, Fabio Paternò[⊠], and Carmen Santoro

CNR-ISTI, HIIS Laboratory, Via Moruzzi 1, 56124 Pisa, Italy
{s.gallo,m.manca,a.mattioli,f.paterno,c.santoro}@isti.cnr.it

Abstract. The rapid pervasive diffusion of Internet of Things technologies has opened up many opportunities for people to directly personalise the behaviour of surrounding objects and devices based on the dynamic events that can occur. To this end, several tailoring environments have been proposed supporting the end-user creation of trigger-action rules. Such tools can support different composition paradigms. In this paper we present a study that analyses three composition paradigms (graphical wizard, block-based, and conversational) to better understand how well they support rule creation activities. In order to make the analysis consistent we considered three implementations of such composition paradigms supporting the same set of triggers and actions. We have carried out a first user study in order to gather empirical feedback for substantiating our analysis, which provides indications of the pros and cons of each approach.

Keywords: Internet of Things · Trigger-action rules · Tailoring environments

1 Introduction

Over the past decade, we have witnessed an increasing diffusion of the Internet of Things (IoT) and related technologies, with the number of connected "things" (devices and physical objects) expected to reach 35 billion worldwide in 2021. Such a pervasive technological trend has opened up new possibilities in terms of end-user development. A variety of events can dynamically be detected in IoT settings and many connected objects and devices can be activated accordingly. This has stimulated growing interest in Trigger-Action Programming (TAP), where triggers can be events and/or conditions, and the actions indicate the functionalities to activate. Several commercial tools supporting this approach are available, such as IFTTT[1] and Zapier[2].

However, while creating personalization rules through such environments is relatively simple, often users either cannot specify the intended behaviour because of limitations of the language supported by the considered tool, or, even when they can, they obtain rules whose performance does not generate the expected behaviour. Brackenbury

---

[1] https://ifttt.com/.
[2] https://zapier.com/.

© Springer Nature Switzerland AG 2021
D. Fogli et al. (Eds.): IS-EUD 2021, LNCS 12724, pp. 53–70, 2021.
https://doi.org/10.1007/978-3-030-79840-6_4

et al. [2] discuss a number of potential bugs in TAP, and highlight how often the temporal aspects of both triggers and actions is a crucial source of ambiguity. For example, the difference between events and conditions is often not noticed by users [10], also because many tailoring environments do not clearly highlight that they are two different temporal concepts. Indeed, one of the most known tools in this area is IFTTT, and it does not provide clear indications in this respect, and does not even support rules with multiple triggers. One further problem is that several tailoring environments do not provide the possibility of creating rules that are activated if some event does not occur in a given period of time (they do not support the NOT operator associated with a trigger). Overall, it seems that designing tailoring environments for TAP that are able to address such issues and offer satisfying usability is still an open issue, and deserves further investigation. One aspect that can be important to consider is the composition paradigm to support the development process of trigger-action rules. By composition paradigm we mean how the tailoring environments guide the rule development process: how they present the relevant concepts and interact with users.

For such reasons we have conducted a study that considers tailoring environments that on the one hand provide support for the problematic aspects mentioned above (clear distinction between events and conditions, support of NOT operator, possibility to compose multiple triggers and actions), and on the other hand support different composition paradigms. The goal is better understanding the pros and cons of each solution, and more generally to provide useful indications for designers and developers of tailoring environments for IoT settings. In particular, the composition paradigms considered in this paper are: graphical wizard, where users can create the rules through various selections performed on logically organised lists of options; block-based, where the puzzle metaphor is used to enable users to put together the elements composing the rules; and conversational, in which a chatbot in natural language asks user information, receives answers, and provides requests for clarification.

In the paper after discussion of related work, we introduce the three tailoring environments considered. Then, we report on a study carried out with a number of students without or with limited experience in programming, who created rules with different structures with the three considered tailoring environments. We then discuss the lessons learnt, and draw some conclusions and indications for future work.

2 Related Work

A first comparative study [12] analysed three Android apps (Tasker, Atooma, and Locale) for creating context-dependent behaviours in terms of expressiveness and usability, and found that the environment supporting the widest set of expressions for specifying rules (Tasker) was also the one that was found to be the most difficult to use (highest performance time, error numbers, and unsuccessful performance numbers). Then, a study [4] carried out a literature review on the design and evaluation of tools for smart home control, and an experimental study in which three tools (Tasker, IFTTT, Atooma) were compared in order to identify the interaction mechanisms that end users appreciate most. On the basis of the obtained results, some design implications for the development of tools for smart home control and management were proposed. Another comparative user study between IFTTT and Atooma was reported in [3]. It involved students who used them in small groups. Participants observed that IFTTT provided more services for composition than Atooma, which was found easier to use and intuitive, and also able to combine multiple triggers. Overall, such studies mainly focused only on solutions following the graphical wizard approach.

More recently, a design space to compare tools for end-user development of IoT and/or robotic applications has been put forward [14]. It is composed of various logical dimensions that highlight the aspects to analyse and consider, such as the type of metaphor used for representing the relevant concepts and the programming style adopted for creating the desired behaviour. A comparison between composition paradigms for trigger-action rules was introduced in [8]. They considered two wizard-based tools (one with more guidance than the other) and one based on the graph metaphor. One of the results of the comparative study revealed that the visual data-flow paradigm downgraded both user performance and satisfaction. Thus, we decided to no longer consider such paradigm in our study, and expand our analysis to two rather different paradigms (conversational and block-based).

Conversational interfaces seem a promising approach. Valtolina et al. [15] reported on a study evaluating the benefits of a chatbot in comparison to traditional GUI, specifically for users with poor aptitude in using technologies. They considered applications in the healthcare and smart home fields, and found that for the user experience the chatbot application appears to be better than the GUI-based one. Another relevant work exploring the use of chatbots is CAPIRCI [1], a multi-modal web application supporting end users to define tasks to be executed by collaborative robots. In general, the conversational interaction style has received limited attention for supporting creation of trigger-action rules. InstructableCrowd [9] is a framework which enables users to converse with the crowd through their phone and describe a problem. Then, it provides a graphical interface for crowd workers to both chat with the user, and compose a rule with a part connected to the user's phone sensors, and a part connected to the user's phone effectors in order to solve the problem. HeyTap [6] allows users to communicate their personalization intentions, which are used, along with related contextual and semantic information, to recommend rules that are able to map the abstract user needs to entities among those in the available dataset. Overall, such work has not focused on the use of chatbots for creating trigger-action rules since in InstructableCrowd the rules are created through a graphical interface, while HeyTap uses the chatbot to receive parameters for recommending rules from an existing dataset. An exploration of using chatbot to create trigger action rules is in [11] but it only considers single trigger – single action rules, and does not distinguish between events and conditions. Thus, in the paper we provide an original comparative analysis of three composition paradigms: one is based on a graphical wizard that aims to guide the users by selecting available options shown graphically (TAREME [5][3]), one follows the puzzle metaphor to support the composition activity (BlockComposer [13][4]), and the last one adopts a conversational style.

---

[3] https://tare.isti.cnr.it/RuleEditor/login.

[4] https://giove.isti.cnr.it/demo/pat/.

3   The Tailoring Environments

The three tailoring environments considered in the study were configured in such a way to support the same triggers and actions, and the same operators, according to the same language. In this way they were able to express the same rules, and thus we avoided that greater capabilities of one tool could influence the user perception of its usability and usefulness. The triggers considered refer to three contextual dimensions: user, technology, and environment; while the actions considered state changes of home appliances, or the generation of reminders, alarms, or the activation of Alexa services.

The tool supporting the graphical wizard composition (TAREME) is visually structured into two main parts, one for triggers and one for actions, and one sidebar providing feedback on the progress achieved in creating the rules. Both the trigger and action parts are organized in terms of main categories, which, when selected, unfold their subcategories, and it is possible to iterate until the basic elements with their attributes are visualised. The puzzle metaphor has been used in different environments (e.g. smartphones [7], robots [16]). In this case the tool considered (BlockComposer) is structured into a lateral panel from which the elements can be selected and dropped into the main area, while the composition operators are available in the bottom part. The elements for composing the rules in the lateral panel are hierarchically organized as well. There is a block element associated with the rule that has to be completed in the composition process.

The tool supporting the conversational interface is RuleBot, which has been implemented with DialogFlow. It has been obtained by defining an intent for each possible trigger and action, and the corresponding entities allow the identification of the terms in the intents. Some contexts have been defined in order to direct the conversation in such a way that users enter the necessary information. After the chatbot welcomes, the user can enter a possible trigger or action, and then the chatbot provides feedback, and asks for the remaining information to complete the rule (an example in Fig. 1). When the user input corresponds to one of the defined intents, DialogFlow checks the presence of the necessary entities, and send them to a Node.js server, which will then generate the natural language description of the rule created. In the supported conversations users can delete the last item entered, and asks for a summary of the rule so far created.

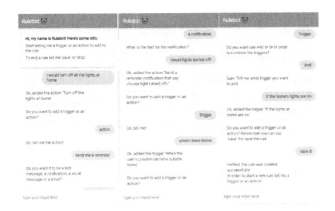

Fig. 1. Example of dialogue with the conversational interface.

4   User Study

We carried out a user test to better assess strong and weak points of the three approaches for programming automations via trigger-action rules by non-professional developers.

4.1   Participants

The participants for this test were recruited in a course of a Digital Humanities degree. Twenty-three users (55.6% females) with age ranging between 22 and 55 (mean $= 27.22$, std. dev. $= 8.17$) were involved in the user study. Their knowledge of programming languages was categorized into five different levels from no knowledge to very good knowledge: 1: No knowledge in programming; 2: Little Knowledge (which means: knowledge of HTML, CSS, and basic knowledge of a programming language, such as JavaScript); 3: Medium Knowledge (knowledge of a programming language, basic knowledge of another language, such as PHP or Java or C++); 4: Good Knowledge (good knowledge of the known languages); 5: Very Good Knowledge (knowledge of development languages at a professional level). In our analysis, from the initial 27 participants, we excluded the data of 4 participants because they had good or very good knowledge of programming languages. As such, all the 23 participants had a knowledge of programming languages between no knowledge and medium knowledge. In particular, 5 of them (22%) declared no programming experience, 11 (48%) had little experience, 7 (30%) reported a medium level in programming experience.

4.2   Test Organisation

The test was introduced in a course lesson given by teleconference because of the pandemic crisis. The students received a brief introduction to the study, the three tools, and the trigger-action rule structure, as well as an explanation of the main features of the three tools, and a short introductory video for each. The students were required first to login to the three tools and then familiarize themselves with each for some time. Then, the students had to write down (using natural language) five rules that had to follow a predefined structure, and then these rules had to be specified using each of the three tools. The rules had to comply with the following structures indicating the number of elements, whether events or conditions should be considered, and the type of contextual aspect and action to consider:

- Elementary trigger (technology) + elementary action (reminder)
- Elementary trigger (including the NOT operator) + composed action (alarm, light)
- Composed trigger (event+condition: environment+environment) + elementary action (reminder)
- Composed trigger (conditon+condition: environment+technology) + composed action (alarm, light)
- Composed Trigger (event+condition: user+technology) + composed action (light, reminder)

Such rules were presented to participants in the same order. The idea was to progressively increase the complexity of the rules, which was mainly connected with two aspects: a higher number of triggers and actions to specify implied a more complex rule, and we assumed that a trigger that needs the inclusion of a NOT operator would be more difficult than a trigger that does not need it.

After receiving the introduction to the exercise, the students were free to complete the tasks autonomously by using the three tools. They were free to choose in which order to use the tools. In the last phase they had to fill in an online questionnaire asking for some socio-demographic information (age, gender), and also indicating their expertise in programming. In addition, using a 5-point Likert scale (1 = Strongly disagree, 5 = Strongly agree) they also had to rate how much they agreed on statements concerning some aspects of the proposed environments, and provide observations on positive/negative aspects they noticed on the assessed systems, and recommendations for possible improvements. We asked them to provide honest feedback, saying that the test is an evaluation of the tools and not of their performance, and that any issue they could find would be useful to improve the tools. The students had to complete the test and the questionnaire remotely, as soon as they could. Thus, the possibility of social pressure when filling in the questionnaire was very low.

4.3   Questionnaire Results

Question 1. I found it easy to edit the "trigger" part of a rule using the user interface of the TAREME tool (Median = 4; Min = 2; Max = 5)
The vast majority of people liked the intuitiveness of the tool. In particular, its hierarchical representation was appreciated for its immediacy, and the support it offers in progressively refining the level of detail in the specification of the contained elements. In the composition process, the two main parts of a rule (the one dedicated to triggers and the one dedicated to actions) were judged easily distinguishable, and the layout was appreciated for its clarity. Two users pointed out that, after a minimal phase of familiarization, using the tool (i.e. for editing the triggers) is easy. Another user pointed out that, while editing a trigger, sometimes it can happen that its parent node is no longer visible, and in such cases the user might lose the context. Another highlighted that not all the trigger names are equally clear and self-explanatory. One user pointed out that the set of available triggers should be extended, while another found the use of IF vs. WHEN within the tool not immediately clear. Finally, one user pointed out that the natural language feedback appearing on the top, though useful, could be improved.

Question 2. I found it easy to edit the "trigger" part of a rule using the user interface of the Block Composer tool (Median = 4; Min = 2; Max = 5)
A significant part of users (10) clearly expressed their appreciation towards Block Composer. They found it intuitive and usable, and especially liked the idea of using the jigsaw metaphor to guide the rule specification process. One of them particularly liked the availability of a lateral, compact menu that can be expanded as needed: this allows users to have a 'clean' view of the main panel (by hiding what is not currently relevant). Another one found BlockComposer as very pleasant to use, also appreciating the sound

that is rendered when a block gets composed. One user pointed out that the movement of the blocks is not always 'fluid' when using a desktop PC with a mouse, compared to touch-based tablets. One highlighted that the size of the characters used for rendering the names of the triggers, as well as the distance between the associated UI elements should be increased. However, one user did not find the jigsaw metaphor particularly intuitive: he said that sometimes the various pieces seem to go "out of control". One user, while appreciating the overall intuitiveness of the tool, pointed out that, when adding new blocks, they are placed in a position that is not always visible to users (i.e. in the top-left part), which forced her to scroll the main panel to find the new element.

Question 3. - I found it easy to edit the "trigger" part of a rule using the user interface of the RuleBot tool (Median = 3; Min = 1; Max = 5)
Six users explicitly said that RuleBot is easy to use even though some of them complained that it is not always able to correctly recognize user intent. One user found it easy to edit the "trigger" part of a rule, while another reported it to be very easy and convenient to use the chatbot especially for those not very familiar with technology. A pair of users declared to have had some initial difficulties that disappeared after a quick familiarization with the tool. However, several users pointed out that, while on the one hand the interaction with the chatbot is quick, on the other hand the considered chatbot did not always correctly understand the input given by the user. One complained about the 'rigidity' with which it sometimes works (i.e. not being very flexible in the sentences it can recognize). A pair of users complained that the sentences to use for interacting with the chatbot need to be precise and that, in order to be understood, it is necessary for the user to properly organise them in the format expected by the chatbot. In addition, another user reported that sometimes the chatbot asks questions that seem unrelated to the current conversational context, and which the user needs to answer to continue the interaction (this likely happens when the user is less aware of the current point of the dialogue in the rule composition process, and thus interprets the chatbot's questions as unrelated to the current context, which might not be the case).

Question 4. I found it easy to compose two "triggers" of a rule using the user interface of the TAREME tool (Median = 4; Min = 2; Max = 5)
On the one hand, the majority of participants (around 15 users) declared having found this task quite easy. On the other hand, practically all of them highlighted that the button dedicated to add the operators, as being placed in a lateral bar in the left-hand part of the window, results not particularly intuitive and visible. One of them further added that this becomes particularly challenging when the window is resized, since the lateral menu can even become hidden (in extreme cases); this same user highlighted that, if one just focuses on the central panel of the main window, it is not clear how to include operators. One of them suggested placing a dedicated button in the central part of the window.

Question 5. I found easy composing two "triggers" of a rule by using the Block Composer (Median = 3; Min = 2; Max = 5)
Seven users explicitly declared to like the way in which BlockComposer supports the combination of triggers. Nevertheless, some aspects were judged as problematic. A user found this tool not intuitive to use when combinations of triggers are to be created, as it

is not immediately clear that another block should be added to specify the composition operator. Another user reported difficulties in moving the elements and in the fact that the operators are not very visible in the UI. To this regard, seven users complained about the limited visibility of operators within the UI (since – they noted – they are placed in the bottom part of the UI). However, at the same time most of them declared that this issue is ameliorated by the fact that an alert notification is given to users when it is necessary to include an operator to compose triggers. One user complained that the elements in the UI (i.e. the 'trigger' blocks) are rendered sometimes too close each other, which could create confusion in the layout. A pair of users reported that sometimes it seems that the tool did not correctly frame some pieces together.

Question 6. I found it easy to compose two triggers of a rule using the user interface of the Rule Bot tool (Median = 4; Min = 1; Max = 5)
The majority of users (16) appreciated the easiness with which it is possible to compose two triggers with the RuleBot. Many users highlighted that this is because it is directly the chatbot that suggests the user to combine a new trigger with a previously specified one, also highlighting the available operators. The remaining users complained that the chatbot needs specific statements to recognize correctly the user's input, thus showing limited flexibility. In this regard one user reported to have unsuccessfully tried to provide the chatbot with two triggers at once (not supported by this tool at the test time).

Question 7. I found it easy to edit a "trigger" that uses the "not" operator using the user interface of the TAREME tool (Median = 4; Min = 2; Max = 5)
The vast majority of users (around 20) found this very intuitive in TAREME. For the few remaining users, it seems that their difficulties were at a more conceptual level. For instance, some of them did not understand that, in order to verify that an event is not occurred, an associated interval of time should be specified to indicate the temporal period when it should not occur.

Question 8. I found it easy to edit a "trigger" that uses the "not" operator using the user interface of the BlockComposer tool (Median = 4; Min = 1; Max = 5)
The vast majority of users found intuitive to carry out this task using BlockComposer. As for the remaining users, one user complained that the checkbox for including the NOT operator was not very visible, another one had some difficulties with specifying the associated time interval.

Question 9. I found it easy to edit a "trigger" that uses the "not" operator using the user interface of the RuleBot tool (Median = 4; Min = 1; Max = 5)
15 users gave overall quite positive comments, not having encountered specific difficulties in carrying out this task. The rest of the users pointed out that the chatbot did not always immediately recognize the negation.

Question 10. I found the distinction between event and condition simple when editing the "triggers" of a rule using the user interface of the TAREME tool (Median = 4; Min = 2; Max = 5)

The vast majority of users (19) found this quite intuitive, using TAREME. As for the remaining ones, a pair of users noted that, while setting an event or a condition using TAREME is intuitive, the tool should better support users in understanding (at a conceptual level) the underlying concepts associated with events and conditions. A pair of other users said that the difference between the two, as rendered just by the keywords "IF" and "WHEN" are not immediately understandable: one of them however added that having available explicitly in the UI the information about the kind of trigger associated with each keyword (conditions for "IF" and "events" for WHEN) was helpful.

Question 11. I found the distinction between event and condition simple when editing the "triggers" of a rule using the user interface of the BlockComposer tool (Median = 4; Min = 2; Max = 5)
The vast majority of users (19) declared that the tool allows them to accomplish such task in a quite easy manner, since every time the selection of the most suitable option (between events and conditions) is required by the user, the tool first explains the distinction (showing a short explanation), and then it allows the user to select the correct one. As for the remaining participants, one user declared that this distinction was clear only after having completed all the parts of the concerned rule, i.e. after having the possibility to read the whole rule.

Question 12. I found the distinction between event and condition simple when editing the "triggers" of a rule using the user interface of the Chatbot tool (Median = 3; Min = 1; Max = 5)
Eleven users reported that this part is sufficiently intuitive. Most of them said that they appreciated the fact that, if the user does not explicitly use 'IF' or 'WHEN' within a trigger when it is being created, the chatbot explicitly asks the user whether the newly added trigger should be considered as an event or a condition. As for the remaining users, one of them pointed out that this distinction is not sufficiently highlighted in the tool: in his view it seems somewhat "expected" that the user should know this difference. Other five users reported some difficulties in understanding this difference.

Question 13. I found it easy to edit the action part of a rule using the user interface of the TAREME tool (Median = 4; Min = 3; Max = 5)
Almost the totality of users (20) said that the task is very easy and intuitive, as the tool offers a clear, simple and coherent UI for specifying the action part of a rule using TAREME. The other users did not report any specific difficulties: most of the time they just highlighted some aspects that they found not completely clear in the UI, for instance some of them did not understand the reason why the receiver of a message is required by the tool only for emails or sms and not for e.g. vocal notifications (this was due because in the latter case it was assumed that the person currently using the associated application -e.g. Alexa- will receive the notification).

Question 14. I found it easy to edit the action part of a rule using the user interface of the BlockComposer tool (Median = 4; Min = 2; Max = 5)

Also for BlockComposer, the part dedicated to specifying the action was judged intuitive to be used by practically all of the participants. One user added that using different colours for visualizing triggers and actions makes easy to identify the action part.

Question 15. I found it easy to edit the action part of a rule using the user interface of the RuleBot tool (Median = 4; Min = 1; Max = 5)
Nine users found the interaction with the chatbot for editing rules sufficiently satisfactory. However, most of the remaining users complained that the chatbot does not always understand the input provided by the user and often the user is forced to use as much as possible specific sentences for achieving better results. One user did not appreciate the way in which currently it is possible to edit a rule with this tool. Another user found not very clear the possibility to undo an interaction using the tool.

Question 16. I found it easy to compose two actions within a rule using the user interface of the TAREME tool (Median = 4; Min = 2; Max = 5)
The vast majority of users (19) found this task very easy using TAREME. As for the remaining users, one user highlighted that there is no specific operator to use for composing actions using this tool (differently from what is currently done with triggers). Alongside the same line, one user reported that it is not completely clear whether the tool considers (by default) the second action to be carried out just after the first one. A pair of users highlighted that the lateral menu on the left part of the tool might get hidden when the user significantly resizes the window.

Question 17. I found it easy to compose two actions within a rule using the user interface of the BlockComposer tool (Median = 4; Min = 3; Max = 5)
Six users reported that the element (a block) dedicated to specifying the composition of actions (through the "sequential" and "parallel" operators) could be better highlighted in the UI (currently it appears in the footer of the page). A pair of users reported some difficulties in realizing that, to compose two or more actions, a further block is needed. The remaining users reported that overall this task was easy to carry out with this tool.

Question 18. I found it easy to compose two actions within a rule using the user interface of the RuleBot tool (Median = 4; Min = 1; Max = 5)
Almost all users appreciated the support offered by the tool for combining actions. Some of the others highlighted that it sometimes does not correctly interpret the input provided by the user. One user pointed out that in the first place one could be tempted to provide the two actions at once (at the time of the test not supported by the tool, which asked them one by one).

Question 19. The way rules are built using the TAREME tool is fast/efficient (Median = 4; Min = 2; Max = 5)
Almost all the participants found this tool efficient, quick, and easy to use. Some of them appreciated the lateral bar in the left-hand part, however it was noted that it might get

hidden in some cases. Some users especially appreciated the possibility to have feedback of the rule composed in natural language on the top part of the window.

Question 20. The way rules are built using the BlockComposer tool is fast/efficient (Median = 4; Min = 2; Max = 5)

The majority of users found this tool easy to use. The jigsaw metaphor exploited was found very intuitive. However, some of them noted that sometimes the blocks are moved in a way that is not extremely 'fluid'. One user suggested including the specification of the rule in natural language, beyond the block-based specification. Another user highlighted that the process of creating a rule using it is a bit affected (in terms of efficiency) by the time needed to drag the various elements in the central, main panel.

Question 21. The way rules are built using the RuleBot tool is fast/efficient (Median = 4; Min = 1; Max = 5)

Several users expressed appreciation for this tool. However, many of them highlighted that by using this tool the process of creating rules is not very efficient as sometimes the chatbot is not able to interpret the input provided by the user, therefore its flexibility in that should be increased. One user suggested better highlighting the terms according to which a user is more likely to have the input correctly interpreted.

Question 22. Overall, I found the interaction with the user interface of the TAREME tool satisfactory (Median = 4; Min = 1; Max = 5)

The vast majority of the users liked this tool and found it structured, clear, and satisfactory in its use. The distinction between triggers and actions was found clearly visible and increased the clarity of the tool. Users also appreciated the availability of the natural language description of rules. One user suggested improving the lateral menu (in the left-hand side), to avoid that it gets hidden when the user resizes the window.

Question 23. Overall, I found the interaction with the user interface of the Block-Composer tool satisfactory (Median = 4; Min = 3; Max = 5)

This tool was found easy, intuitive and pleasant to use by many users, even "entertaining" by some of them. However, further improvements could be done in the support provided for editing rules. In addition, sometimes the various blocks do not immediately frame each other. A user said that a quick phase of familiarization might be needed to understand how to place the pieces to build a rule.

Question 24. Overall, I found the interaction with the user interface of the RuleBot tool satisfactory (Median = 3; Min = 1; Max = 5)

Almost half of users expressed overall appreciation for the tool, and found it easy to use, even though a quick phase of familiarization might be needed. One user suggested improving the tool in handling possible user errors (e.g. adding the possibility of undoing the last action), or better handling situations in which the user needs to edit a rule. However, most of the complaints regarded the limited ability of the bot in understanding the inputs by the user. In addition, some users reported that they sometimes preferred to re-build a rule from scratch instead of modifying it.

Question 25. Which of the 3 composition styles did you find most suitable for editing rules in this context, and why? (wizard = 13, BlockComposer = 9, RuleBot = 1)
TAREME was found the most intuitive, efficient and easy to use especially when considering unskilled users. Its ease of use was due to its clear structure, and the simplicity with which it is possible to edit the various parts of a rule. In particular, the lateral bar was appreciated in that it provides a convenient and helpful summary of the current point reached in the process of creating a rule. BlockComposer was appreciated for the intuitiveness of the metaphor used, which allows users to mentally 'visualize' the rule that is being currently created, one user reported. One user especially liked the pleasant effect of concretely moving and connecting the various blocks. Another one liked the fact that BlockComposer guides the user in the creation of rules, and it is also easy to fix errors. Just one user selected the RuleBot as the most suitable tool for creating rules, saying that this system was the one that allowed him to create the rules in the quickest manner.

Question 26. Which of the 3 composition styles did you find least suitable for editing rules in this context, and why? (TAREME = 2, BlockComposer = 6, RuleBot = 15)
The answers associated with this question highlighted that users did not much like the composition style exploited in the considered chatbot, which was judged as the least suitable one among the three tools. The chatbot was found as the least suitable one for various reasons: somewhat imprecise, requiring more interactions, thus not very efficient; with some features requiring improvements (e.g. the possibility to edit a rule); sometimes it does not understand the input provided, or it just partially understand it because such input needs to be provided according to specific syntactical 'guidelines' that were received as rather 'rigid'. Finally, the support aimed to handling possible user errors needs improvements, the chatbot sometimes just limits its assistance to just repeating the same question. A pair of users judged TAREME as the most unsuitable one, as it requires the highest number of steps to define a rule. BlockComposer was found to be a bit too complicated in its interactions, and overall not very intuitive.

Figure 2 shows a summary of the ratings gathered for the evaluated aspects. Finally, we also performed a chi-square test to analyse possible dependencies between the programming knowledge of participants and the tool they preferred, but we did not find any significant result.

4.4 Analysis of Rules Correctness

The rules generated by the participants were analysed, with the purpose of better grasping the strong and weak points of each composition paradigm. This investigation was performed through the analysis of the discrepancies between the behaviours that participants expected from the rules, as expressed in their natural language description written textually at the beginning of the test, and the actual behaviours implemented with the rules created through the tailoring environments. To this regard, it is worth pointing out that the rules considered for the analysis were all syntactically correct, also in case of rules created using the conversational tool (i.e. the analysed rules did not contain errors

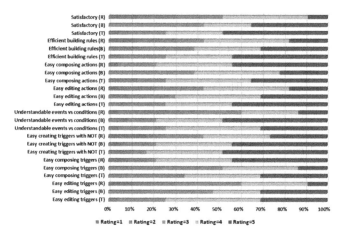

Fig. 2. Stacked bar chart summarizing the usability ratings.

related to natural language understanding issues). Indeed, when the conversational tool was not able to correctly understand the user input (i.e. was not able to match a user's input to an intent for which it was trained for), it asked further questions to the user in order to properly match their input to one of the available intents, until the user was finally satisfied by the rule and then saved it.

Before starting the rule composition using the editors, participants were asked to provide a natural language textual description of the behaviour that they wanted to obtain. Such natural language descriptions were subsequently manually translated into a non-ambiguous structure. For example, from a rule explained in natural language as "When the user's footsteps count is less than 1999 from 12:00 and 18:00, send a notification and start an activating light scene in the living room", we obtained the non-ambiguous form "not Event (steps) with time constrain (start time - end time), Action (notification), Action (living room activating light)". This was done to facilitate the later comparison with the rules obtained by the students with the tools.

Four categories of errors were identified within the rules and thereby involved in the analysis: incorrect definition of triggers and of actions; incorrect association of a trigger with an event vs a condition; incorrect application of the negation operator; incorrect use of composition operators (and/or) to combine different triggers. For each error, a weight was assigned following the severity scheme defined in Table 1, where 1 point indicates a severe error and 0.5 a moderate one. Classifying an error as "severe" or "moderate" was made depending on the "distance" between what was specified in natural language and the content of the rule created, and on its consequences. For example, a moderate trigger/action type error is, in the rule "When the user is in bed and the bedroom light level is daylight, send a notification to the user and turn off all the lights in the bedroom", using the trigger "bed movement" instead of "bed occupancy". In the same rule, not using any bed-related or light-related trigger is instead considered a severe error.

An example of moderate event/condition error is using two conditions in the rule "When (event) a person is in the bathroom for more than thirty minutes and if (condition)

Table 1. Criteria adopted for computing the error scores.

Error type	Trigger/action	Event/condition	Negation	Trigger operators
Severe	Missing or completely different rule element	The wrong specification makes the rule completely different/non-functioning	Missing operator or applied to a wrong trigger	Wrong operator
Moderate	Different but related rule element	The behaviour of the rule has partial overlap with the intended one	Incorrect time specification	/

the bathroom light is on, send a voice alarm and text message as a reminder to check the bathroom". In this case, the rule will still activate, but not only under the specific situation intended by the user. A severe error is instead using two events in a trigger because this rule will never be activated.

A moderate negation error is not inserting the reference time interval in the rule "When medicine has not been taken between 07:00 and 08:00 and the user is inside the house, do turn on the kitchen light and set its colour to red", while a severe error is not using the negation operator at all, or applying it to the "user position" trigger. All the errors that involved an incorrect application of the logical operators between triggers were considered severe.

We analysed the 345 rules produced by the participants (5 tasks carried out using each of the 3 editors). The obtained average error score considering all the tasks performed per participant is 0.72 (std. dev. 0.81) for the Wizard-based editor, 1.26 (std. dev. 1.38) for the Block-based and 1.02 (std. dev 0.85) for the Conversational-based. The Wizard-based editor obtained a total error score of 16.5, the Block-based of 29, and the Conversational-based of 23.5. Looking at the score per task graph (Fig. 3, right side) we see a higher score for the Block-based editor, especially on the first 2 tasks.

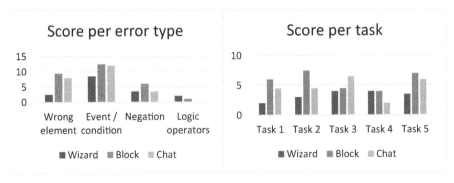

Fig. 3. Comparison of the error scores by error type and by task

From a comparison of the error scores with respect to the different paradigms (Fig. 3, left side), we can obtain some preliminary insights. Logical operators between triggers were well applied by participants, and errors were found only in 3 occurrences out of 207 rules which included these operators. Errors in the choice between event and condition were the most common errors in all the paradigms. Errors of this kind can be found in 51 out of 345 total rules, with a compound error score (the sum of the scores associated with the considered errors) across all editors of 33. The choice of the correct triggers and actions appears to be more problematic with the conversational and the block paradigms. This type of error is present in 25 out of 345 rules, with a compound error score of 20. Many of these errors consist in the choice of a related rule element, e.g., bathroom lights instead of bedroom lights. Lastly, some issues in the application of the negation operator are present in all the composition paradigms, but especially in the block-based editor. This class of error affected 21 out of 69 rules that required this behaviour, with a compound error score of 13. However, most of the errors of this type (16 out of 21) are of the moderate type, hence related to the timing aspects of the negation (i.e. not inserting the required timing constraint, or indicating a rule that will be activated when the selected *trigger condition* becomes different from the specified one in a time interval instead of when the *trigger event* does not occur in that time interval).

The wizard composition style was more effective in particular from the point of view of the selection of the correct elements. This could be because in this style the composition is precisely guided, therefore when users select an element it is used only for the current rule. This is not always true for BlockComposer where it is possible to move several blocks in the work area, use some of them for one rule, and then reuse them for the next rule. This, on the one hand, can be convenient for those familiar with the tool, but it may have led to some confusion and use of wrong blocks. As for the conversational approach, the difficulties in selection can be consequent to the user not always having clear the state of the rule under construction, and to the difficulties of interpreting the natural language. One consideration regarding the block environment is the mismatch between the perception of understanding the concepts of events and conditions (very good, see the answers to question 11), and the errors of this type actually found in the rules (more than in other editors). It could be an indication that the method used to present this difference is not very effective in conveying this concept (although in this case it would be a problem in the explanation, and not in the style of composition).

5 Discussion

The study has been useful to indicate some pros and cons of the various approaches. We considered users who were not initially familiar with the set of triggers and actions proposed. One issue that emerged was that when users are unaware of the available triggers and actions provided by the tailoring tools, a visual representation that directly offers the possibility of navigating across the available options is more immediate than a conversational interface, which can also be rendered vocally, and therefore does not immediately present all the available options also to avoid becoming tedious. On the other hand, when it is clear what should be done, the conversational interface can be more efficient than the other composition paradigms, especially with simple rules (one trigger, one action), whose description can be more easily recognised by the chatbot. When users have to build more complex rules, then the visual approaches tend to be more effective in guiding them, as they provide more interaction control just using their visual features, thereby limiting the possibility of error. The wizard seeks to have the user enter the missing info, and the block-based editor shows in the puzzle elements the parts that still need to be connected with a missing piece. BlockComposer was a bit affected (in terms of efficiency) by the time needed to drag the various elements in the central, main panel. Overall, the participants appreciated that the relevant concepts are clearly indicated in all the approaches. Some issues were still detected concerning exact understanding of some of them. For example, some users did not immediately understand that a trigger specified using a NOT operator needs to be accompanied by the definition of a time interval, which is essential to indicate when the lacking event should be checked. Likewise, explicitly using different terms for indicating events and conditions was useful to make users aware that they are different concepts, but in some cases such distinction was not yet completely understood.

To summarise we can say that TAREME was found intuitive, fast and easy to use, and it leads to making few mistakes, also because the user interface contains various support widgets (natural language feedback, rule sidebar). However, more steps are required to compose the rules than in other editors, thus it could be tedious for a frequent user. BlockComposer supports an intuitive metaphor, which leads to a clear view of the rule, pleasant interaction, a feeling of "hooking" the pieces, but the drag-and-drop interaction was not always easy, especially with small blocks, and it led to more errors. RuleBot is fast in rule creation, is able to clearly distinguish between events and conditions but it is necessary for the user to "align" with the way of understanding of the chatbot, and often it is necessary to have additional interactions (i.e. dialogues) to have the chatbot properly understand the user's intent. Moreover, it needs extensive training to interpret the various possible ways of expressing the rules, and lacks a continuous feedback of the status of the rule during its composition.

Some findings are in line with results reported by previous work [10], i.e. the difference between events and conditions is an abstraction that users are not always able to correctly exploit when writing rules: this remains true regardless of the type of composition paradigm used, which further confirms the fact that the main difficulty is at a more conceptual level. Other findings can be useful to improve/extend the support and guidance offered by users in specific situations that have been shown as more problematic for them. For instance, a conversational rule editor tool, when detecting some breakdowns in the conversation while users are building a complex rule, could automatically provide users with information about the point at which they are, as well as better explain the reason why the bot is asking further questions to users (i.e. to mitigate some inaccuracies or ambiguities), with the goal of increasing their awareness, which should also positively impact in the end the quality of their interactive experience.

6 Conclusions and Future Work

The study presented based on the user feedback and an analysis of the rules actually created through three different tools provides some useful indications about how to design support for each of them, and when and how a composition paradigm can be more effective. For example, a chatbot is certainly efficient when the terms and the structure used in the user input match well with what it expects. For novice users, a visual wizard is more effective since it provides more support on how to proceed and possible options.

As future work, we are considering the development of a new version of the chatbot that is also able to understand more complex users' input entered in one single interaction in order to see whether this can improve the user experience. We also plan to carry out further empirical studies, also with direct observation of users while interacting with the tailoring tools, to identify and provide further indications regarding the design and use of different compositional paradigms.

Acknowledgments. This work is partially supported by the Italian Ministry of University and Research (MUR) under grant PRIN 2017 "EMPATHY: EMpowering People in deAling with internet of THings ecosYstems".

References

1. Beschi, S., Fogli, D., Tampalini, F.: CAPIRCI: a multi-modal system for collaborative robot programming. In: Malizia, A., Valtolina, S., Morch, A., Serrano, A., Stratton, A. (eds.) IS-EUD 2019. LNCS, vol. 11553, pp. 51–66. Springer, Cham (2019). https://doi.org/10.1007/978-3-030-24781-2_4

2. Brackenbury, W., et al.: How users interpret bugs in trigger-action programming. In Proceedings of the 2019 CHI Conference. ACM, New York (2019). Article no. 552, 12 pages

3. Cabitza, F., Fogli, D., Lanzilotti, R., Piccinno, A.: Rule-based tools for the configuration of ambient intelligence systems: a comparative user study. Multimedia Tools Appl. **76**(4), 5221–5241 (2016). https://doi.org/10.1007/s11042-016-3511-2

4. Caivano, D., Fogli, D., Lanzilotti, R., Piccinno, A., Cassano, F.: Supporting end users to control their smart home: design implications from a literature review and an empirical investigation. J. Syst. Softw. **144**, 295–313 (2018)

5. Corcella, L., Manca, M., Nordvik, J., Paternò, F., Sanders, A.-M., Santoro, C.: Enabling personalisation of remote elderly assistance. Multimedia Tools Appl. **78**(15), 21557–21583 (2019). https://doi.org/10.1007/s11042-019-7449-z

6. Corno, F., De Russis, L., Monge Roffarello, A.: HeyTAP: bridging the gaps between users' needs and technology in IF-THEN rules via conversation. In: Proceedings Advanced Visual Interfaces AVI 2020, Salerno, Italy. ACM, New York (2020). 9 pages

7. Danado, J., Paternò, F.: Puzzle: a visual-based environment for end user development in touch-based mobile phones. In: Winckler, M., Forbrig, P., Bernhaupt, R. (eds.) HCSE 2012. LNCS, vol. 7623, pp. 199–216. Springer, Heidelberg (2012). https://doi.org/10.1007/978-3-642-34347-6_12

8. Desolda, G., Ardito, C., Matera, M.: Empowering end users to customize their smart environments: model, composition paradigms and domain-specific tools. ACM Trans. Comput.-Hum. Interact. **24**(2) (2017). Article no. 12, 52 pages

9. Huang, T.H.K., Azaria, A., Bigham, J.P.: InstructableCrowd: creating IF-THEN rules via conversations with the crowd. In: Proceedings of the 2016 CHI Conference Extended Abstracts, (CHI EA 2016), pp. 1555–1562. ACM, New York (2016)

10. Huang, J., Cakmak, M.: Supporting mental model accuracy in trigger-action programming. In: Proceedings of the 2015 ACM International Joint Conference on Pervasive and Ubiquitous Computing (UbiComp 2015), pp. 215–225. ACM, New York (2015)
11. Lago, A., Dias, J., Ferreira, H.: Managing non-trivial internet-of-things systems with conversational assistants: a prototype and a feasibility experiment. J. Comput. Sci. **51**, 101324 (2021)
12. Lucci, G., Paternò, F.: Understanding end-user development of context-dependent applications in smartphones. In: Sauer, S., Bogdan, C., Forbrig, P., Bernhaupt, R., Winckler, M. (eds.) HCSE 2014. LNCS, vol. 8742, pp. 182–198. Springer, Heidelberg (2014). https://doi.org/10.1007/978-3-662-44811-3_11
13. Mattioli, A., Paternò, F.: A visual environment for end-user creation of IoT customization rules with recommendation support. In: AVI 2020: Proceedings of the International Conference on Advanced Visual Interfaces, pp. 1–5, September 2020. Article no. 44
14. Paternò, F., Santoro, C.: End-user development for personalizing applications, things, and robots. Int. J. Hum. Comput. Stud. **131**, 120–130 (2019)
15. Valtolina, S., Barricelli, B.R., Di Gaetano, S.: Communicability of traditional interfaces VS chatbots in healthcare and smart home domains. Behav. Inf. Technol. **39**(1), 108–132 (2020)
16. Weintrop, D., et al.: Evaluating CoBlox: a comparative study of robotics programming environments for adult novices. In: Proceedings of the 2018 CHI Conference. ACM (2018). Paper 366, 12 pages

Devices, Information, and People: Abstracting the Internet of Things for End-User Personalization

Fulvio Corno, Luigi De Russis, and Alberto Monge Roffarello^(⊠)

Politecnico di Torino, Corso Duca degli Abruzzi 24, 10129 Turin, Italy
{fulvio.corno,luigi.derussis,alberto.monge}@polito.it

Abstract. Nowadays, end users can take advantage of end-user development platforms to personalize the Internet of Things. These platforms typically adopt a *vendor-centric* abstraction, by letting users to customize each of their smart device and/or online service through different trigger-action rules. Despite the popularity of such an approach, several research challenges in this domain are still underexplored. Which "things" would users personalize, and in which contexts? Are there any other effective abstractions besides the *vendor-centric* one? Would users adopt different abstractions in different contexts? To answer these questions, we report on the results of a 1-week-long diary study during which 24 participants noted down trigger-action rules arising during their daily activities. Results show that users would adopt multiple abstractions by personalizing devices, information, and people-related behaviors where the individual is at the center of the interaction. We found, in particular, that the adopted abstraction may depend on different factors, ranging from the user profile to the context in which the personalization is introduced. While users are inclined to personalize physical objects in the home, for example, they often go "beyond devices" in the city, where they are more interested in the underlying information. Our findings identify new design opportunities in HCI to improve the relationship between the Internet of Things, personalization paradigms, and users.

Keywords: End-User Development · Internet of Things · Trigger-action programming · Abstraction · Diary study · Context

1 Introduction

Through a network of physical objects always connected to the Internet, and a multitude of online services such as social networks and news portals, the Internet of Things (IoT) already helps society in many different ways, e.g., through applications ranging in scope from the individual to entire cities [6]. Smart devices and online services, in particular, are increasingly pervading the environment and are often utilized together [21], therefore opening up new possibilities for end-user personalization. In this context, End-User Development (EUD) empowers users to program the joint behaviors of their devices and services in various

© Springer Nature Switzerland AG 2021
D. Fogli et al. (Eds.): IS-EUD 2021, LNCS 12724, pp. 71–86, 2021.
https://doi.org/10.1007/978-3-030-79840-6_5

areas, like the home, the car, or for a healthy lifestyle. Several works in the literature (e.g., [14,16,18]) demonstrate the effective applicability of EUD techniques for personalizing different contexts, particularly for the smart home [12,20]. In the broader IoT context, end users can nowadays personalize their ecosystems of devices and services by using cloud-based EUD platforms like IFTTT[1] and Zapier[2], typically by composing trigger-action rules like

"IF the entrance *Nest* security camera detects a movement, THEN blink the *Philips Hue* lamp in the Kitchen."

Such platforms, however, present their own set of issues, e.g., in terms of interoperability [9] and expressiveness [17]. Within them, in particular, users are forced to compose trigger-action rules with a unique, *vendor-centric* abstraction, with which they must specifically refer to every single device or online service needed to execute the intended behaviors. While such an approach allows users to have a fine-grained control, it forces them to define several rules to program their ecosystems, i.e., every device or online service needs to be programmed in a specific way. Furthermore, it requires users to know in advance any involved technological detail, e.g., the manufacturer or brand of all the involved "things." A number of previous works tried to overcome the aforementioned issues by focusing on the underlying tools [16], notations [3], and/or visual programming paradigms [13]. Despite these recent efforts, several research questions about end-users' personalization needs and attitudes are still underexplored.

Which "things" would users personalize, and in which contexts? What are the most effective alternatives to the contemporary *vendor-centric* abstraction? Would users adopt different abstractions in different contexts? To answer these questions, we report on the results of a 1-week-long diary study in the style of a contextual inquiry with 24 participants living in 16 households. The study consisted of two semi-structured interviews and a period of time in which participants noted down trigger-action rules arising during their daily activities. In the study, we encouraged participants to think of scenarios, both regarding their "physical" and "virtual" worlds, in which they would have liked to personalize the behaviors of their devices and online services, and we gathered more than 200 trigger-action rules composed by the participants during the week of study.

Results show that users would define triggers and actions by adopting *different abstractions* in *different contexts*, with personalization needs that go beyond the smart home and include other smart environments and the "online" world as well. Participants of our study, particularly in the case of programming experts and tech-enthusiasts, used a *device-centric* abstraction to personalize different IoT entities, ranging from domestic appliances to car accessories. Through an *information-centric* abstraction, instead, participants went beyond physical devices by shifting their focus to the underlying information, e.g., to personalize their personal plans and appointments, news, and messages. Participants also

---

[1] https://ifttt.com/, last visited on April 20, 2021.
[2] https://zapier.com/, last visited on April 20, 2021.

envisioned their direct involvement in trigger-action rules by defining *people-centric* behaviors. With triggers such as *"when I enter home in the evening"* or *"if me and my friends have free time"*, for example, they explicitly positioned themselves (and other people) *inside* the personalization. An analysis of the contexts in which participants envisioned their personalizations further demonstrates that users would adopt multiple abstractions. We found, for example, that participants mostly used *people-to-information* rules for their health and wellbeing, by connecting a trigger that directly involves the individual to an action for obtaining or manipulating an information. In the smart home context, instead, participants extensively used *device-to-device* rules to customize the joint behavior of different devices or systems. Furthermore, participants used *information-to-information* rules to personalize information when the context was the city or their "online" world.

To encourage further research on the evolving fields of End-User Development and Internet of Things, we release the dataset collected during the study[3]. Furthermore, we discuss our results by identifying new design opportunities in HCI to improve the relationship between the Internet of Things, personalization paradigms, and users. Adapting EUD interfaces to different abstractions may reduce the gap between expectations and reality, thus breaking down barriers and increasing the adoption of EUD for an effective personalization of the IoT.

2   Background and Related Works

The core idea of adopting end-user development for IoT personalization is to empower users to take advantage of *ecosystems of interoperable smart objects and services* [1], by letting them combine flexibly, i.e., according to their situational needs, the behavior of different entities [13]. In this context, platforms such as IFTTT and Zapier have become popular [17]. Through Web editors, users can typically define trigger-action rules, i.e., they can define sets of desired behaviors in response to a specific event. Trigger-action programming is indeed one of the most popular programming paradigm adopted in EUD: it has been largely used for introducing personalization in different contexts, e.g., the smart home [12,20], and it offers a very simple and easy-to-learn solution for creating IoT applications, according to Barricelli and Valtolina [1]. For these reasons, in our study, we chose the trigger-action programming paradigm to explore end-users' abstractions in personalizing their IoT ecosystems.

Despite their growing popularity, existing platforms for IoT personalization present their own set of issues. The expressiveness and understandability of IFTTT rules, for instance, have been criticized since they are rather limited [17,20,21]. By discussing metaphors and programming styles for EUD, in particular, Paternò and Santoro [19] state that the possibility to compose complex events and actions is limited in contemporary platforms for IoT personalization, and they propose a new design space to include several additional aspects, with a particular focus on different kinds of (contextual) triggers and

---

[3] The dataset is available at https://bit.ly/3gmU1Ec.

actions. In platforms like IFTTT and Zapier, indeed, users are forced to compose trigger-action rules with a unique, *vendor-centric* approach. This clearly poses interoperability challenges, as users are required to know in advance any involved technological detail to execute the intended behaviors. In the forthcoming IoT world, however, new "things" will not always be knowable a priori [22] but they may appear and disappear at every moment, e.g., as with public services in a smart city. As a result, little social and practical benefits of End-User Development in the IoT have emerged [13]. A number of previous works tried to overcome the aforementioned issues. Baricelli and Valtolina [1], for instance, proposed an extension of the trigger-action paradigm that incorporates recommendation systems, other users, and the social dimension. Brich et al. [3] reported on the comparison of two different notations, i.e., rule-based and process-oriented, in the smart home context, showing that trigger-action rules are generally sufficient to express simple automation tasks, while processes fit well with more complex tasks. Desolda et al. [13] reported on the results of a study to identify possible visual paradigms to compose trigger-action rules in the IoT, and presented a model and an architecture to execute them. Ghiani et al. [16] proposed a method and a set of tools to personalize the contextual behavior of IoT applications. Differently from the described approaches, where the focus is on the underlying tools, notations, and/or programming paradigms, we focus on the different abstractions that users would adopt to personalize their devices and services.

Previous work mainly explored end-users' personalization needs and abstractions in limited scenarios, e.g., the smart home [3,20], analyzed rules of existing platforms *off-line* [21], or explored pre-built conceptual models in a few minutes with a questionnaire prompt [7]. In our work, we claim that multiple abstractions besides the *vendor-centric* one are possible and needed to empower users personalize their IoT ecosystems, and that such abstractions may depend on the context in which the personalizations are introduced. Only few recent works explore the personalization of IoT ecosystems through the lens of abstraction. Ur et al. [20], for instance, found that the way users express triggers ranges from events related to sensors to more abstract behaviors that involve multiple devices. In their study, the authors asked participants to "imagine that you have a home with devices that are Internet-connected and can therefore be given instructions on how to behave," therefore adopting a device-oriented abstraction [7]. By exploring triggers and actions that go beyond devices, instead, Corno et al. [8] proposed EUPont, an ontological representation of End-User Development in the IoT for creating context independent IoT applications based on the users' final goals. Instead of turning on a Philips Hue lamp or opening the bedroom's blinds, for example, with EUPont users can directly ask the system to *illuminate* the room. Despite the aforementioned works, it is still unclear which abstraction users would prefer, and whether such an abstraction depends on the context in which the personalization is introduced. As demonstrated by the work of Clark et al. [7], the way a system is presented to the user can have a priming effect on the initial mental models formed by users. Stemming from such an assumption, which highlights how critical it is to consciously choose abstractions in the design phase, we decided to explore abstractions in IoT personalization *in-the-wild*, with the aim of going beyond the contemporary *vendor-centric* approach.

3   Diary Study

We devised a diary study in the style of a contextual inquiry to end-users' personalization needs and adopted abstractions in the IoT. Although diary studies suffer from the problem that they are tedious for the recorder, they have high ecological value as they are carried out *in situ*, in the users' real environments [11], and they can offer a vast amount of contextual information without the costs of a true field study [4]. Our aim was to investigate:

(a) how far-reaching are end-users' needs in personalizing the IoT;
(b) whether other abstractions besides the contemporary *vendor-centric* one are possible, and
(c) whether the adopted abstraction(s) depend on the context in which the personalizations are introduced.

Participants. Due to the sensitive nature of the study, consisting in multiple home visitations, we recruited 24 participants from our social circle through direct e-mails and messages. To motivate participants for the study, we drew a prize worth more than 250 € among those who accepted. We tried to balance the population with respect to the following characteristics: age, gender, living situation, and occupation. The mean age of the participants (15 male and 9 female) was 31.71 years ($SD = 11.47$, $range = 19$–57). Overall, 18 participants lived in a shared household, i.e., in couple or with more than 2 other inhabitants, while the remaining 6 participants lived alone. The participants' occupations reflected a very varied population. Our study involved office workers (7), students (6), primary school teachers (3), farmers (3), factory and construction workers (3), an entrepreneur, and an airplane pilot. We also asked participants to answer some initial questions about their technological affinity. On a Likert-scale from 1 (Very Low) to 5 (Very High), participants stated their level of technophilia ($M = 3.83$, $SD = 1.09$) and programming experience ($M = 1.58$, $SD = 0.92$). Only 2 participants out of 24 had already used platforms like IFTTT.

Rule Notation and Composition Kit. To allow participants to define IoT personalizations in their daily lives, we created a *composition kit* with which users could freely note down trigger-action rules arising during their daily activities at home or outside. We chose to adopt the trigger-action paradigm due to its simplicity and its popularity in the context of End-User Development [1]. As done by Brich et al. [3] in the smart home context, we built a pen and paper kit to avoid artificially restricting the elicitation process to a specific user interface. The *composition kit* consisted on a home-made book and a pen (Fig. 1(a)).

To express trigger-action rules in the study, we defined a *rule notation*. To focus on the research goal without introducing unnecessary complexity for end users, we adopted the simplest form of the trigger-action programming approach, i.e., each rule contains exactly one trigger and one action. As suggested by Ur et al. [20], we allowed participants to enrich each trigger and action with multiple restrictions. In particular, the rule notation is inspired by the work of Desolda et al. [13], where the authors chose to follow a *5W* model for defining triggers and actions. The original *5W* model is adopted in several domains, such as journalism and customer analysis, to analyze the complex story about a fact through the following keywords: **W**hat, **W**ho, **W**hen, **W**here, and **W**hy. We adapted the model in our notation by specializing the meaning of each keyword to our domain, and by replacing the **W**hy with the **W**hich keyword (Fig. 1(b)). In particular, **W**hat is used for describing the trigger or the action, while **W**ho, **W**hen, **W**here, and **W**hich are used as social, temporal, spatial, and technological constraints, respectively. To compose trigger-action rules, the book contained 20 pages with the *rule notation* template (Fig. 1(b)). Furthermore, it contained a brief manual, and some rule examples (Fig. 1(c)).

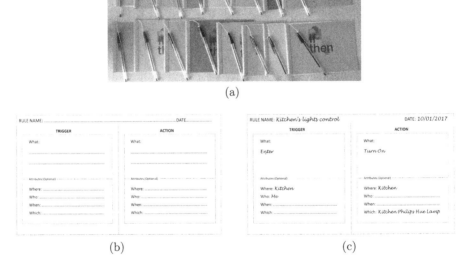

Fig. 1. Figure 1(a) shows the kits we used for the diary study, composed of a booklet and a pen. Figure 1(b) shows the template reported on the 20 book's pages for composing trigger-action rules, while Fig. 1(b) reports one of the rule example reported in the book. In the reported examples, we intentionally used different abstractions to avoid biases.

Study Procedure. To start the study, we set up a first appointment at the participants' home[4]. The appointment took about 30 min. At the beginning, participants were introduced to the general idea of EUD in the IoT. First, the IoT paradigm was introduced, along with some examples of devices and online services. Then, participants were taught about the trigger-action programming approach and the adopted *rule notation*, with some practical examples of trigger-action rules in different contexts and with different levels of abstractions. Finally, we gave the *composition kit* to the participants: they were instructed to take the kit with them in all their daily activities, and to record as many trigger-action rules as possible until the second appointment one week later. At the end of the study, we revisited participants in their home for a second appointment that took about 30 min. At the beginning of the appointment, participants were asked to show the trigger-action rules they had defined by explaining their mental process retrospectively. The focus of this phase was to understand whether the noted down trigger-action rules were correctly representing the ones participants envisioned, and to identify which abstractions participants used. Then, we concluded the study with a debriefing session. Our aim was to understand why participants used a given abstraction, and to investigate whether participants were aware of the implications of using a particular abstraction. All home appointments were audio-recorded. In case of households with more than one inhabitant, the two appointments were conducted separately.

4 Results

Thanks the study, we collected 233 freely recorded trigger-action rules and more than 25 h of audio recording. In this study, we report on the different abstractions adopted by our participants in their trigger-action rules, we describe the contexts in which the participants' personalizations have been envisioned, and we study the relationships between these contexts and the adopted abstractions. We support qualitative outcomes with quantitative results. To further explore our data, we also divide participants in four groups, on the basis of *a*) their *programming expertise*, i.e., by considering experts those participants that declared a programming experience greater than 3, and *b*) their *enthusiasm towards technology*, i.e., by considering enthusiasts those participants that declared a technophilia greater than 3 (in both cases, out of a Likert-scale of 5). Results are shortly discussed where necessary, while insights and new design opportunities are presented in the next section.

On average, each participant contributed to the study with 9.71 rules ($SD = 3.74$). Programming experts tended to record more rules with respect to participants with limited programming experience ($M = 11.34$, $SD = 4.04$, *vs.* $M = 9.47$, $SD = 3.75$, respectively). The technophilia, instead, did not affect the number of collected rules: both tech-enthusiasts and non enthusiasts recorded, on average, a very similar number of rules ($M = 9.81$, $SD = 3.43$, *vs.* $M = 9.50$, $SD = 4.57$, respectively).

---

[4] The study was conducted before the COVID-19 pandemic.

4.1 Personalizing the IoT Through Different *Abstractions*

To explore which abstractions end-users would adopt in personalizing their IoT ecosystems, we firstly analyzed the recorded triggers and actions, along with the participants' explanations collected in the final appointment, with the aim of determining clusters. To classify triggers and actions, in particular, we adopted the categorization proposed by Clark et al. [7] in the smart home context, according to which a personalization may fall in one these categories:

Device-centric A personalization whose subject is the physical medium with which it is executed. In our context, device-centric triggers and actions specified a device either directly in the **W**hat field or in the **W**hich field. A device-centric trigger, in particular, represents an event that is recognized by a physical object, while a device-centric action is the execution of an automatic behavior on a physical object. Participants, for example, used a device-centric abstraction to detect when the *garage door* closes (P1), to monitor the *car's* speed (P15), or to discover when there is an electrical failure in the *home lighting system* (P6).

Information-centric A personalization whose subject is the underlying information, regardless of the physical medium with which it is manipulated. In our context, information-centric triggers and actions specified such an information either directly in the **W**hat field or in the **W**hich field. A data-oriented trigger, in particular, represents an information that becomes available, while a data-oriented action is an information to be automatically obtained. Participants, for example, used an information-centric abstraction to monitor *their university exams* (P2), to detect when a *dangerous web site* has been visited (P14), or to manage *Facebook's notifications* (P12).

When rules were expressed in an ambiguous way, we used the qualitative data collected during the home appointments to disambiguate participants' intentions. During such a process, we found a large group of triggers that did not follow a device-centric nor information-centric abstraction. While these triggers resembled the "fuzzy triggers" discovered by Ur et al. [20] in the smart-home context, they also shared an additional characteristic, i.e., all of them envisioned a direct involvement of the participant in the personalization. We therefore defined an additional abstraction:

People-centric A personalization where users, their actions, and/or feelings are at the center of the interaction, independently of any physical and virtual medium. In our context, people-centric triggers had typically an empty **W**hich field, and they explicitly mentioned an individual or a group of individuals either directly on the **W**hat field or in the **W**ho field. Participants, for example, used a people-centric abstraction to trigger an event whenever *they arrive* at home (P8), to monitor *family members* (P20), or for more futuristic ideas, e.g., to detect when *they are hungry* (P20).

Participants demonstrated to prefer the *device-centric* abstraction when defining triggers (103 times), but they consistently used the *information-centric* and the *people-centric* abstraction, too (70 and 60 times, respectively). In defining actions, instead, participants adopted the *device-centric* and the *information-centric* abstractions in a similar way (121 and 112 times, respectively). Interestingly, although we could easily imagine people-oriented actions (e.g., "wake me up"), we did not find any collected actions that followed such an abstraction. We did not find any significant statistical difference on the adopted abstractions between participants' groups, i.e., programming experts *vs.* non experts and tech-enthusiasts *vs.* non enthusiasts, although interesting qualitative trends emerged. For what concerns triggers, programming experts and tech-enthusiasts demonstrated on average their preference towards including devices in their personalizations. Programming experts, for example, recorded on average 6.00 *device-centric* triggers ($SD = 5.29$), while they used the information-centric abstraction 2.67 times on average ($SD = 2.16$) and the people-centric abstraction 2.33 times on average ($SD = 2.08$). On the contrary, people with limited programming experience and enthusiasm used the 3 different abstractions in a similar way. Non-enthusiast participants, for example, recorded on average 3.36 *device-centric* triggers ($SD = 3.29$), 2.87 *information-centric* triggers ($SD = 2.03$), and 3.12 *people-centric* triggers ($SD = 2.23$). Such results seems to suggest that people that already know how to program and love technology prefer to maintain control over their IoT ecosystems. When considering actions, instead, differences are less prominent and no explicit trend emerges: independently of their programming expertise and technophilia, participants defined actions both with the *device-centric* and the *information-centric* abstraction.

The abstractions used by participants for defining triggers and actions lead to different types of rules. Table 1 describes the retrieved rule types and presents some examples. From *device-to-device* rules, i.e., rules with both the trigger and the action expressed with a *device-centric* abstraction, to *people-to-device* rules, i.e., rules with a *people-centric* trigger and an *information-centric* action, participants personalized their IoT ecosystems in very different ways.

4.2   The Right Abstraction for the Right *Context*

By looking at the collected trigger-action rules, and, in particular, by analyzing the **W**here fields, we found that participants introduced personalizations in different contexts. By means of 94 different trigger-action rules, participants often personalized the behaviors of their home, thus confirming the user's interest in home automation [3]. In 20 cases, in particular, participants defined rules to control home appliances, ranging from the coffee machine to the fridge. In some cases, participants referred to multiple appliances in the same rule. P19, for example, defined the following rule: *"[if] the dishwasher, the washing machine, and the oven are all turned on at the same time, [then] a limiter automatically deactivates other not essential appliances, to avoid failures in the home lighting system."* This highlights a gap between end-users' mental models and the contemporary *vendor-centric* abstraction. The latter, in fact, typically allow users to program one appliance at a time. Other prominent rules in the smart home

Table 1. The abstractions used by participants lead to different types of rules, from *device-to-device*, where rules involve devices, only, to *people-to-information*, where triggers that directly involve users are used to obtain or manipulate information. The reported rules have been rephrased for the sake of readability.

	Description	Examples
Device to device	Rules to execute an action over a physical entity when something happens or is detected by another physical entity	"[If] the *tensiometer* detects that the soil is dry, [then] turn on the *irrigation system*" (P11)
Device to information	Rules to obtain or manipulate an information when something happens or is detected by a physical entity	"[If] the *sensor* detects that it's raining, [then] warn me through a *WhatsApp message* or a *SMS*" (P18)
Information to device	Rules to execute an action over a physical entity when a new information is available	"[If] the *weather conditions* change while I'm driving, [then] the *car radio* starts playing songs that better fit with the new conditions" (P6)
Information to information	Rules to obtain or manipulate an information when another information is available	"[If] my *bank account* exceeds a threshold, [then] propose me safe *financial investments*" (P11)
People to device	Rules to execute an action over a physical entity when an individual perform a generic action or her conditions change	"[If] *I'm hungry* at night, [then] lock *the fridge* and the food storage" (P3)
People to information	Rules to obtain or manipulate an information when an individual perform a generic action or her conditions change	"[If] *I wake up*, [then] read the *newspaper headlines*" (P12)

context were recorded to control lights (12), doors and windows (9), and the temperature of the environment (7). Also in this case, participants specified triggers and actions in different ways. With the rule *"[if] the temperature on the thermostat drops below a given threshold, [then] set the thermostat temperature to a predefined value,"* for instance, P15 referred to a specific device (the thermostat) both in the trigger and in the action. Instead, the rule *"[if] my daughter is coming home in the weekend, [then] automatically warm her room"* of P21 generically referred to the heating system of his daughter's room. Despite the popularity of the home context, participants also personalized other smart environments, such as their gardens and courtyards (25), their car (23), and their workplace (17). The car, in particular, was mentioned in rules with different purposes. In this rule of P15, for instance, the car is considered as the main focus of the personalization: *"[if] my boyfriend or I exceed the speed limit by car, [then] decrease the car speed within the limit."* This rule of P3, instead, considers the car as a specific context: *"[if] I'm using the smartphone while I'm driving, [then] block it."* In addition to environments under their strict control, e.g., the home and the car, participants also envisioned rules in the city context (19 times), thus defining triggers and actions that involve environments, devices, and services that could be potentially accessed by all the citizens. P19, for instance, would like to be notified on her smartphone when pollution exceeds a given threshold, while P22 would like to be warned when there is a nearby car accident. Besides "physical" environments, we found that participants' rules frequently involved their online world (36 times) and their health and wellbeing (19 times). With rules such as *"[if] I publish a post on a social, [then] post it on all the other social networks"* (P4) and *"[if] my car insurance is about to expire, [then] perform a market research on the web"* (P14), participants personalized social networks, news, and their "online" information in general. For their health and wellbeing, instead, participants often defined automatic notifications to be received whenever their health parameters changed, e.g., *"[if] I have some hearth problems, [then] send me a notification"* (P12).

We also studied the relationship between the context and the type of the rule. Our aim was to investigate whether the adopted abstraction depended on the context in which the personalization was introduced. Figure 2 shows how many times (in percentage) participants used a given rule type in a specific context.

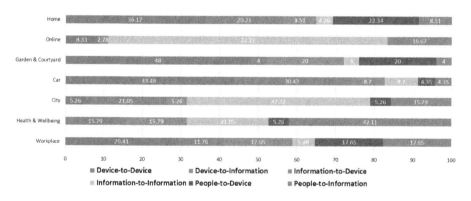

Fig. 2. How many times (in percentage) participants used a given rule type in a context. While *device-to-device* rules were prominent in the home context, participants were more interested in information rather than devices in the city context. Furthermore, participants defined *people-centric* triggers in all the contexts, especially in their workplace, their home, and for their health and wellbeing.

By analyzing the figure, interesting patterns emerge:

- In the home, garden & courtyard, car, and workplace, i.e., the "physical" contexts under their strict control, participants extensively used *device-to-*

device rules (36.17%, 48%, 43.48%, and 29.41%, respectively). In such contexts, also *information-centric* and *people-centric* triggers and actions were typically associated with physical devices or systems, while *information-to-information* rules, i.e., personalizations involving information, only, were rarely used (4.26% in the home, 4% in the garden & courtyard, 8.7% in the car, and 5.88% in the workplace).

– In the city, participants were more interested in information rather than devices. Only 5.26% of the rules were of type *device-to-device*. On the contrary, participants defined *information-to-information* and *device-to-information* rules in 47.37% and 21.05% of cases, respectively. Furthermore, while in the other physical environments the *people-centric* abstraction was frequently associated to devices, in the city participants preferred *people-to-information* rules (15.79%).

– Not surprisingly, the *information-centric* abstraction was prominent in the online context, and it appeared in the 91.67% of the related rules in total. *Information-to-information* rules, in particular, were the most common, and were defined 72.22% of cases.

– Participants used the *people-centric* abstraction in all the contexts. With the exception of the car (8.7%) and the online context (16.67%), all the other contexts were personalized through *people-centric* behaviors in more than 20% of cases. In the majority of the rules for the health & wellbeing context (47.37%), for example, participants used *people-to-information* (42.11%) and *people-to-device* (5.26%) rules. *People-to-information* rules were also frequently used in the workplace (17.65%), in the online context (16.67%), and in the city (15.79%). In other contexts such as the home and the garden & courtyard, the *people-centric* abstraction was more often involved in *people-to-device* rules (22.34% and 20%, respectively).

5   Design Opportunities for Personalizing the IoT

We believe that our findings may have a significant impact on the design of new interfaces for personalizing the IoT. By knowing the abstractions end users would adopt and in which contexts, researchers and designers may propose new solutions to break down barriers and increase EUD adoption in the IoT.

Adapting to Different Abstractions. Researchers and designers in the field of end-user personalization in the IoT need to be aware that users would define their trigger-action rules by adopting *different* abstractions depending on their programming experience, their enthusiasm towards technology, and the contexts in which the personalization is introduced. Instead of using a single, *vendor-centric* approach, participants of our study ranged from a *device-centric* abstraction, with which they "programmed" their physical entities, to other abstractions that go beyond physical devices, i.e., *information-centric* and *people-centric*. With *information-centric* triggers and actions they focused on the underlying information, while with *people-centric* triggers participants explicitly positioned themselves (and other people) *inside* the personalization. This variety of adopted abstractions highlights a huge gap with the contemporary EUD solutions, and opens the way to new design opportunities. By embracing different abstractions as a part of their system design space, in particular, designers may explore *adaptive* interfaces. The way a system is presented to the user, in fact, can have a priming effect on the initial mental models formed by users [7], thus influencing how they update their understanding of it based on newly-acquired knowledge [2]. Different strategies could be adopted. On the one hand, novel EUD solutions could provide users with the possibility of choosing the preferred abstraction. On the other hand, they could explicitly prime the user towards a specific abstraction. By reasoning on the "user profile," for example, an EUD interface could empower programming-experts in personalizing specific devices, while it could assist users with no or limited programming experience in personalizing their IoT ecosystems through *information-centric* and *people-centric* behaviors. As reported in our work, such an adaptation should also consider the context in which the personalization is introduced. To customize users' environments, e.g., homes or workplaces, designers of EUD interfaces should empower users in easily personalizing physical components, be they single devices or more complex systems. For other contexts, instead, EUD interfaces may be automatically adapted to different abstractions. When customizing the "online" context, for example, EUD interfaces could shift their abstraction towards the underlying information, while they might allow users in defining *people-centric* triggers for their health & wellbeing.

Sharing User's Preferences and Habits. Similarly to previous works exploiting a similar methodology (e.g., [3]), we only observed few rules (5, 2.15%) impossible to be executed, at least in the near future, with contemporary technology. All of them included "futuristic" triggers like *"when I'm hungry"* or *"when I'm curious about something."* The usage of a constraint-free study methodology, however, poses questions about the technical feasibility of the composed rules. While a trigger defined with the contemporary *vendor-centric* abstraction can be monitored via a specific device or online service, indeed, this is not true for *people-centric* triggers, for example, as they could be executed and adapted in different ways at run-time. The *"when I enter home"* trigger, for instance, could be monitored through a door that has been opened, or through a security camera detecting movements, among the others. When asked, in the final appointment, whether they would accept an intelligent system to automatically execute these "generic" triggers and actions, 17 participants out of 24 (70.84%) answered yes, at least in some cases. This seems to be partially in conflict with previous works in the smart home context [5, 10] that demonstrated that users do not want to lose control over the system. P14, for example, said: *"I want the lights to be automatically turned off, I don't care how to detect that I left the room ."*

Participants, however, pointed out that they would accept automated solutions for simple use cases, only, e.g., to control lights and temperature, and clearly excluded fully automated solutions. P24, for example, said: *"I don't want a black box: for generic triggers and actions, I would like the possibility to interact with the system, to define my preferences and eventually change the system's choices."* Also other participants envisioned an interaction with the system with the aim of sharing their preferences and habits. We claim that such an interaction is fundamental to *guide* the execution of generic behaviors, thus avoiding black-box solutions and maintaining a certain degree of control over the system. This is particularly true for the *people-centric* abstraction, with which our participants went beyond devices and information by defining triggers and actions that strongly depended on their tastes and feelings, e.g., *"when I'm hot"* (P3) and *"set my ideal water temperature"* (P22).

6   Limitations

There are some limitations to be considered in our work. While we balanced our participants according to different characteristics, e.g., occupations, programming experience, and tech-enthusiasm, our study involved a small sample of 24 users, and all our participants came from the same cultural background. Further analysis involving larger and varied samples are needed to assess the generalizability of our findings to other populations. As such, our study provides a sample of typical size for qualitative studies. Another limitation is related to the study design. The examples adopted in the initial appointment, in particular, may have influenced the abstractions participants adopted. The rule notation as well may have biased participants. Results, however, highlights consistent differences in the adopted abstractions. Finally, it has to be kept in mind that a diary study as the one we devised does not allow for making any assumptions about how seriously users would engage with real-world devices, systems, and online services, that are obviously a lot harder to set up and maintain than a piece of paper. Nevertheless, using a diary empowered our participants to be creative without any restriction, and allowed us in pursuing our goal, i.e., eliciting the abstractions end users would adopt with no regard for current technological constraints.

7   Conclusions

The expected growth of the Internet of Things opens new possibilities for end users: they can already personalize their devices and services on the basis of their personal needs. End-users personalization is particularly important since people are often forced to improvise, in order to tackle with unexpected changes in their life. Moreover, users would like to address these changes creatively, while adapting existing solutions to solving their issues at hand [15,20]. Contemporary EUD platforms in the IoT, however, present their own set of issues, and as a consequence, different gaps between users' expectations and reality emerge [13].

   In this work, we tried to close these gaps by exploring, directly with end users, the *abstractions* they would adopt in personalizing their IoT ecosystems.

The way a system is presented to the user, in fact, can have a priming effect on the initial mental models formed by users, and the abstraction used by a system is strictly related to its adoption [7]. By reporting on the results of a diary study with 24 participants, we show that users would adopt different abstractions by programming devices, information, and people-related behaviors, and we demonstrate that the adopted abstraction may depended on different factors, ranging from the user profile, e.g., her programming experience, to the context in which the personalization is introduced. While users are inclined to personalize physical objects in the home, for example, they often go beyond devices in the city, where they are more interested in the underlying information. Furthermore, through *people-centric* triggers, users would explicitly position themselves (and other people) *inside* the personalization, independently of the context.

Our findings point to new design opportunities in HCI to improve the relationship between the Internet of Things, personalization paradigms, and users. By embracing different abstractions as a part of their system design space, designers may explore EUD interfaces that go beyond the contemporary *vendor-centric* approach, able to adapt their abstractions and to share users' habits and preferences.

References

1. Barricelli, B.R., Valtolina, S.: Designing for end-user development in the Internet of Things. In: Díaz, P., Pipek, V., Ardito, C., Jensen, C., Aedo, I., Boden, A. (eds.) IS-EUD 2015. LNCS, vol. 9083, pp. 9–24. Springer, Cham (2015). https://doi.org/10.1007/978-3-319-18425-8_2

2. Bibby, P.A., Payne, S.J.: Instruction and practice in learning to use a device. Cogn. Sci. **20**(4), 539–578 (1996). https://doi.org/10.1207/s15516709cog2004_3

3. Brich, J., Walch, M., Rietzler, M., Weber, M., Schaub, F.: Exploring end user programming needs in home automation. ACM Trans. Comput.-Hum. Interact. **24**(2), 11:1-11:35 (2017). https://doi.org/10.1145/3057858

4. Broom, A.F., Kirby, E.R., Adams, J., Refshauge, K.M.: On illegitimacy, suffering and recognition: a diary study of women living with chronic pain. Sociology **49**(4), 712–731 (2015). https://doi.org/10.1177/0038038514551090

5. Brush, A.B., Lee, B., Mahajan, R., Agarwal, S., Saroiu, S., Dixon, C.: Home automation in the wild: challenges and opportunities. In: Proceedings of the SIGCHI Conference on Human Factors in Computing Systems, CHI 2011, pp. 2115–2124. ACM, New York (2011). https://doi.org/10.1145/1978942.1979249

6. Cerf, V., Senges, M.: Taking the internet to the next physical level. IEEE Comput. **49**(2), 80–86 (2016). https://doi.org/10.1109/MC.2016.51

7. Clark, M., Newman, M.W., Dutta, P.: Devices and data and agents, oh my: how smart home abstractions prime end-user mental models. Proc. ACM Interact. Mob. Wearable Ubiquit. Technol. **1**(3), 441–4426 (2017). https://doi.org/10.1145/3132031

8. Corno, F., De Russis, L., Monge Roffarello, A.: A high-level semantic approach to end-user development in the Internet of Things. Int. J. Hum. Comput. Stud. **125**, 41–54 (2019). https://doi.org/10.1016/j.ijhcs.2018.12.008

9. Corno, F., De Russis, L., Roffarello, A.M.: A high-level approach towards end user development in the IoT. In: Proceedings of the 2016 CHI Conference Extended Abstracts on Human Factors in Computing Systems, CHI EA 2017, pp. 1546–1552. ACM, New York (2017). https://doi.org/10.1145/3027063.3053157

10. Costanza, E., Fischer, J.E., Colley, J.A., Rodden, T., Ramchurn, S.D., Jennings, N.R.: Doing the laundry with agents: a field trial of a future smart energy system in the home. In: Proceedings of the SIGCHI Conference on Human Factors in Computing Systems, CHI 2014, pp. 813–822. ACM, New York (2014). https://doi.org/10.1145/2556288.2557167

11. Czerwinski, M., Horvitz, E., Wilhite, S.: A diary study of task switching and interruptions. In: Proceedings of the SIGCHI Conference on Human Factors in Computing Systems, CHI 2004, pp. 175–182. ACM, New York (2004). https://doi.org/10.1145/985692.985715

12. De Russis, L., Corno, F.: HomeRules: a tangible end-user programming interface for smart homes. In: Proceedings of the 33rd Annual ACM Conference Extended Abstracts on Human Factors in Computing Systems, CHI EA 2015, pp. 2109–2114. ACM, New York (2015). https://doi.org/10.1145/2702613.2732795

13. Desolda, G., Ardito, C., Matera, M.: Empowering end users to customize their smart environments: model, composition paradigms, and domain-specific tools. ACM Trans. Comput.-Hum. Interact. (TOCHI) 24(2), 12:1-12:52 (2017). https://doi.org/10.1145/3057859

14. Dey, A.K., Sohn, T., Streng, S., Kodama, J.: iCAP: interactive prototyping of context-aware applications. In: Fishkin, K.P., Schiele, B., Nixon, P., Quigley, A. (eds.) Pervasive 2006. LNCS, vol. 3968, pp. 254–271. Springer, Heidelberg (2006). https://doi.org/10.1007/11748625_16

15. Fischer, G., Giaccardi, E., Ye, Y., Sutcliffe, A.G., Mehandjiev, N.: Meta-design: a manifesto for end-user development. Commun. ACM 47(9), 33–37 (2004). https://doi.org/10.1145/1015864.1015884

16. Ghiani, G., Manca, M., Paternò, F., Santoro, C.: Personalization of context-dependent applications through trigger-action rules. ACM Trans. Comput.-Hum. Interact. (TOCHI) 24(2), 14:1-14:33 (2017). https://doi.org/10.1145/3057861

17. Huang, J., Cakmak, M.: Supporting mental model accuracy in trigger-action programming. In: Proceedings of the 2015 ACM International Joint Conference on Pervasive and Ubiquitous Computing, UbiComp 2015, pp. 215–225. ACM, New York (2015). https://doi.org/10.1145/2750858.2805830

18. Lee, J., Garduño, L., Walker, E., Burleson, W.: A tangible programming tool for creation of context-aware applications. In: Proceedings of the 2013 ACM International Joint Conference on Pervasive and Ubiquitous Computing, UbiComp 2013, pp. 391–400. ACM, New York (2013). https://doi.org/10.1145/2493432.2493483

19. Paternò, F., Santoro, C.: A design space for end user development in the time of the Internet of Things. In: Paternò, F., Wulf, V. (eds.) New Perspectives in End-User Development, pp. 43–59. Springer, Cham (2017). https://doi.org/10.1007/978-3-319-60291-2_3

20. Ur, B., McManus, E., Pak Yong Ho, M., Littman, M.L.: Practical trigger-action programming in the smart home. In: Proceedings of the SIGCHI Conference on Human Factors in Computing Systems, CHI 2014, pp. 803–812. ACM, New York (2014). https://doi.org/10.1145/2556288.2557420

21. Ur, B., et al.: Trigger-action programming in the wild: an analysis of 200,000 IFTTT recipes. In: Proceedings of the 34rd Annual ACM Conference on Human Factors in Computing Systems, CHI 2016, pp. 3227–3231. ACM, New York (2016). https://doi.org/10.1145/2858036.2858556

22. Zaslavsky, A., Jayaraman, P.P.: Discovery in the Internet of Things: the Internet of Things (ubiquity symposium). Ubiquity 2015, 21–210 (2015). https://doi.org/10.1145/2822529

Help Me Create Smart Things: How to Support Design and Art Students at a Distance

Rosella Gennari[(⊠)] [iD], Eftychia Roumelioti [iD], and Secil Ugur Yavuz [iD]

Free University of Bozen-Bolzano, Piazza Domenicani 3, 39100 Bolzano, Italy
gennari@inf.unibz.it, Eftychia.Roumelioti@stud-inf.unibz.it,
Secil.UgurYavuz@unibz.it

Abstract. Design and art students learn in workshops and through practical activities. They are not usually experienced in physical computing. However, this is fundamental for creating smart things, part of our internet-of-things world and hence of creative design and art work. Moreover, these students' creativity was severely hampered due to the COVID-19 pandemic: used to working on practical projects by interacting with different sorts of material, they were forced to learn in a new setting, at distance. This paper reports on a workshop which was run with design and art students, led by researchers in human computer interaction and industrial design. The workshop, held at a distance in a single day, did not assume any programming experience. It relied on a game tool, which was re-purposed for the workshop, by following a meta-design approach. The workshop challenged design and art students to explore and create smart things, by playing the game. Data were collected with multiple methods and analysed so as to study the creativity of students' products and extract useful lessons for designing with design and art students or practitioners, also at a distance.

Keywords: Technologies and infrastructures for end-user development · Cultures of participation and meta-design approaches · Supporting creative work through end-user development · Smart thing · IoT

1   Introduction

Students of Unibz have a unique Bachelor's study programme, which introduces them to different forms of design and art. Along their 3-year study course, they work on various projects in studios, dedicated to "images", "space", "interaction" and "exhibit" in Art, and "product" and "visual communication" in Design major. Students of the third year focus on the development of their final project based on what they have learnt in one of the four studios. Students of the last year are thereby used to learning in workshops and creating projects starting from the first year. Although they have computing courses such as 3D modelling

© Springer Nature Switzerland AG 2021
D. Fogli et al. (Eds.): IS-EUD 2021, LNCS 12724, pp. 87–101, 2021.
https://doi.org/10.1007/978-3-030-79840-6_6

and other design software, their study programme does not offer physical computing courses, in particular, which would enable them to create smart artefacts.

Smart things, on the other hand, are everywhere nowadays. Work of design and art embraces technology also in the form of smart things, e.g., the so-called popable creations and installations by Qi and Buechley [18]. The research reported in this paper aimed at giving design and art students of Unibz, in their last Bachelor's year, new design possibilities related to smart thing design. It aimed at exploring how to tackle the challenge of opening up for them this world in a single-day workshop, without demanding any background in computing, in general, or physical computing, in particular. It eases thus the "tension between technical skills and creativity" [22].

The exploratory research, reported in this paper, intercepted a second challenge, which all students faced in 2020, due the COVID-19 pandemic: how to conduct product-related workshops at a distance. Limitations imposed by the pandemic made the challenge more critical for design and art students of the last year, who had grown used to creating products by working in studios and interacting, experimenting and tinkering with different sorts of material.

The work reported in this paper offered these students a workshop centred around SNaP. This was designed for enabling teens, without computing background, to explore and learn how to design simple smart things at a distance. The tool uses visual metaphors, based on cards, and a highly interactive game environment, which guides users across the design process, till the automated generation of programs for interactive prototypes of smart things.

By following a meta-design approach, the tool was rapidly re-purposed for the design and art students, and an at-a-distance workshop was organised around it. The workshop asked students to create their own smart things, in a day, at a distance. Researchers, participating in the workshop, considered how students used the tool in order to extract useful lessons from its usages in a new context.

The underlying research question of the workshop was as follows: *would the tool support design and art students' creativity?* Qualitative data were collected with multiple methods and results were triangulated for extracting useful lessons in relation to the creativity of the resulting smart things, and the design of tools for creating smart things with design and art students, also at a distance.

The paper starts by briefly outlining the relevant features of SNaP. It reports on strictly relevant related work, concerning the assessment of product creativity and meta-design. Afterwards, the paper comes to its core matters. It presents the workshop design, with its participants and protocol, besides the data collection and research question in details. It continues reporting on the data analysis. It concludes by reflecting on the results of the workshops and extracts lessons for future work concerning tools for design and art students or practitioners.

2   Background on the SNaP Tool

SNaP is a tool for designing simple smart things, made of a thing (e.g., a bench), one input with associated actions (e.g., a button to press) and one output with associated reactions (e.g., a LED strip to light up in different colours). The tool is as an online HTML5 game, which can be used with any modern web browser.

SNaP adopts a card-based metaphor. Some decks of cards serve to represent the main components of smart things: besides things to be made smarts, SNaP contains decks of technology cards for input and output devices. Moreover, SNaP offers so-called mission cards which give possible goals that smart things can accomplish in a nature park environment.

The tool enables users to interact in four main manners, illustrated in Fig. 1 and 2. SNaP enables users to drag cards on the board for conceptualising smart things, e.g., the mission card of exploring the park, the bench card as thing, the button card as input, the LED strip card as output. See the top of Fig. 2. The tool enables users to describe their ideas of a simple smart thing with a semi-controlled natural language, with a condition for the input and a behaviour for the output, e.g., if the button is pressed then the LED strip lights up in orange. She the bottom of Fig. 1.

Moreover, the tool generates graphical representations of users' ideas, assembled and described in the board, which users can further revise or download. See the top of Fig. 2. Last but not least, the tool generates, automatically, programs for their simple smart thing conceptualised in a board. The program has an infinite loop with a conditional, related to the description in natural language of the idea. Such programs are rendered with visual blocks of the Makecode programming environment for the micro:bit board, a programmable physical computing board with on-board or plug-in input and output devices, such as buttons or LED lights [16,17]. See the bottom of Fig. 2. Users can then continue programming in Makecode or run a simulation of physical prototypes with them.

3   Related Work

3.1   Creativity and Its Evaluation

Creativity has been extensively researched and discussed in Human Computer Interaction (HCI) research and beyond [12]. Defining creativity is a difficult topic that cannot be fully captured with a single approach and within one discipline [20]. In general terms, creativity is considered a multifaceted construct, involving different abilities, skills and techniques that can draw on critical judgement, imagination and often intuition [15].

Guilford considered creativity as a form of problem solving through two types of cognitive operations: (i) divergent thinking, the process of creating many, varied ideas through the association and recombination of individual elements and (ii) convergent thinking, the process of "making sense" of the multiple ideas and converging into a single, concrete outcome, by means of reflections [13]. Instead Rhodes distinguished creativity along the so-called four p-categories: (1) the creative place, (2) the creative person, (3) the creative product, and (4) the creative process. Definitions of creativity usually reflect at least one of these four cognitive categories [19,21]. In this paper, we focus on creative products, namely ideas of smart things by design and art students.

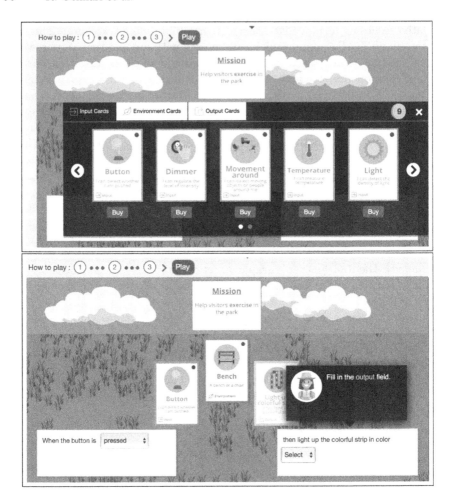

Fig. 1. Users buying cards from the input deck (top) and using them in their board for conceptualising a simple smart thing idea (bottom)

Whether and how product creativity can be assessed is another issue under debate. A comprehensive assessment of the creativity of products requires considering also the process or person responsible for them and, in general, contextual factors [3,14,23]. In light of that, creativity can be best assessed by adopting a holistic perspective, within a qualitative research or mixed-method research framework. When relying on one of these frameworks, Treffinger et al. suggest a multi-method assessment of creativity [24]. This draws upon many different sources of data and frequently includes measurement sources; then qualitative data can be coded and quantified over, and thus treated statistically. This paper adopts a qualitative framework with a multi-method assessment of the creativity of design and art students' products, which considers some qualitative data as measurement sources.

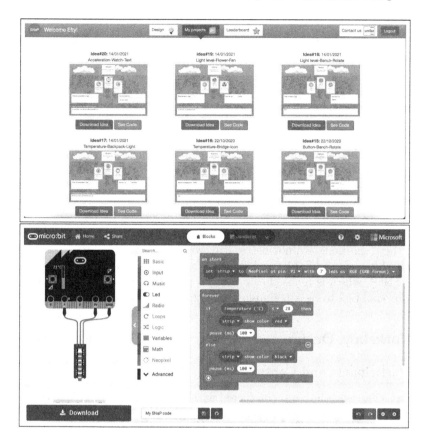

Fig. 2. Ideas generated by a user with downloadable images (top), and an example of the automatically generated program for an idea with Makecode blocks and physical simulation

In order to 'measure' the creativity of design and art students' products, this paper considers dimensions often correlated to creativity. Example dimensions are novelty, feasibility and elaboration [4,6,8]. Among them, elaboration refers to the details and richness of a product, broadly conceived (e.g., idea, artefact, software), in response to given stimuli [1,2,13]. This paper adopts and measures an indicator of elaboration of students' smart thing ideas, correlated to their creativity: the number of components in their smart thing ideas.

3.2 Meta-design

Meta-design is a conceptual framework rooted in end-user development. One of the leading assumptions of meta-design is that the usage of a novel technology or its usage in a novel context cannot be anticipated during development, e.g., different users may use technology in unexpected ways. Therefore meta-design focuses on the emergence of design rather than pre-planning, and recommends that researchers embrace unexpected usages [9,10]. Thereby it is an approach suitable for assessing the usage of the SNaP tool in a novel context, as in the workshop reported in this paper, given that the tool was never used with design and art students previously.

Meta-design also aims at creating a design space within a culture of continuous innovation, in which all stakeholders (e.g., researchers and users) participate, albeit with potentially different roles [9]. In this manner, meta-design benefits from a give-and-take paradigm, where users learn and contribute through personally or socially meaningful activities and, in return, design also grows and evolves with the contributions of all [11]. This is also the case of the workshop reported in this paper, in which students were invited to use SNaP in order to create smart things and take inspiration from its usages.

In order to accommodate the emergence of design and a continuous shared innovation, meta-design recommends "underdesigned solutions" [5]. In other words, these solutions are not necessarily with limited capabilities, rather they are malleable and modifiable, and suitable for a rapid evolution. This is also the case of SNaP, which is realised as a vertical prototype exploring basic functionalities for enabling to design simple smart things at a distance.

4   Workshop Design

4.1   Participants and Context

Context. The workshop was conducted within a semester-long course with third year's students of the Design Bachelor's programme. The tangible outcome of the course is a physical product, which each student creates for a given context. The context was the local park train station, given as a briefing to students: "Mind the Gap! Ideas for a better quality of stay at the local train station".

Participants. The one-day workshop was moderated by the design course lecturer together with two HCI researchers, experts of physical computing.

There were in total 8 students participating in the workshop and course, 2 males and 6 females. The participant students had a briefing about physical computing the week before the workshop, so as to introduce the idea and basic terminology of smart thing design. However, none of them declared to have any experience of programmable electronics except in one case, of a student who had "tried Raspberry Pi with Scratch but never managed to learn how to make it work on my own or understand it".

4.2   Research Questions and Data Collection

Research Questions. Products are students' ideas of smart things. The underlying research question of the workshop was related to the usage of a tool like SNaP for creating such products: *would it support design and art students' creativity?* The general question was divided into two specific research questions:

R1. What smart thing ideas would design and art students elaborate on with the tool?

R2. How would design and art students use the tool?

Data Collection. Qualitative data were collected in order to answer the two specific research questions, **R1** and **R2**. Such choice helps discover how participants construct their own view or meaning of an experience, in relation to 'what' and 'how' questions [7].

R1. For tackling the what-**R1** question, data were collected at two main points in time:

1. before the workshop with SNaP;
2. after the workshop with SNaP.

Such data are students' artefacts documenting ideas (visual representations, filled-in SNaP boards) and students' unstructured interviews about their ideas, conducted by the lecturer and HCI experts. In the interviews, strong emphasis was placed on gathering personal comments and opinions directly from the students.

R2. For tackling the how-**R2** question, different qualitative data were used. The lecturer reported in a diary her observations during the entire workshop, documenting how students approached and used SNaP. Such data were integrated with unstructured interviews around the tool with the HCI experts, held in conclusion to the workshop, besides students' visual representations of their smart thing ideas. Again, the interview strived to elicit students' views and gain an insight on their own approach to the tool.

4.3 Protocol

Due to COVID-19 related restrictions and regulations, the workshop was conducted online, at a distance. Students could not experience physically how to build mock-ups or prototypes by themselves in order to test their ideas, as in the in-presence version of the course. Therefore SNaP was employed to enable students to explore the main components of smart things at a distance, ideate smart things with on-line cards, and test how their smart things would play out on their own, by relying on the programs automatically generated by SNaP and simulated in the Makecode programming environment. The workshops was divided into sessions, explained in the following.

Introduction and Exploration. The workshop started with the HCI experts who introduced themselves, their research and how SNaP works for circa 15 minutes. Then students introduced themselves and explained whether they had any experience in physical computing or smart thing design, and their ideas of smart things for their course projects in case they had them.

Ideation and Reflection. In the second session, students started using SNaP. They were invited to use it freely. For instance, although SNaP already offers things which can be found in or around a train station (such as benches, trees, public lighting), students were free to choose other things or add their own, e.g., closer to their projects in case they had matured them.

After an initial ideation of c. 1 h, in which students were rapidly generating as many ideas as possible with SNaP, they shared their ideas in a collective reflection exercise with the lecturer and the other students. Each student had 3–4 ideas. This reflection served to select one idea per student. This idea was further developed by the students themselves, starting off with SNaP again.

Prototyping and Reflection. At home, on their own, students used SNaP in order to generate the programs for their refined ideas. Students could run programs in Makecode which enabled them to simulate and test mock-ups of their ideas. Afterwards, students shared their work with the lecturer, who had micro:bit in her location. The lecturer downloaded the programs for student's smart things on micro:bit boards and showed students how these would "physically" play out. For building physical mock-ups, the lecturer used green and low-cost material, such as cardboard, or everyday things like a cup, a pen and a vase. She was guided by the students, as if the students' commands were moving the lecturer's hands in building the physical mock-ups. In this manner, students could experience both the simulations of their ideas in Makecode, as well as small-scale physical mock-ups of these ideas. This experience became a physical extension of the digital game and added an additional dimension to the learning process. Experiencing the ideas as small interactive mock-ups helped students to experience sensor-actuator relations in a real-life setting.

After testing the physical prototypes, students spent one more hour to work on their scenarios for explaining how the smart things work, and created visual representations of the scenarios. At the end of the workshop, the students shared their work with the lecturer and the HCI experts in a 2-h session online. They illustrated their scenarios and visual representations, and they also engaged in dialogues concerning their smart things and how they used SNaP for creating.

5   Results

5.1   Elaboration of Smart Thing Ideas

Data collected for tackling the **R1** question became measurement sources of the elaboration of student's products, that is, their smart thing ideas. As indicators of elaboration, researchers considered: (1) the number of things, (2) the number of inputs, (3) the number of outputs of each student's idea.

SPSS 26 for Windows was thus used for computing descriptive statistics and executing tests concerning such indicators. In general, as the descriptive statistics in Table 1 shows, all students explored and experimented with the technology SNaP opened up for them, in the form of inputs and outputs.

A Wilcoxon signed-rank test returned that the SNaP-based workshop elicited a statistically significant difference in the number of input and output devices, related to technology, present in smart thing ideas ($Z = -2.047$, $p = .041$ for input, and $Z = -2.565$, $p = .010$ for output), and no statistically significant change in the number of things ($Z = 1.857$, $p = .063$).

Table 1. Statistics related to the number of things, inputs, outputs before and after using SNaP

	Number of things		Number of inputs		Number of outputs	
	Before	After	Before	After	Before	After
Mean	.88	1.62	.63	2.13	.38	2
St. Dev.	.36	.74	.92	.99	.52	.54
Minimum	0	1	0	1	0	1
Maximum	1	3	2	4	1	3

Content analysis was used by the lecturer and HCI experts in order to further analyse data related to smart thing ideas. They reflected and focused on the level of elaboration of student's ideas prior to using SNaP. The content analysis was conducted independently and then jointly discussed. The following patterns emerged.

The students (three), who had a vague idea of smart things for the chosen context before using SNaP, explored all decks of SNaP cards (missions, things, inputs, outputs) and changed their ideas accordingly. For instance, a student changed completely her vaguely defined idea of a "GPS to trace the bike if stolen, QR code to unlock the bike with colours". Her conclusive smart thing was a smart bench, which gave rise to a multi-species interaction: the smart bench was enabling a communication between the tree and the person in the park. Her visual representation emphasises that her smart thing includes others-than-humans, it is not human-centred, as the tree is the central focus element. In the conclusion to the workshop, explaining her idea, the student commented as follows: "We forget how magic nature is and so I was just thinking of how to place it in the centre [of our attention] like in a movie". She got inspired by one of the missions of SNaP and its things (tree, bird houses, bench), which led her elaboration around technology.

All other students except one, who had a refined smart thing idea before using SNaP, elaborated further on it with input and output devices. This situation is illustrated in Fig. 3, concerning a signage system. The student was using a QR code before using SNaP because she "had no idea of what other technology could be used" except what she knew of "Alexa, smartphones or the like". After using SNaP, she replaced the QR code with a microphone for detecting sound, a pressure sensor, buttons, and a distance detector, which she illustrated in her storyboard with images and SNaP cards. Only in one case, a student with an elaborated idea did not elaborate on it but started off a new idea by using all SNaP cards.

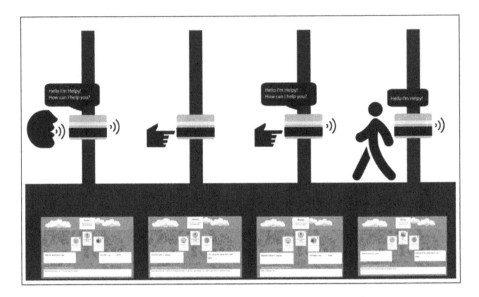

Fig. 3. The SNaP cards and description of a smart signage system by a student, and how the usage of this smart thing was narrated with a storyboard with several inputs and outputs from SNaP.

5.2   Unexpected Usages of the Tool

All students immediately learnt how to use SNaP; none of them asked for support concerning its usage after it was introduced by HCI experts. The following reports a content analysis of the lecturer's notes besides students' interviews and visual representations, for answering the **R2** question—how students used the tool during the workshop. Analyses are reported separately per type of usage, focusing on unexpected usages.

Free Exploration. Students, with a vague idea of a smart thing before SNaP, used it for scaffolding the ideation process by randomly combining cards. One of them declared that "all my ideas started from its cards for inspiring". Another said he chose missions of SNaP to start the ideation, and then he continued "playing and randomly putting together [input, environment, output] cards" in order to open up his imagination. In the end, he generated ideas for (at least) two different playful smart things, namely, a smart bench detecting and leaving temperature traces of passers-by, and a street-sign interacting and playing with passers-by. Figure 4 shows his idea of a smart bench. The idea was conceived and conceptualised with SNaP cards, as shown on the left. Then the student illustrated how to interact with this smart thing by referring to SNaP cards for the main components of this smart thing, as shown on the right side of the figure.

Technology at Different Levels. Some students, who elaborated on their initial ideas, used SNaP in order to explore input and output devices, and what kinds of interactions they enable. For instance, a student, working on a smart column for a train station, explored and discovered different sensors to embed into her smart thing with SNaP. Some students did not stop with SNaP: they continued exploring and elaborating with the Makecode environment, accessed with the program generated automatically by SNaP. By tinkering with the program, they explored other possibilities related to the chosen input and output devices. A student declared that "SNaP opened up new [technology related] possibilities", she would not have discovered otherwise. Another student said: "SNaP helped me think about the technology in my daily life, like with sliding doors" and "I never thought there is technology there for input and output".

Visual Representations and Beyond. What observed in relation to Fig. 4 seems to be a general trend: in the visual narration of their smart things, students referred to SNaP cards, for input and output devices, and continued using them in their presentations in order to clarify how the input and output devices would enable the interaction.

Another interesting usage emerged in students' visual representations. The SNaP tool, currently, enables them to generate boards for ideas and programs for simple smart things: each board or program refers to a single input and a single output for a thing. The visual representations of students went beyond such limitation and used several SNaP boards or referred to cards creatively, overcoming it. Figure 3 shows an example of this usage: the student used different boards with different cards for input and output in order to narrate the interaction visually with her smart thing.

In one case, the exploration of input and output devices, opened up by SNaP, went beyond the digital aspects of smart things. The scaffolding of SNaP helped a student imagine different scenarios for her main smart thing. During the workshop the student elaborated on her public seating unit with a digital game board for children to play tic-tac-toe while waiting for a train. This idea later was embedded in the student project in an analogue version, as a blackboard for drawing attached to the seating unit for children. Therefore, the workshop with SNaP gave rise to an idea that was translated from a digital to an analogue setting.

6   Reflections and Recommendations

The workshops collected qualitative data. Some were used as measurement sources for the elaboration of students' products, which is often associated to their creativity. All data were further analysed in order to discover patterns in smart thing ideas by students and in order to investigate unexpected usages of the tool, so as to answer the **R1** and **R2** research questions, respectively. Conclusive reflections are reported in the following. Related recommendations, for tools à la SNaP, are extracted for future work.

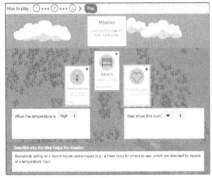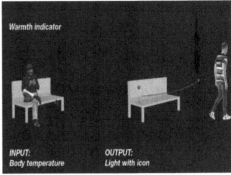

Fig. 4. The SNaP cards and description of a smart bench by a student, and how the cards were used in the student's storyboard.

6.1 Elaboration of Smart Thing Ideas

A Wilcoxon signed-rank test returned a statistically significant difference in the number of input and output devices that students discovered with SNaP and put to use in their smart thing ideas during the workshop. Such a difference is taken as an overall indicator that students were creative from the technology viewpoint, in that they elaborated on their ideas of smart things with inputs and outputs: all of them significantly changed the number of input and output devices for their smart things, after using SNaP.

A content analysis of students' ideas revealed two patterns. Students, who had a vague idea for a smart thing before the workshop, tended to use all SNaP cards and elaborate novel smart things. All others, except one, used mainly technology cards for input and output for elaborating on ideas.

The statistical analysis and the follow-up content analysis of student's smart thing ideas suggest the following answer to the **R1** question: all students elaborated on smart thing ideas with the technology they discovered thanks to SNaP cards, independently of whether they had got a refined or vague idea for a smart thing before using SNaP. This result suggests the following recommendation for future tools à la SNaP:

> *Tools for design and art students should unveil for them the main technology components of a smart thing (e.g., input and output devices).*

6.2 Unexpected Usages of the Tool and Recommendations

A content analysis was also conducted on the lecturer's diary notes and interviews of students at the end of the workshop, besides students' visual representations. The analysis gives three main answers to the **R2** question, related to the usage of the tool. In the following, these are reflected over and related recommendations are put forward.

Free Exploration. First of all, SNaP was used as a creativity trigger for starting off the ideation process of design and art students when ideas were vague. In this case, they used all cards and tended to "play and randomly put together cards" for "inspiration" and conceiving novel ideas of smart things. Secondly, when students had refined ideas of smart things to start with, they tended to elaborate on their ideas and explore technology with SNaP, not knowing what type of technology is behind smart things, beyond what is popular, e.g., microphones, QR codes. As they declared, also their creativity was triggered because SNaP unveiled for them input and output devices of smart things and how they can be used. Such usages suggest the following recommendation:

Tools for design and art students should enable them to randomly assemble components of simple smart things and incrementally explore a range of them when ideas evolve in elaboration.

Technology at Different Levels. Moreover, SNaP was used by design and art students to explore technology at different levels. While some students explored mainly cards and developed some scenarios based on their combinations, other students started with them and then continued with the Makecode environment so as to further understand technology and elaborate on their ideas accordingly. Such usages lead to the following recommendation:

Tools for design and art students should enable them to explore technology components of smart things with both visual conceptual representations and physical/simulated interactive prototypes.

Visual and Physical Representations. However, all students used or referred to SNaP input and output cards in their visual narratives. It seems that once discovered how they work, students tend to use them in a functional manner in their projects. Moreover, they did not seem constrained by the restraints of the SNaP tool, which enables them to generate a program with a simple if-then-rule for a smart thing. For instance, in their visual representations, they used more than one SNaP dashboards in storyboard representations, when they wished to use more than one input or output in their idea. Even more interesting, in one case, the idea generated with SNaP was even translated from a digital setting to an analogue one. Such result suggests that design with SNaP does not necessarily remain a mere exploration of technology, but that it can have an impact on the students' analogic artistic production. Moreover, the use of everyday objects, like cardboards or other artefacts found at home to create interactive mock-ups, can be integrated in the creative process to give more physicality to the physical computing workshops held at distance. These usages are translated in the following recommendation:

Tools for design and art students should generate and enable to reuse visual and physical representations of components of smart things, which students can embed into their visual representations or projects of smart things.

7   Conclusions

This paper presented a workshop for enabling design and art students to create smart things at a distance. The workshop centred around the SNaP tool. Following a meta-design approach, the use of the tool was rapidly re-purposed and adapted for the needs of design and art students. It collected different qualitative data, which were analysed with two main lenses: the creativity of students' products; the usages they made of the tool. Results were deeply reflected over, and lessons were distilled for designing future tools for creating with design and art students. Limitations of the work are mainly due to its qualitative nature. However the rich data set which was collected and analysed enabled researchers to extract useful reflections and design recommendations for possible bespoke tools/instruments to be developed for design and art students or practitioners to work on creative projects embedding ideas of smart things.

References

1. Amabile, T.M.: Social psychology of creativity: a consensual assessment technique. J. Pers. Soc. Psychol. **43**(5), 997–1013 (1982). https://doi.org/10.1037/0022-3514. 43.5.997

2. Baer, J.: Domain specificity: introduction and overview. In: Baer, J. (ed.) Domain Specificity of Creativity, pp. 1–16. Academic Press, San Diego (2016). https://doi. org/10.1016/B978-0-12-799962-3.00001-X

3. Barbot, B., Besancon, M., Lubart, T.: Assessing creativity in the classroom. Open Educ. J. **4**, 58–66 (2011). https://doi.org/10.2174/1874920801104010058

4. Besemer, S.P.: Creative product analysis matrix: testing the model structure and a comparison among products-three novel chairs. Creativity Res. J. **11**(4), 333–346 (1998). https://doi.org/10.1207/s15326934crj1104_7

5. Brand, S.: How Buildings Learn: What Happens After They're Built. Penguin, London (1995)

6. Christiaans, H.H.C.M.: Creativity as a design criterion. Creativity Res. J. **14**(1), 41–54 (2002). https://doi.org/10.1207/S15326934CRJ1401_4

7. Creswell, J.: Research Design: Qualitative, Quantitative, and Mixed Methods Approaches. SAGE Publications, Thousand Oaks (2009)

8. Demirkan, H., Afacan, Y.: Assessing creativity in design education: analysis of creativity factors in the first-year design studio. Des. Stud. **33**(3), 262–278 (2012). https://doi.org/10.1016/j.destud.2011.11.005. https://www.sciencedirect. com/science/article/pii/S0142694X11000986

9. Fischer, G., Giaccardi, E.: Meta-design: a framework for the future of end-user development. In: Lieberman, H., Paternò, F., Wulf, V. (eds.) End User Development. HCIS, vol. 9, pp. 427–457. Springer, Dordrecht (2006). https://doi.org/10. 1007/1-4020-5386-X_19

10. Fischer, G., Herrmann, T.: Meta-design: transforming and enriching the design and use of socio-technical systems. In: Wulf, V., Schmidt, K., Randall, D. (eds.) Designing Socially Embedded Technologies in the Real-World. CSCW, pp. 79–109. Springer, London (2015). https://doi.org/10.1007/978-1-4471-6720-4_6

11. Fogli, D., Giaccardi, E., Acerbis, A., Filisetti, F.: Physical prototyping of social products through end-user development. In: Díaz, P., Pipek, V., Ardito, C., Jensen, C., Aedo, I., Boden, A. (eds.) IS-EUD 2015. LNCS, vol. 9083, pp. 217–222. Springer, Cham (2015). https://doi.org/10.1007/978-3-319-18425-8_19

12. Frich, J., Mose Biskjaer, M., Dalsgaard, P.: Twenty years of creativity research in human-computer interaction: current state and future directions. In: Proceedings of the 2018 Designing Interactive Systems Conference, DIS 2018, pp. 1235–1257. ACM, New York (2018). https://doi.org/10.1145/3196709.3196732

13. Guilford, J.P.: Creativity: a quarter century of progress. In: Taylor, I.A., Getzels, J.W. (eds.) Perspectives in Creativity (1975)

14. Horn, D., Salvendy, G.: Consumer-based assessment of product creativity: a review and reappraisal. Hum. Factors Ergon. Manuf. Serv. Ind. 16(2), 155–175 (2006). https://doi.org/10.1002/hfm.20047

15. Kupers, E., Lehmann-Wermser, A., McPherson, G., van Geert, P.: Children's creativity: a theoretical framework and systematic review. Rev. Educ. Res. 89(1), 93–124 (2019). https://doi.org/10.3102/0034654318815707

16. Micro:bit-Educational-Foundation: Micro:bit educational foundation — micro:bit (2019). https://microbit.org. Accessed 06 Sep 2019

17. Microsoft: Microsoft Makecode (2019). https://makecode.microbit.org. Accessed 06 Sep 2019

18. Qi, J., Buechley, L.: Electronic popables: exploring paper-based computing through an interactive pop-up book. In: Proceedings of the Fourth International Conference on Tangible, Embedded, and Embodied Interaction, TEI 2010, pp. 121–128. Association for Computing Machinery, New York (2010). https://doi.org/10.1145/1709886.1709909

19. Rhodes, M.: An analysis of creativity. Phi Delta Kappan 42(7), 305–310 (1961). https://www.jstor.org/stable/20342603

20. Runco, M.A., Jaeger, G.J.: The standard definition of creativity. Creativity Res. J. 24(1), 92–96 (2012). https://doi.org/10.1080/10400419.2012.650092

21. Said Metwaly, S., Van den Noortgate, W., Kyndt, E.: Approaches to measuring creativity: a systematic literature review. Creativity Theories-Res.-Appl. 4 (2017). https://doi.org/10.1515/ctra-2017-0013

22. Sawyer, R.: Teaching creativity in art and design studio classes: a systematic literature review. Educ. Res. Rev. 22, 99–113 (2017). https://doi.org/10.1016/j.edurev.2017.07.002

23. Shah, J.J., Smith, S.M., Vargas-Hernandez, N.: Metrics for measuring ideation effectiveness. Des. Stud. 24(2), 111–134 (2003). https://doi.org/10.1016/S0142-694X(02)00034-0

24. Treffinger, D., Young, G., Selby, E., Shepardson, C.: Assessing creativity: A guide for educators (2002)

Personalization in a Paper Factory

Marco Manca(iD), Fabio Paternò(iD), and Carmen Santoro(⊠)(iD)

HIIS Laboratory, CNR-ISTI, Pisa, Italy
{marco.manca,fabio.paterno,carmen.santoro}@isti.cnr.it

Abstract. The purpose of this work is to explore the potentialities of a personalization platform in industrial settings. We report on a case study in the paper factory domain, in which the industrial aspects identified with relevant experts through interviews have been simulated and connected with a personalization platform. A first user test has been carried out with a representative set of users, which has provided useful and encouraging feedback in terms of the potentialities of the approach in industrial settings.

Keywords: End user development · Internet of Things · Industry 4.0

1 Introduction

Today's industrial environments are becoming highly dynamic, with shorter product life cycles and delivery times, requiring increased levels of innovation and customization. Such requirements call for rapidly responding systems that can adjust to required changes in processing functions and production, and meet customization demands on a timely basis. Industry 4.0 is the current response to these complex scenarios: by combining different technologies and software, it aims to enable seamless and flexible production, thus signifying the disruptive power of digitalization in industrial plants. For instance, thanks to the Internet of Things (IoT), a key enabling technology of Industry 4.0, the way in which operations and processes are carried out is radically changing. What in the past was 'closed' inside factories, stored in different local 'data silos' (i.e. one for each machinery producer), and managed using devices based on proprietary/non-standard communication protocols (which kept them rather isolated and inflexible), now is increasingly handled through more standard approaches, promoting easy connectivity and interoperability between the devices, sensors and actuators available in firms. This will offer unprecedented access to real-time data on products and processes, and more informed decisions taken across the whole enterprise (from technicians, to front-line operators to top managers), potentially leading to continuous factory optimization.

In the manufacturing sector, while the availability of up-to-date information at all levels (i.e. from technical processes, to individual equipment components, to associated production and business processes) for a better factory control is becoming paramount [17], turning this vision into reality is extremely challenging. Not only because in these contexts there is a plethora of processes, IoT assets, information sources and up-to-date as well as legacy machines to manage, but also because the integration, maintenance,

D. Fogli et al. (Eds.): IS-EUD 2021, LNCS 12724, pp. 102–118, 2021.
https://doi.org/10.1007/978-3-030-79840-6_7

and control of software is usually responsibility of Information Technology (IT) experts. Therefore, when manufacturing workers identify that a change is needed to the software controlling some processes (e.g. because in a specific situation a different behavior is needed), they strongly depend on the IT department to implement it. However, current software development cycles are not always able to respond quickly to the dynamic needs of factories, then this situation could introduce significant delays and increase costs. Thus, it is becoming clear that applications whose behaviour depends on context cannot be completely "hard-coded" at design time by professional developers, since they cannot predict all the possible situations of use and whether the results produced will actually be meaningful, as they often lack the knowledge that usually only domain experts have. This scenario seems a suitable application area for End-User Development (EUD), which aims to provide domain experts with effective tools to build solutions to the problems they face every day, by empowering them to develop and iterate autonomously on needed customizations without including IT experts at each stage.

In the context of IoT-based applications, EUD approaches that exploit the trigger-action paradigm have demonstrated particularly promising [2, 9], thanks to their compact and intuitive structure which directly links dynamic events or conditions of the current context to actions to execute when the rule is triggered. Several applications from the academic and industrial fields have shown that the trigger-action paradigm could be easily understood also by people without specific programming skills [15], since its use does not require specific algorithmic knowledge, or abilities in the use of complex programming structures: users have just to specify the rules that indicate the desired effects (e.g. in terms of changes to the state of devices, appliances and user interfaces) when specific situations occur. Such approaches have been applied to different domains ranging from rehabilitation [14], robotics [16], smart homes [4], Ambient Assisted Living [10], and finance [5]. However, to the best of our knowledge, so far industrial contexts have been considered only in a limited manner with regard to EUD themes.

In this paper, considering the increasingly emergent trend of Industry 4.0 we focused our attention on applying a EUD trigger-action approach to an industrial scenario in the paper sector, to investigate to what extent the concepts associated with this approach could be found suitable for addressing current issues in such Industry 4.0 scenarios, and easily exploited by domain experts for personalizing the behaviour of a factory according to events and situations occurring in it. The contribution of this work is to show how a solution based on trigger-action rules can be used to make such personalization easier for people who are not professional software developers. In order to show this, we extended an existing EUD platform to support triggers and actions relevant in an industrial context and then we assessed the solution through a remote usability study in which real experts in the considered sector had to specify relevant rules. We also provided participants with the possibility to see the effects of the interactions with the EUD tool, by executing some rules using simulated prototypes.

The structure of the paper is as follows. In the next section we describe related research, then in Sect. 3 we report on some interviews with stakeholders, which have been carried out to identify relevant requirements. In Sect. 4 we describe the case study considered, while in Sect. 5 we detail the solution to support experts of this domain to personalise their applications. In Sect. 6 we describe a user study that we carried out involving relevant stakeholders in the paper sector, also providing a discussion of the main results gathered. Then we conclude, describing our future plans in this area.

2   Related Work

According to [1], the application domain of business and data management is one of the most frequent in which End User Development or End User Programming techniques have been applied (24% of total). This is also because it was the historical domain where the idea of tailoring digital artefacts by end users at use time was born, by exploiting spreadsheet programming [3]. An interesting recent work [12] describes a systematic literature mapping study analysing the main EUD strategies used by organizations, as well as the benefits and barriers to their adoption. The benefits they identify can be classified into human factors and organizational factors, whereas the barriers can be related to people, processes and technologies. In particular, on the one hand, support for decision-making, reduced dependence on IT, increased end-user productivity and increased end-user satisfaction are the most mentioned benefits of EUD adoption. On the other hand, lack of training for end-users, lack of support for end-users and the need for technological support were the most cited barriers.

In the business domain, a common approach is to use workflow-based technologies to define and execute business processes, with established standards being BPEL and BPMN. However, such approaches focus just on business process, whereas Industry 4.0 settings are typically more complex, as they involve a variety of heterogeneous physical IoT devices, digital resources, services and activities, which can change their course based on events occurring on them or in the operator's context. As an attempt to bridge the gap between physical IoT devices and business processes, [8] suggested employing process models to define the process layer of IoT applications and enact them through a process engine. However, while workflow-based approaches facilitate the integration of different systems, they require quite strong programming skills, so being unsuitable for unprofessional developers.

A key component of Industry 4.0 is its human-centricity, which Romero et al. [13] concretized in the *Operator 4.0* concept. It refers to smart and skilled operators of the future, who will be assisted by automated systems providing a sustainable relief to their physical and mental stress, and enabling them to better leverage on their creative skills without compromising production objectives. The authors propose an Operator 4.0 categorization, arguing that one operator could incorporate one or several others, differentiated between: Super-Strength Operator (e.g. using exoskeletons), Augmented Operator (e.g. using augmented reality tools), Virtual Operator (e.g. using a virtual factory), Healthy Operator (e.g. using wearable devices to track well-being), Smarter Operator (e.g. using agent or artificial intelligence for planning activities), Collaborative Operator (e.g. interacting with cobots), Social Operator (e.g. sharing knowledge using a social network) and Analytical Operator (using Big Data analytics).

Fogli and Piccinno [7] highlight that there is a gap between what Industry 4.0 promises, and how Operators 4.0 will be called on to change their work practice, suggesting that the integration of EUD with Industry 4.0 enabling technologies might help workers to evolve more smoothly into the various types of Operator 4.0. For instance,

Super-Strength Operator can be included in Augmented Operator by assuming exoskeletons as a form of augmentation that must be (physically) personalized to the user, while Smarter, Healthy and Social Operators can be embraced in IoT Operator, who, through EUD, should be able to manage the entire IoT ecosystem. Thus, the enabling technologies of Industry 4.0 should be tailored to the work context and the type of operator *by users themselves*, supported by suitable EUD tools developed according to meta-design [6], as it not only focuses on technologies, but can also sustain the cultural transformation needed to address the future complexity of workplaces.

Other examples that focused on EUD applied to industrial environments involve robotics. While robots have not yet become commonplace in homes, collaborative robots work with humans in factories with increasing frequency. In [16] the authors introduce Robot Blockly, a block-based programming interface for a single-armed industrial robot, showing that novices with no prior programming experience successfully wrote programs to accomplish basic robotics tasks. However, as acknowledged by authors themselves, it was just a preliminary investigation in the potential of block-based programming for industrial robots. Recent commercial automation platforms such as IFTTT[1] or Zapier[2] also allow users to integrate different IT systems in an easy and flexible manner, without having programming skills. However, they typically allow users to define rather simple rules, and have been just limitedly considered for integration in business scenarios so far (e.g. Zapier integrates Customer Relationship Management).

In sectors such as the manufacturing industry, tailoring issues have been addressed even less till now. To this regard, Wieland et al. [18] propose MIALinx, a lightweight and easy-to-use integration solution for SMEs using *if-then* rules that connect occurring situations in manufacturing environments (e.g. machine breakdowns) with corresponding actions (i.e. an automatic maintenance call generation). To this goal, MIALinx connects sensors and actuators according to rules defined in a domain-specific and easy manner, to enable rule modelling by domain experts. In their approach, rules involve available sensors and actuators in the current production environment, and they are then transformed to be managed and executed using existing rules engine (e.g. Jess or Drools). In a more recent paper [11] the user interface of MIALinx has been presented. It was installed and tested in an industrial plant and in a lab dedicated to research on future working places: first test results show that it usually takes less than 30 s to create a rule after a short introduction (less than 5 min). However, no further details on these tests are provided in [11] to fully appreciate the validity of the solution. To sum up, by analysing the state of the art there is a lack of solutions that apply EUD approaches in an Industry 4.0 manufacturing context (paper factories in our case), also gathering feedback from real stakeholders. This work aims to contribute to fill this gap.

3 Domain Analysis and Requirements Elicitation Through Interviews

We interviewed stakeholders of the paper sector preferably having a managerial view, to identify relevant requirements, to better understand current practices and challenges,

---

[1] https://ifttt.com/

[2] https://zapier.com/

and to identify events and actions relevant for customization. They were recruited from the network of the members of a project funded by the Tuscany Region (Italy). Initially contacted by phone, they received via email a brief introduction and a document on personal data processing and informed consent, to fill in and sign. Interviews were remotely conducted on: *i) Information on stakeholders* (user's age, gender, familiarity with technology, experience in the sector, role/tasks) and their *companies* (goals, size); ii) *Adoption of IoT/Industry 4.0 and currently used methods; iii) Relevant events/sensors; iv) Relevant actions/actuators; v) Challenges* (e.g. aspects that pose problems, situations to improve). We involved 5 subjects (1 woman; AVG age $= 51.2$; SD $= 3.8$; Min $= 45$; Max $= 55$), overall quite familiar with technology, and working in companies all located in the Lucca area, one of the largest Italian districts in this sector.

Stakeholders. One stakeholder (M, 52) is responsible of the IT department for a company (300+workers in Lucca) that builds undulators (the machines producing undulated cardboard, typically used for packaging). Another one (M, 53) works in a paper mill (200+workers in Lucca) producing undulated cardboard: he has 37+years of experience in this sector, currently managing safety. Another stakeholder (F, 45) is the IT director of a paper mill (200+workers only in Lucca). Another one (M, 51) is the administrator of a small transport company (~40 people): his activities range from managing warehouses, customers, to administration and even safety. The last one (M, 55) is the General Director of a paper converting company (~65 workers in Lucca).

Adoption of IoT/Industry 4.0 Technologies. In the firm producing undulators, they already use predictive maintenance. The paper mill producing undulated cardboard is technologically heterogeneous: modern and legacy equipment co-exist, with several costly machines, difficult to replace. Also, they do not strongly leverage on Industry 4.0 technologies yet. Even the idea of using web TVs (already available in some plants) to send messages to operators was hindered by the top floor for security reasons. In the transport company, they recently purchased a trolley which updates automatically the warehouse's inventories by "firing" barcodes on items; to move goods, they also have elevator carts which automatically register entry/exit via barcodes. The other stakeholder working in a paper mill also reported that Industry 4.0 adoption is still at an early stage: while they already use many sensors, they would eager to have further support such as predictive maintenance or self-correcting equipment. They have both 'old' machines (dating to the '80s, for which they use sensors to "retrofit" them), and newer ones measuring i.e. paper humidity, strength, and grammage (a measure of paper 'thickness', used to define different paper types). The stakeholder working in the transport company reported that they would like to have sensors to detect risky situations (i.e. when ground personnel are not properly separate from forklifts), which currently is not the case. The paper converting company just started adopting Industry 4.0: one of their newer lines has its composing machines (i.e. winders, cutters) connected with the management system, thus operators can get data in real-time. They are also installing a predictive maintenance system.

Events. In the company building undulators, relevant events include monitoring the quality of the produced equipment and the production speed. In one paper mill, situations to detect include the characteristics of the produced board (cameras and sensors are already used to control starch, glue, humidity), anomalies (i.e. unglued sheets), number of produced items, temperature of the equipment. In the other paper mill, relevant events include e.g. the consumption of raw material (in terms of e.g. water, steam, starch) and also its quality (i.e. humidity, amount of contained ashes or plastic). The situations to monitor reported by the stakeholder working in the transport company include controlling cost/revenue ratio (i.e. they would like to suitably handle more up-to-date information, whereas now reports are sent every 3 months), and whether activities are carried out in accordance with safety regulations. In the paper converting machine company, relevant aspects include those related to machinery (i.e. state, production speed, temperature), paper grammage, number of tears in paper rolls, roll length and diameter.

Actions. In the company producing undulators, actions include those that operate on parts of the equipment (i.e. cylinders, pistons, valves, servomotors). Alarms or notifications are sent in case of anomalies, or when the equipment is poorly working. In paper mills, notifications are sent to users in case of anomaly via sounds or lights, or using monitors on the lines. Also, one of the most serious alarms is issued when a machine stops, while warnings occur e.g. when the "recipe" currently used (i.e. the mixture of ingredients used to produce a particular product) is going to change. In the paper transport company, audible or visual alarms are already sent in "man-down" situations (by using dedicated devices), or to personnel on moving carts (who may not see well their surroundings). However, the user points out that it is important to limit such alarms to truly risky situations. This was also confirmed by the stakeholder working in the paper converting machine company, who reported that while acoustic and flashing signals are already used to highlight anomalies, often such alarms do not correspond to truly dangerous situations, thus in such cases it is needed that human operators check them.

Current Challenges and Personalization Scenarios. In the firm producing equipment for papermaking there is the challenge of improving the satisfaction of operators, whose tasks nowadays are often reduced to rather passive roles (i.e. visual monitoring), as well as improving factory efficiency (i.e. increasing production while decreasing the need of maintenance stops). Also, to supervise production, the IT team developed an application providing the company with real-time data about the equipment they produce, and their customers with various reports about the equipment they use, also allowing them to modify autonomously specific parameters according to their needs (by acting on a database), without the need of manufacturer's intervention. For paper mills, one challenge is to avoid paper breaking (depending on the contract, there is a maximum number of admitted tears in the same paper roll). When this situation occurs, they have to avoid both customer's 'downgrading' of the product (due to too many 'joints' in the same roll) and wasting material. In particular, in these situations she would like to set that e.g. dispensers (feeding the line with the ingredients) automatically stop, and specific warnings reach concerned people with associated reporting of the problem. She also would need more sensors on the lines, to improve checks *in-line* (i.e. in real time), and not *off-line* (i.e. in laboratories), as it occurs today. In the paper converting machine company, a challenge is enhancing the quality control: currently the data about e.g. product defects or equipment efficiency come on a sample basis and at a later stage (since machines work in a continuous cycle), while they would need them continuously, to enable suitable prompter reactions. The stakeholder working as a safety officer in a paper mill mentioned several scenarios that can benefit from personalisation: their undulators need to be configured based on dynamic plant's factors (e.g. internal temperature, humidity); he also would like to get real-time info on trucks' flow at plant's gate to send tailored navigation info to concerned drivers.

To sum up, while the companies where the interviewees work are overall at an initial stage in adopting Industry 4.0/IoT for various apparent reasons (i.e. investments needed to replace machines/infrastructure, difficulties in managing IoT-related security issues), their managers seem well aware of the opportunities that these technologies could bring to them in terms of e.g. having an integrated, real-time view of the system to enable continuous optimization. In this scenario, the proposed personalization approach targeting non-technical people (like them) was judged particularly relevant and indeed concrete personalization scenarios came up during the interviews, which also provided useful information for the design of our solution in the considered domain.

4   The Case Study Considered

The case study focuses on a paper factory. Paper production is basically a process in which a fibrous raw material is first converted into pulp, which is then converted into paper. To this aim, wood chips are first processed so that the unusable part of wood (i.e. lignin) is separated from useful fibres (i.e. cellulose), which are broken up through water within 'pulpers' to produce pulp, the main ingredient of paper. Pulp then feeds a continuous "paper machine", together with the other ingredients that define the "recipe" used to deliver a specific product (e.g. 'paper' is distinguished from 'carton board' since it has a lower basis weight or 'grammage'). Paper machines are endlessly moving belts that receive a mixture of pulp and water and make excess water drain off (by suction, pressure, or heat). The continuous paper sheet (called 'web') coming out of this machine is wound onto an individual spool, to become a 'parent reel' (or 'jumbo roll', see Fig. 1). Since the reel width is fixed for each paper machine, next, another machine (a 'winder') cuts the reel into rolls of smaller diameter, using as little material as possible to minimize trim losses. For cut-sheet paper products, rolls are loaded onto a 'sheeter', which unwinds them and slices the paper into sheets of desired size, which are then wrapped and loaded onto vehicles for shipment to customers/distribution centres. While jumbo rolls are the output of paper mills, they in turn represent the input of paper converting companies, which transform them into e.g. napkins, envelopes, tissue.

5   The Architecture of the Solution

To address the requirements identified in the paper domain we extended an existing platform [9] previously applied to other sectors (i.e. smart home, Ambient Assisted Living), to support the triggers and the actions relevant to the industrial context considered. The architecture of the solution is shown in Fig. 2. The idea is that the applications used by a worker to control and manage the paper factory (i.e. for monitoring the production, for acting on parts of the production equipment, for managing emergency situations within the plant, for supporting data analysis and reporting), should be able to adapt their behaviour in a context-dependent manner, reacting to the events occurring in the

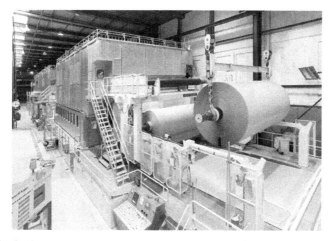

Fig. 1. A paper machine with jumbo rolls in the foreground (from VOITH)

surrounding context, and applying the actions specified in rules defined by 'end user developers', who, in our case, are mainly experts in the paper sector.

The Rule Editor is the EUD tool they should use to specify such behaviour, following a trigger-action paradigm. Once rules are created via the Rule Editor, those that the user wants to consider for actual execution in the current context are sent to a module called "Rule Manager", which subscribes to another module, the Context Manager, to be informed when relevant events occur in the current context. More specifically, the Context Manager consists of a Context Server receiving the context updates, and several Context Delegates, which are lightweight software applications able to communicate with sensors and appliances to receive info about their state, and consequently forward such information to the Context Server, by exploiting REST-based calls on HTTPS. In our solution, since it was problematic to perform the experimentation in a real industrial setting, two simulators have been developed to simulate the occurrence of events and actions, respectively (further details will be provided later on in this section). The Context Manager receives the data coming from sensors, and stores them in a uniform format used for all the devices, appliances and machines belonging to the considered context. The applications in turn subscribe to the Rule Manager to be informed when an action should be carried out. Whenever an event specified in a rule occurs, the Rule Manager receives a notification from the Context Manager, selects the actions associated with the triggered rule and sends them to the subscribed applications. The applications have to interpret the received actions, then sending via MQTT the associated commands to the devices, appliances, actuators involved in the actions. This in some cases could also involve additional roles (e.g. a message is sent to another factory worker).

As mentioned before, we also developed two simulator prototypes. The one dedicated to events simulated situations occurring on production lines (by using it, the user can monitor the state of the production lines and also change relevant parameters associated with its composing equipment i.e. the weight of paper trim losses detected at the end of the production cycle), and also the occurrence of emergency situations (such as the

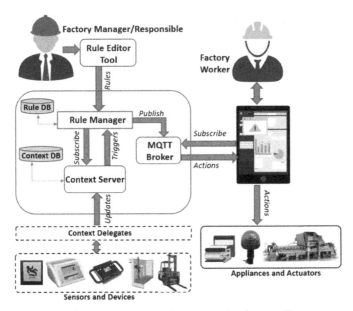

Fig. 2. The platform architecture (Color figure online)

'man-down' alarm, which in real scenarios is typically issued by dedicated devices that detect worker's falls). As for the actions, on the one hand the simulator provided a view of the factory, which included elements such as coloured semaphores highlighting specific situations on production lines (i.e. a red semaphore indicates a situation that needs further attention). On the other hand, actions such as sending alarms/reminders via email/SMS were not simulated, but actually supported by the prototype.

5.1 The Tailoring Environment for the Paper Industry Domain

The Rule Editor supports trigger and action selection by displaying the available ones organised in logical hierarchies that can be configured according to the needs of he considered domain. In this case the configuration considered, as reference, an exemplary paper mill. The triggers refer to three contextual dimensions (*User*, *Technology*, *Environment*), while the actions considered state changes of factory appliances, or the generation of reminders and alarms. In particular, in this case study the *User* dimension covers aspects associated with workers, who can be of three types: managers, front-line operators (working 'on the floor'), and technicians (i.e. those in charge of equipment maintenance). Their specification is refined into "Physical aspects" and "Position". The first one is to identify situations where workers are moving or not (such as the well-known "Man-Down" event). The current position of users can be specified in absolute terms (via GPS) or according to some "points of interest" within the factory (e.g. "Raw Material Warehouse", "Production Line 1", "Pulper").

The *Environments* element is refined according to key environments/departments of the factory (e.g. Raw Material warehouse, Finished Product warehouse, Production Department, Offices). All are characterised by typical environmental properties such as light level, noise, smoke, pollution, humidity. In addition, warehouses also have 'Entry Speed' and 'Exit Speed', namely the rate at which raw material (resp.: finished product) enters/exits a warehouse, and also the "capacity" currently reached in each warehouse (i.e. empty, almost empty, almost full, full). The warehouses can be internal or external, according to whether they are managed within the company or not.

Regarding the *Technology* dimension, the following elements have been considered: Pulper (the machine that produces pulp from cellulose), Desiccator (which dries excessive water from the paper web), Weight Scale (at the end of the production cycle, it measures paper trim losses), Elevator (the cart moving materials within the plant). Of course, we also considered Production Lines as another key technology. All of them have the following attributes: "Efficiency" (a value in percentage terms, defining the efficiency of the equipment) and "Status" (whether the equipment is working, in pause or is stopped). The Production Lines (see Fig. 3) consider additional aspects: Entry Speed (the speed at which raw material is consumed), Exit Speed (the speed at which the final product is delivered), Jumbo Roll Weight (the weight of the reel produced at the end of the production cycle), Paper Grammage (the basis weight of the paper), Paper Waste (the paper trim losses measured by the weight scales at the end of the production line), and Order Type (the type of "job" currently managed by the production line, refined in terms of Type of Customer and Type of Product Requested, thus specifying the customer who commissioned a specific order and the type of product requested).

Actions have been refined into Alarms, Reminders, and actions on the Production Lines. Alarms and Reminders are refined basically using the same fields: the text to send, the notification mode (i.e. mail, SMS, push notification), repetition times, and the recipient (i.e. a phone number or a mail address depending on the notification mode). The other actions aim to change the state of a line (stop, start, pause), or change the light of the semaphore associated with the production line (red, green, yellow), and also modify the recipe used for feeding the production line.

Finally, to more properly cover the needs of the considered domain, in the Rule Editor we enabled different "views" of the hierarchies of triggers and actions, depending on the type of user who accesses it. Indeed, access to the Rule Editor also implies the possibility to have the control of particular equipment/machinery of the company, which of course must be allowed only to specific roles. Thus, beyond the "responsible" role (who can access the whole hierarchies) there is also an "external operator" role, who can access only a portion of triggers and actions, namely those operating on the specific entities this role can manage (i.e. a subset of warehouses). Finally, rules can also be shared with others, using a public rule repository.

6   User Study

The goal of the test was to get feedback from real stakeholders on the potentialities of the platform and the approach. The test was remotely conducted. Potential participants were recruited from the network of the members of a Regional project, trying to involve non-technical personnel (i.e. heads of departments, managers). They were first contacted by phone/email to ask for their willingness to participate. Then, they received an email detailing the test structure (also including info on the processing of personal data and the

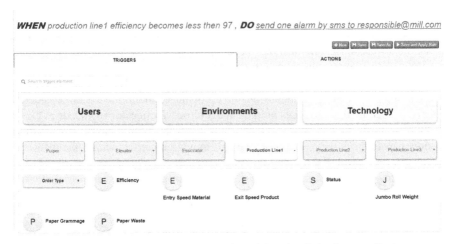

Fig. 3. The Rule Editor for the considered domain (Color figure online)

request for informed consent), its objectives, and main functionalities of the Rule Editor and of the simulators (also with a short video). We sent them also the tasks, the links to the tools and the simulators to use for the test (with associated credentials), and to the online questionnaires to fill in anonymously after the test: the SUS Questionnaire, and further ad-hoc questions about the approach and the tool. The metrics considered were errors (how many and of which type), and task success categorised as it follows: complete success: the user has not made any mistake; failure: the user gave up or did not complete the task; minor problems: the user made one or two errors; major problems: the user made more than two errors. We considered an error a difference between the rule defined by the participant and its correct specification. Possible errors on trigger specification are: i) use of an event instead of a condition and vice versa; ii) use of a trigger element other than the one expected (i.e., use a trigger that involves the "dryer" element instead of one involving the "pulper"); iii) selection of an incorrect attribute within a trigger (i.e. instead of specifying "inside" an environment (i.e. a department) specify "outside" it; iv) inclusion of an additional trigger, not required by the rule; v) a missing trigger. Except for the first type (which deals with the event/condition distinction, peculiar to triggers), similar types of errors were considered for actions.

6.1 Tasks

Tasks were identified to allow users to evaluate different aspects of the approach (trigger/action composition, events vs. conditions), and were proposed according to increasing difficulty levels (progressively asking to do more, and respecting more constraints).

- *Task1*: Write in your own words 2 rules you consider relevant in the paper sector.
- *Task2*: Using the Rule Editor, build a rule that you consider significant, containing 1 trigger and 1 action. Save the rule as "task2".

- *Task3*: Using the Rule Editor, build a rule you consider significant, containing 2 triggers (combined through AND or OR), and 1 action. Save the rule as "task3".
- *Task4*: Using the Rule Editor, specify: "As soon as the temperature of the Production Dept. exceeds 30 degrees while the operator is within it, send an alarm SMS to 0011223344". Save the rule as "task4".
- *Task5*: Using the Rule Editor, create two rules:

  - *Task5.1* As soon as paper waste on Production Line1 turns out to be less than 30 kg, a green light is turned on. Save it as "task5_1".
  - *Task5.2* In situations in which the weight of paper waste on Production Line 1 turns out to be equal or beyond 30 kg, a yellow light turns on and an e-mail is sent to your mailbox. Save it as "task5_2".

After creating Task5's rules, users had to activate them in the Rule Editor, use the event simulator to set the context in which the rule is triggered, then check that the executed actions (displayed in the action simulators) were those expected.

6.2 Participants

The test user group is made up of real users (i.e. experts in the paper sector), familiar with using web applications, but no additional skills were required. Six participants were involved in the test (1 woman), all different from those involved in the interviews. Before the test, the participants had never used the applications to test in the trial. The average age of the participants was 45.3 years (min = 40; max = 53, SD = 4.7). Three participants have a high school Diploma, 2 users have a Master's Degree (one in Physics, another in Aeronautical Engineering), the latter has a Bachelor's degree in Electrical Engineering. Three participants declared to have no knowledge of programming languages, the others had limited/low knowledge, one user declared to have good knowledge of industrial programming languages. All users have good familiarity with the web. Their companies range from the production of tissue, to production of paper converting machines, to developing services for automation/industrial applications. Most of them have 50–250 employees, one company has more than 500 employees. One user is the head of the company's IT department, another is the sales manager for machine components; another participant deals with the sale of spare parts, another with the planning and coordination of maintenance and warehouse management, another deals with solutions for predictive maintenance, the last user is responsible for company's quality and safety. Most users have more than 10 years of experience in the paper industry, with 50% having more than 15 years. 5 users never used any tools for customizing applications before the test (one user mentioned the Voith OnCare tool).

6.3 Results

In Task1 users were asked to report two rules in natural language, which they considered significant. Examples of rules created are: If number of knife cuts = X, send to maintenance the following text "number of knife cuts = X, blade change required; If the traffic light associated with the line signals a reel deviation > 10 kg, send a warning via email; If a man-down is detected, call the safety officer. If reel diameter = 10 m, send message to production asking to change the reel". By analysing the rules, users generally exploited a rather simple structure (one trigger, one action). Three out of the 6 involved users referred to man-down scenarios in their rules, whereas the actions were generally of notification/alarm/warning type. Task2 required to build a (1 trigger, 1 action) rule the user considered significant (from Task2 onwards users were required to use the Rule Editor). All the rules built by users included sending an alarm as an action. Three rules correctly included an event trigger whereas in the other rules a condition trigger was used: the latter, when combined with an instant action (i.e. sending an alarm), would result in repeatedly sending the notification, a situation that does not always correspond to a desired one. However, all users at maximum experienced minor problems with Task 2. Example of rules are: IF operator is laying down, DO send one alarm by mail to sistema@company.com; When production department temperature becomes more then 40 C, do send 3 alarms by mail to maintenance@mill.com; When production line1 efficiency becomes less than 80%, do send one alarm by SMS to 123456789. Task3 required to build a rule containing 2 triggers (combined through AND or OR), and one action. Examples of rules created were: i) When production department smoke becomes more than 100 AND operator is near production_line_1, do send one alarm by SMS to 123456789; ii) When production department noise becomes more than 98 OR production department humidity becomes more then 95, do send three alarms by mail to manager@mill.com; iii) If production line2 paper grammage is 17 AND production line2 paper waste is more than 10, do send alarm by mail to quality@farm.com. Most of the times the AND operator was used to combine the triggers, only twice the OR was used. Alarm type notifications were included as an action type, while the most used types of triggers were of Environment type and of User type. Most users completed Task3 successfully, in the worst cases with one or two errors, and no failure was reported. In Task 4 the majority of users (66.7%) experienced minor problems or successfully completed the task. For Task 5.1, all the users either experienced minor problems or successfully completed it. Task 5.2 was the most affected by errors: however, it was the most complex one, as it required both the specification of a structured rule (2 triggers, 2 actions) and its actual execution (using the simulators). Across all the tasks, the error in which conditions and events were used incorrectly was the most frequent one (38.2% of the total), followed by the one in which an attribute different from the one expected was used (23.5%). The average of the global values obtained by SUS (i.e. the average level of satisfaction of the sample) was 68.8, thus denoting a more than acceptable usability. Additional questions were included to collect feedback on other aspects of the solution presented. Some questions (Q1–Q5, see Fig. 4) involved providing a score using a scale from 1 to 7 (1 = not very useful/appropriate; 7 = very useful/appropriate), and also a motivation for it. The other questions gathered qualitative feedback e.g. on the most positive and negative aspects of the approach, and willingness to adopt it. As it can be seen from Fig. 4, overall users appreciated the usefulness of the approach. A user stated that since it is not possible to program "a priori" all the events occurring in a complex industrial environment such as a paper mill, a dynamic handling like the one proposed is extremely useful. Two users particularly appreciated its usefulness for managing safety and production: one noted that the control of the variables manipulated by production processes well suits with a trigger-action logic to promptly act on critical situations through corrective actions. Another user highlighted, as one of its main advantages, that the approach can benefit numerous aspects of the management of a paper factory, from handling anomalies and emergencies to quality control and logistics. Both the hierarchy of triggers and of actions were overall well received, although some participants suggested further expanding the available choices. The description of the rules in natural language was appreciated by the users, one of them stated: "*Those who specify the rule behaviour are often unskilled users, then the use of natural language simplifies rule understanding*". One highlighted that this can be useful to make the rule behaviour more easily understandable also to people different from the ones who created them, thereby serving as a useful communication mean. For the event/condition distinction, they judged it "clear and concise" and "simple to use". However, when it came to actually exploit it within rules, it seems that not all of them completely grasped it, as well as the importance of the impact that a misuse of it could have at rule execution time.

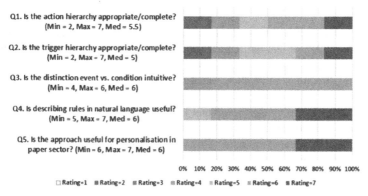

Fig. 4. Chart with user ratings on some aspects of the Rule Editor tool

Among the positive aspects of the tool (Q6), the simplicity of use and the clarity of its parts were indicated. One user reported the good potential of the solution in his own company, another user found the possibility to specify alerts through various channels very interesting. As for negative aspects (Q7), one user would have preferred more options for triggers/actions, another said that he would have preferred additional mechanism (i.e. flowcharts) for displaying rules. When asked whether in their companies they already faced similar customization needs (Q8), two users affirmatively replied: one pointed out that they are using a Manufacturing Execution System that integrates functions to send emails or feed SQL tables in a manner suitable also for unskilled users. Another one reported that they are creating a dashboard both at the management level and at the level of the single production plant to handle the underlying processes in a facilitated manner. Another user reported that they are considering this type of issues for situations such as downtime and/or emergencies. Two stated that these issues have not yet been addressed in the company. The last one is not aware of any initiative within his company, in this regard.

There was also a question about whether they would recommend the use of a tool like the one proposed in their company (Q9): four users answered positively. A user stated that the proposed tool could be a "plus" to be included in the automation package associated with the machines. Another user found the tool intuitive as it only requires the minimum level of understanding of if-then constructs. Two users stated that the tool has certainly good potential for exploitation in IoT and I4.0 scenarios and would be useful in their companies even though it should be further adapted to consider the multitude and the variety of objects and appliances that can be found in companies working in this domain. One especially found a high potential in making more understandable the policies that are in place in a factory also to not strictly technical people. Further suggestions to improve the tool/approach (Q10) were to include graphics (such as Zabbix[3], one said) to improve the monitoring view offered to users, and to provide a sort of "production line layout" where triggers are also visualised through their actual position on the machines.

7   Discussion

From the data collected it emerges that the tool was generally appreciated by users, even if the limited number of test participants does not allow generalization of the gathered data, but to consider them only qualitatively e.g. as indicative of possible opportunities and promising directions, or problematic areas encountered.

One of the positive data—and encouraging for any future development of the platform is that, despite the participants never had the opportunity to use the tool before the test, they were able to use it with good results, also expressing high appreciation on its potentiality in the paper domain. This is especially relevant considering that the participants were real professionals, mostly senior managers operating within paper-related companies, thus having limited time available to devote to activities not strictly connected with their own work.

The proposed approach was found promising to them not only because it supports personalisation of the functioning of a complex, context-dependent system like the one typically found in companies working in this sector, and without requiring from users specific programming skills. Also because, by using rules, which are also rendered using natural language, the approach supports easy communication between different stakeholders, as it allows for externalizing the knowledge of a worker to others, and this knowledge can be easily adapted to fit other scenarios.

Also the fact that the considered approach exploits a uniform interface was particularly appreciated by them, in that it facilitates dynamic optimization of factories to the highly different aspects and scenarios that can emerge in the various involved departments, in an unifying and integrated manner. While the goal of this work was more on assessing the opportunities that introducing such approach could offer to workers in this domain in more general terms, some participants highlighted that the presented tool, while providing a promising innovative direction, should be further adapted to support the needs that can be found in real scenarios e.g. in terms of number/variety of things and appliances. One aspect to this regard would be to provide enhanced visualisations

---

[3] https://www.zabbix.com.

for presenting in an effective and efficient manner the multitude of sensors, things, appliances and actuators that can be available in Industry 4.0 scenarios in a way that remains usable, effective and efficient for the workers. For instance, one option could be to provide users with the possibility to filter the hierarchies of triggers and actions, to take only the elements that are typically of interest for the considered user role. Another one could be to consider even recommending specific elements to users (i.e. when some actuators are often used with specific sensors), which can also represent interesting future work.

8   Conclusion and Future Work

The work presents the application of a trigger-action platform in the paper domain. For this purpose, a set of relevant concepts and requirements have been identified through some interviews carried out with real professionals in the paper domain, which were used to suitably configure the personalization platform for the considered sector. The approach was assessed through a user test with domain experts, which provided encouraging feedback regarding the potential adoption of the proposed approach in industrial settings. Future work will consider extending the personalization tool, and integrating it in industrial settings, also considering the possibility of further, improved visualizations (e.g. considering Augmented Reality –based techniques), as well as carrying out further empirical studies in such contexts of use.

Acknowledgments. We thank Virtualis company for collaboration under the APIC Tuscany Region Project.

References

1. Barricelli, B.R., Cassano, F., Fogli, D., Piccinno, A.: End-user development, end-user programming and end-user software engineering: a systematic mapping study. J. Syst. Softw. **149**, 101–137 (2019)
2. Bellucci, A., Vianello, A., Florack, Y., Micallef, L., Jacucci, G.: Augmenting objects at home through programmable sensor tokens: a design journey. IJHCS **122**, 211–231 (2019)
3. Bricklin, D., Frankston, B., Fylstra, D.: VisiCalc, software arts (1979). http://www.bricklin. com/history/intro.htm
4. Caivano, D., Fogli, D., Lanzilotti, R., Piccinno, A., Cassano, F.: Supporting end users to control their smart home: design implications from a literature review and an empirical investigation. J. Syst. Softw. **144**, 295–313 (2018)
5. Elsden, C., Feltwell, T., Lawson, S.W., Vines, J.: Recipes for programmable money. In: Proceedings of CHI 2019 Systems, Paper 251, pp. 1–13. ACM, New York (2019)
6. Fischer, G., Giaccardi, E.: Meta-design: a framework for the future of end-user development. In: Lieberman, H., Paternò, F., Wulf, V. (eds.) End User Development. HCIS, vol. 9, pp. 427–457. Springer, Dordrecht (2006). https://doi.org/10.1007/1-4020-5386-X_19
7. Fogli, D., Piccinno, A.: End-user development in industry 4.0: challenges and opportunities. In: Malizia, A., Valtolina, S., Morch, A., Serrano, A., Stratton, A. (eds.) IS-EUD 2019. LNCS, vol. 11553, pp. 230–233. Springer, Cham (2019). https://doi.org/10.1007/978-3-030-24781-2_21

8. Friedow, C., Volker, M., Hewelt, M.: Integrating IoT devices into business processes. In: Matulevičius, R., Dijkman, R. (eds.) Advanced Information Systems Engineering Workshops. CAiSE 2018: Lecture Notes in Business Information Processing, vol. 316, pp. 265–277. Springer, Cham (2018). https://doi.org/10.1007/978-3-319-92898-2_22

9. Ghiani, G., Manca, M., Paternò, F., Santoro, C.: Personalization of context-dependent applications through trigger-action rules. ACM. ToCHI **24**(2), 1–33 (2017)

10. Jaschinski, C., Ben Allouch, S.: Listening to the ones who care: exploring the perceptions of informal caregivers towards ambient assisted living applications. J. Ambient Intell. Humaniz. Comput. **10**(2), 761–778 (2018). https://doi.org/10.1007/s12652-018-0856-6

11. Lucke, D., Steimle, F., Cuk, E., Luckert, M., Schneider, M., Schel, D.: Implementation of the MIALinx user interface for future manufacturing environments. Procedia CIRP **81**, 606–611 (2019)

12. Modesto, A.S.C., da C. Figueiredo, R.M., Ramos, C.S., de S. Santos, L., Venson, E., Pedrosa, G.V.: Organizational strategies for end-user development—a systematic literature mapping. Informatics **8**(1), 15 (2021)

13. Romero, D., et al.: Towards an operator 4.0 typology: a human-centric perspective on the fourth industrial revolution technologies. In: Proceedings of CIE46, Tianjin, China (2016)

14. Tetteroo, D., et al.: Lessons learnt from deploying an end-user development platform for physical rehabilitation. In: Proceedings of CHI 2015 Conference, pp. 4133–4142. ACM, New York (2015)

15. Ur, B., McManus, E., Yong Ho, M.P., Littman, M.L.: Practical trigger-action programming in the smart home. In: Proceedings of CHI 2014, pp. 803–812. ACM, New York (2014)

16. Weintrop, D., Shepherd, D.C., Francis, P., Franklin, D.: Blockly goes to work: block-based programming for industrial robots. In: IEEE 2017 Blocks and Beyond Workshop, Raleigh, USA, pp. 29–36. IEEE (2017)

17. Wieland, M., et al.: Towards a rule-based manufacturing integration assistant. Procedia. CIRP **57**, 213–218 (2016)

18. Wieland, M., et al.: Rule-based integration of smart services using the manufacturing service bus. In: SmartWorld/SCALCOM/UIC/ATC/CBDCom/IOP/SCI 2017, San Francisco, CA, USA, pp. 1–8 (2017)

Learning Domain Knowledge Using Block-Based Programming: Design-Based Collaborative Learning

Renate Andersen[1(✉)], Anders I. Mørch[2], and Kristina Torine Litherland[2]

[1] Department of Primary and Secondary Teacher Education, Oslo Metropolitan University, Oslo, Norway
renatea@oslomet.no
[2] Department of Education, University of Oslo, Oslo, Norway
{andersm,kristitl}@iped.uio.no

Abstract. Block-based programming languages have lowered the threshold to computer science (CS), providing a powerful (low threshold-high ceiling) arena for early CS education and engagement in STEM subjects. This paper presents results of an empirical study in three schools; involving 43 pupils aged 12–16 using MakeCode with Microbit (a microcontroller), basic physical objects, and Zoom video communication as a shared learning environment. Using design-based research (DBR) together with teachers, we created technology-rich learning materials and tasks in math, biology, and physics and organized a series of project-based learning activities wherein pupils met three hours per week for 16 weeks during two semesters. Recorded Zoom meetings serve as our data. We thematized and transcribed the video material of selected groups' online activities and used verbal interaction analysis and visual artefact analysis as our methods. Our results include a new analytical framework, design-based collaborative learning (DBCL), achieved by adopting concepts from computer-supported collaborative learning (CSCL) and end-user development (EUD), specifically domain-oriented design environments (DODE). Our empirical findings are: 1) block-based programming in a collaborative context, 2) block-based programming as part of a DODE, 3) block-based programming integrated with school subjects, and 4) block-based programming as an explorative design method.

Keywords: Block-based programming · Computer-supported collaborative learning · Design-based collaborative learning · Design-based research · Domain-oriented design environment · End-user development · Programming in school

1 Introduction

In the Nordic countries, it has been suggested that programming and computational thinking (CT) in K–12 should not be taught as a separate subject but as part of a more comprehensive twenty-first century skills approach sometimes labelled as digital competence [3]. As of the autumn 2020, our country has implemented a curriculum where

D. Fogli et al. (Eds.): IS-EUD 2021, LNCS 12724, pp. 119–135, 2021.
https://doi.org/10.1007/978-3-030-79840-6_8

programming and CT have been integrated in other subjects, in particular mathematics, natural science, music, and arts and crafts. This unique situation calls for research on the implications of the new, technology-enriched curriculum to determine how it works in practice.

End-user development (EUD) is referred to as a set of methods and techniques that allow people who are nonprofessional software developers to create or modify a software artefact [18], as the opposite of technical development carried out by trained programmers and software engineers. It includes, among others, visual programming [23], domain-oriented design environments [10], and programmable applications [9].

The usefulness of these EUD environments can be assessed according to access, flexibility, and purpose. *Access* means the extent to which the EUD environment provides a gentle slope to modification and programming [21, 28]. *Flexibility* refers to the extent to which the tools are low threshold and high ceiling, allowing a large number of interesting artefacts to be created [9, 23, 24]. Furthermore, access and flexibility should be measured against *purpose* (e.g., solving technical problems, practicing computational thinking, or learning science, technology, engineering, and mathematics (STEM) topics) [10]. Our aim is to understand block-based programming as a tool for explorative learning of STEM topics. Therefore, we asked the following research question: What characterizes block-based programming as an explorative design space to learn STEM topics in an online collaborative setting?

The rest of the paper is organized as follows. First, empirical studies of block-based programming are discussed. Next, end-user development and collaborative learning are elaborated upon; this results in an analytical framework, which we use to analyze our empirical data. Finally, we discuss our results by comparing them with related work.

2   Related Work

This section presents a review of the literature related to end-user development and learning: block-based programming, domain-oriented design environments, and computer-supported collaborative learning.

2.1   Brief Review of Literature on Block-Based Programming

Block-based programming is a method of programming in which visual code blocks are combined to create and modify animations and games, and to interact with physical objects (sensors, buzzers, motors, lamps, LED displays, etc.). Popular block-based languages are Scratch, Blocky, Agentsheets, Alice, and MakeCode [23, 24]. The idea of blocks to encapsulate software programs goes back to structured programming with notions such as block structure and nesting (blocks inside blocks) to organize code in editors and compiled code in memory. Today's code blocks draw on children's visual metaphors (e.g., jigsaw puzzle; wooden blocks; lego bricks) and computational innovations like drag and drop interfaces and online repositories of code for reuse. They have lowered the threshold to programming and broadened participation to the entire school system. However, the success of block-based programming is hampered when children use block-based languages without understanding the programming concepts underlying the blocks, which may prevent computational thinking from being achieved.

Our own preliminary observation suggests that children refer to block types by color and talk about the "blue block" and "red block" and "red goes inside blue," etc., instead of "loops" and "conditionals" and "conditionals are used in loops." This is supported by technological affordance because blocks snap together to create syntactically correct programs. Researchers have found that primary school children use color, shape, and arguments (parameters in blocks) as visual cues when searching for blocks, and the children pick up both intended and false affordances when programming [8].

Lewis [17] compared the learning outcome of sixth graders' coding of similar tasks in Logo and Scratch and found that the two languages were similar in terms of stimulating continued interest in programming, but differed in how affordances for programming varied for different programming constructs. In particular, Lewis [17] found that children understood loops better in Logo, but conditionals better in Scratch.

Based on a series of examples from the Scratch online community, Brennan and Resnick [4] argued that visual programming is more than writing code and leads children to socializing with peers. The authors suggested that computational practices and computational perspectives should supplement computational concepts (e.g., loops and conditionals) toward an understanding of computational thinking as a mass collaboration phenomenon. The authors found that some students were able to engage in computational practice and reuse code to create a new project without fully understanding the underlying computational concepts. The current study builds on this finding.

Based on empirical studies of middle and high school students' practices with coding in and out of school, Lee et al. [16] suggested a model of computational practice, use-modify-create, which can scaffold children's acquisition of CT concepts. The model entails children going through a progression toward learning computational thinking. In the use stage, they test existing solutions (e.g., playing a game created by someone else). In the modify stage, they begin to modify the game at different levels of complexity. In the create stage, they reuse the acquired understanding and apply it to create something new.

2.2   Domain-Oriented Design Environments: Visual Language vs. Components

Researchers in EUD have been concerned with bringing programming closer to the domain expert users' practices and needs for more than 30 years, along several dimensions. One dimension is general purpose vs. domain orientated technology support, which includes work in EUD that spans visual programming languages [e.g., 6, 23] to component-based design and end-user tailoring [e.g., 21, 27]. This line of work was reviewed in [20] and is here summarized as a conceptual framework, domain-oriented design environment (DODE). In a DODE, a programming language and software components are combined. A DODE is a software application consisting of a domain-oriented user interface that supports design activities within a particular domain [10], and a programming environment in the background that allows end-user developers to modify and further develop the DODE, such as to introduce new components and rules [11]. Users accomplish component-based design when they interact with components in visual builders to select, modify, and connect components using high-level operations rather than writing program code [21, 27]. In a DODE, this is accomplished by the end users when they select components from a palette of parts, which are further edited in a work area, stored in a catalog of examples, and incorporated in future applications by reuse and redesign [10]. Block-based programming languages combine aspects of a high-level programming language and component-based design not unlike a DODE. Therefore, we used DODE in a conceptual framework to understand block-based programming in practical use with research methods from the social sciences.

2.3 Group Cognition Review of Computer-Supported Collaborative Learning

Computer-supported collaborative learning (CSCL) is an interdisciplinary research field in which two or more people learn or attempt to learn something together [7]. The underlying premises in CSCL are that people learn together with the help of a computer and that what they learn together is more than what they could have learned independently [26]. The results of CSCL are shared knowledge and expertise developed by collaborating through the creation of shared artefacts, which can enhance skills in social interaction and collaboration [19]. Thus, the core features of CSCL are: 1) interaction between learners, 2) information sharing, 3) joint meaning making based on negotiation within the group, and 4) developing common artefacts [1, 26]. CSCL research encompasses both co-located and distributed contexts. An empirical study of distributed CSCL referred to as collaborative knowledge creation [1], identified mutual development processes in online collaborative learning. "Mutual development" was first coined in the context of EUD as a joint collaboration process between different stakeholders when they co-create a shared artefact [1, 2]. We use CSCL in order to understand how pupils learn together when working in small groups to create code and physical artifacts to solve subject-specific tasks.

3 Analytical Framework: Design-Based Collaborative Learning

We created an analytical framework derived from central terms in CSCL and EUD. We refer to the combination of EUD and CSCL as design-based collaborative learning (DBCL). Our goal was to understand collaborative learning of knowledge and skills in specific STEM domains (e.g., math, biology, and physics) and to use block-based programming as a method toward that end. From CSCL we focused on the collaborative learning process of creating common artifacts. From EUD we drew on DODEs. This combination of concepts provided a group interaction perspective on domain-oriented design environments, which is new. The concepts in our analytical framework are displayed in Table 1. *Information sharing* is a central element in collaborative learning as it starts all the other processes of meaning making [26]. *Negotiation* is defined as establishing a shared meaning, in which the individual group members have to negotiate multiple personal perspectives to create one that can be shared and to affirm that the meaning is shared [25]. *Group cognition* is a goal of collaborative learning and entails multiple people participating in coherent interactions that achieve cognitive accomplishments that are best analyzed, at least in part, at the group level, rather than attributing contributions and agency entirely to individual minds [25]. *Scaffolding* involves a metaphor in the collaborative learning context describing how teachers and experienced peers support learners by providing feedback and support [12].

Table 1. Concepts of analytical framework.

Analytic concepts from CSCL	Analytic concepts from DODEs
Information sharing (from me to you)	Design unit (DU, separate building blocks to be combined with other DUs)
Negotiation (you and I decide what to focus on)	Rule (knowledge of the relations between two or more DUs to form a more complex DU)
Group cognition (shared meaning)	Argumentation base (a priori shared knowledge)
Scaffolding (help from teacher/senior peer)	Example (a previous solution for reuse)

From DODE [10], we adopted the following components: *Design units* (DUs) are the basic objects in the design environment. They model specific domain objects as standalone components as well as objects that are more technical. *Rules* define domain knowledge and consist of desired relations between domain objects. The rules are triggered by actions and events in the environment. Critics are automated scaffolding based on rules, but this component is outside the scope of our work. *Argumentation base* is the design rationale associated with domain knowledge and represented in the form of arguments for and against adding, removing, or replacing design units. *Examples* are previous solutions created by other users in the design environment, which provide ideas and starting points for new users to reuse and redesign. We used the two sets of analytic concepts in an integrated effort as thematic codes to make sense of the empirical data in our analysis.

4 Methods

In this section, we describe our research design and techniques for data collection and analyses within the umbrella of design-based research (DBR).

Design-Based Research is an educational research tradition focused on both the development of pedagogical practice and the development of theory. In DBR, researchers, teachers, and other stakeholders typically design educational interventions collaboratively. The interventions are situated in authentic educational contexts and are tested and developed through several iterations [14]. Note that the use of design in DBR (design as intervention) is different from the use of design in DODE (design as creation).

Research Design and Participants. We developed and tested a series of technology-enriched classes for gifted pupils to learn block-based programming as an integral part of their course subject. Four iterations are planned over two years, with one intervention per semester. Based on evaluations and feedback, the DBR process iterates. In total up to 100 pupils aged 12–16 will participate, 50 each semester, divided into four classes. Each class is taught by a high school teacher, which means there are also four participating high school teachers in the research project. Each of the four interventions has a different focus concerning the course subject. All of the interventions have the same time perspective: a duration of eight weeks, with a three-hour class each week.

Materials and Procedure. The data derived from the second intervention where the topics were mathematics, biology, and physics, aided by physical components and Microbit. Each week began with the teacher introducing the topic for the half-day and the topic to be learned and then the teacher divided the class into groups (breakout rooms in Zoom) consisting of three to four pupils. The assigned task was to learn one or more domain concepts by using MakeCode as one of the tools. In order to collaborate with the use of different materials, the teachers encouraged the pupils to share their screens with the others to show their partial solutions. In this way, the pupils had common ground for the discussions. The group was the unit of analysis in our research.

(a)   **(b)**

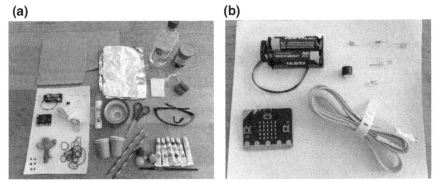

Fig. 1. a) The physical materials the pupils had access to and used in some of the assignments. b) Microbit circuit board with electronic components. We referred to each item as a design unit.

Figure 1a) shows the materials we provided for the pupils participating in the second intervention. Figure 1b), is a picture of the Microbit microcontroller (a small computer) with some sensors that can be connected to it. MakeCode is the block-based programming environment used for writing the code that controls the Microbit.

Selection of Participants and Context of Study. The participants in the study were gifted children, who, through nomination from parents/teachers, applied for participation in the research project. The reason for choosing gifted pupils as participants was their need for differentiated learning. As the pupils were aged 12–16, the intervention covered competence goals aimed at high school pupils, that is, one to four academic years above their actual ages.

4.1 Data Collection

When collecting the empirical data, we used participant observation and video recordings of the participants' screens in Zoom. We collected our data in an online context due to the Covid-19 pandemic. Virtual participatory observation is a technique used in virtual ethnography. Virtual ethnography is a method for analyzing social interactions in an online context. Hine [13] stated that virtual ethnography is an ethnographic approach to the Internet. When conducting virtual ethnography, different techniques can be used, ranging from "fly on the wall" (non-participant observation) to engaging in the social interactions when collecting empirical data [13]. We used a participant observation approach wherein we sometimes asked the pupils to explain what they were doing while programming to initiate social interaction [15]. In total, from Intervention 2, we collected around 70 h of screen recordings of interaction data. The pupils decided whether and when they shared their screens, and toggled their web cameras and microphones at will. Data privacy is an important concern in all research, therefore, we obtained written consent from all the participants' parents/guardians, and the data is stored in encrypted and secure data management servers. In addition, all the extracts presented in this article are anonymized using pseudonyms. The Norwegian center for research data approved this study, ensuring that we collect personal data legally and safely.

4.2 Data Analysis

To analyze the empirical data, the first two authors used a combination of thematic analysis [5] and interaction analysis [15] in a two-step manner. In using this approach, we applied a combination of inductive and deductive coding schemes, defined as an abductive approach [22]. Through collective analysis in data workshops, we focused on the participant's "voice," being inductive, and we also relied on our analytical framework, being deductive.

Thematic Analysis. Thematic analysis is a method for systematically identifying, organizing and offering insight into patterns of meanings (themes) across a dataset [5]. We started by using thematic analysis to comb through our empirical data seeking themes and creating thematic codes that came across as interesting and relevant to the research question. Examples of themes that emerged were block-based programming, collaboration, and programming integrated in the subjects.

Interaction Analysis. Next, we selected empirical data extracts that reflected the themes we wanted to focus on in detail and used interaction analysis to scrutinize the utterances [15]. Interaction analysis is a method for empirical investigation of social interaction between humans and the objects in their environment, including speech, non-verbal actions and the use of artefacts [15].

5 Data and Analysis

In this section, we present empirical data that illustrates how the pupils used blocks to experiment and explore a subject area topic within mathematics, biology and physics. Each section is divided into four subsections: 1) contextualizing the extract, 2) raw data (informants' voices), 3) technology object (software and hardware being composed) and

4) discursive object (a sequence of utterances advancing the groups' common understanding). The transcript notations we used include these symbols: ((*text*)) participants' actions, [*text*] researchers' clarifying comments, (.) long pause in interaction and … pause in interaction. During all the data extracts, one of the pupils shared his/her screen so that the other pupils could see what he/she was working on.

5.1   Verbal Data Extract 1: Simulating a Die

Contextualizing the Data Extract: In the first data extract, the pupils discussed the task of the first assignment, which was to determine how to use the Microbit as a die as part of an exercise related to probability in mathematics. Olivia was sharing her screen (Table 2).

Table 2. Simulating a die.

Turn	Person	Utterance	Analytic Concepts
1.1	Sophia	It is just like… Can the Microbit be used as a die?	Argumentation base
1.2	Olivia	Nothing more than that?	
1.3	Sophia	No, that is all!…	
1.4	Olivia	Should we try making a die then, or what?	Negotiation
1.5	Liam	Okay. Mm. We could actually just do what we did earlier	Example (idea reuse);
1.6	Olivia	Like… On [Microbit] shake… ((pics purple block from pallet)) Then…	Design unit (1)
1.7	Liam	Then you can add "show number"… ((Olivia picks blue block and puts inside the purple block)) and a… In addition, math of course. ((Olivia goes to the math pallet and searches)) Then we have a random number ((Olivia finds the "pick random" block set to default values 0 and 10)) from 1 to 6 or 1 to 10 ((Liam sees the number 10)), but 1 to 6 ((Olivia changes the value from 10 to 6 in the innermost block)). Moreover, this should work like a die	Rule; Information sharing; Design unit (3)
1.8	Olivia	((Tests Microbit by clicking the "shake" button 5 times)) It works! ((tone of voice is happy))	Design unit (4); Group cognition

Fig. 2. Visual artefacts for extract 1: A program composed of four design units that simulates a die when the user clicks the shake button. *Left*: Code after turn 1.7. *Right*: Output of program.

Extract 1 illustrates what we mean by two trajectories of participation: technology object development (Microbit and its code) and discursive object development (collaborative learning conversation). We show how these objects develop in next paragraphs.

Technology Object: When developing the program code, Liam told Olivia what code blocks to choose and she put three design units into the configuration shown in Fig. 2 (left image). MakeCode automated the task of creating a syntactically correct program with the "snap" operation (domain general rule). Liam explained the name of two nested blocks of importance for domain knowledge, "show number" and "pick random" (domain specific rules). Olivia changed the default numbers to match the features of a die (ranging from one to six), using another domain-specific rule. Finally, Olivia tested whether the simulated die worked, now consisting of four design units, as shown in Fig. 2 (left and right). It is clear that the pupils did not meet any big challenges creating the code, but they revealed great joy of accomplishment based on tone of voice.

Discursive Object: The main aim of the tasks was to learn domain knowledge as part of their group work, in this case probability and random numbers. In collaborative learning, an essential part of the process is that individual group members share information in order to demonstrate shared understanding [26]. Sophia thought the problem was easy and stated the common task (argumentation base). Olivia reformulated the task into a question for the group to start their collaborative inquiry. Liam suggested that they could reuse the code they had used in a previous assignment and Olivia shared her MakeCode screen. Olivia talked with Liam while she composed the program. Important information was shared and negotiated by the two group members, such as when Liam stated that the block "show number" should show a random number from 1 to 6, analogous to throwing dice, thus connecting with domain knowledge. In turn 1.7, Olivia said, "It works," referring to the shared visual artifact, a simulated die using Microbit (Fig. 2, right image), which indicated that Liam and Olivia, and perhaps Sophia, had collaboratively created shared knowledge.

5.2 Verbal Data Extract 2: Programming the Microbit to Print Gene Codes

Contextualizing the Extract: This extract is part of a biology topic wherein the pupils were given the task to print out 15 random gene codes. Felix shared his screen so the other group members could see his coding process, but only Matheo engaged with him (Table 3).

Table 3. Programming gene sequences.

Turn	Person	Utterance	Analytic concepts
2.1	Felix	Okay, we are supposed to make a random sequence of 15 [genes]. ((Places the blue "on start" block. Sets a variable "text-list," to include an array. Modifies values in the array block to A, T, C, G.))	Design unit (3); Information sharing
2.2	Felix	[After 1 min of group negotiating the nature of the task] Just try to… or? Yes, we will try. Should we take [this block]? ((Felix picks a new top-level purple input block and places below start block; places a green loop block inside and sets parameter to 15; places a blue output text block inside)) … Mmmm… Yes ((puts a variable "list" block as output, initialized with a "random value" block.))	Negotiation; Design unit (3 + 6); Rule
2.3	Matheo	This whole thing about genes and stuff is quite cool	Rule;
2.4	Felix	Yes, it is fun	
2.5	Matheo	Hang on, I am writing [code]… There, wait Felix, I am still making… Felix, I think I also did it, but the thing is, if you go back to what you had [code]…	Design unit (10)
2.6	Felix	Mm ((Both pupils are working on their code separately.))	
2.7	Matheo	Ehmm then I have… or, you are using the join thing [block]	Information sharing
2.8	Felix	Oh, it is not necessary… it is just…	
2.9	Matheo	What does it do? Does it just make them [the blocks] stick together, like follow each other?	Negotiation
2.10	Felix	Yeah, actually, I do not think you need it. ((Starts to reflect in his own code.))	
2.11	Matheo	Yeah	Group cognition
2.12	Felix	No, you could really just have used (.) ((Tries to understand the construct.))	
2.13	Matheo	I just wrote [coded] show string…	Information sharing
2.14	Felix	Yes, that is really all you need to do	

(continued)

Table 3. (*continued*)

Turn	Person	Utterance	Analytic concepts
2.15	Matheo	Then I do not get those hyphens [to space out the letters output the Microbit] - I just get "ding ding" [the gene letters are written out one after the other without hyphens]	Rule
2.16	Felix	Eh, yeah, yeah, because you do not really need... Yes, he [the teacher] just had hyphens in his code, I think. However, you do not really need the hyphens	Information sharing
2.17	Matheo	Yeah, but can you try running it [the code]? May I see what it looks like?	Group cognition
2.18	Felix	With this? ((Referring to the join block with the hyphen.))	Information sharing
2.19	Matheo	Umm, yes	
2.20	Felix	It just goes like this. ((Points to Microbit simulation)) It just takes forever	Design unit (11)

Fig. 3. Visual artefact table for Extract 2: The program composed of 11 design units displays a random sequence of 15 letter gene codes (here two letters, C & G, are shown in three snapshots).

Technology Object: In turn 2.2, Felix shared his screen and started the task by combining blocks in order to write out the letters A, T, C, and G (abbreviations of the four basic building blocks in an organism's DNA) by initializing an array block. He continued to create the program by searching for blocks to combine the letters randomly. At 10 blocks, he indicated that he had finished by asking: "Does it work now?" (Turn 2.4). The other pupils had worked with their own code, and in Turn 2.7, Matheo asked Felix if he really needed the "join block" because it was not used (or may have had an error). Felix pondered the question, agreed, and changed his code. This illustrates how the pupils helped each other to create the code, despite working on separate versions locally with one being shared as a technology object to talk about (Fig. 3).

Discursive Object: When Felix started to create the program as shown in the previous paragraph and Matheo said that he found this way of working "quite cool" (Turn 2.3), it can be interpreted that the pupils perceived their main focus as the science course, using programming as a tool toward learning science. The two boys agreed that a certain block was not needed after some negotiation, with the effect that shared understanding (group cognition) was achieved after first establishing a shared understanding of the code. The utterances in Turns 2.17–2.20 can be interpreted as a collaborative learning process in which group cognition emerged [25]. Shared understanding was achieved during Turns 2.15–20 (producing 15 gene codes as a random combination of the four basic DNA letters) when Felix elaborated that this could be accomplished by using hyphens between the letters, a point emphasized by the teacher in a previous lecture. This achievement was visualized in the program execution in Turn 2.20.

5.3   Verbal Data Extract 3: Microbit as a Burglar Alarm

Contextualizing the Extract: This extract is part of a physics topic wherein the pupils were given the task to program the Microbit to be used as a burglar alarm. When doing this, the children were asked to use aluminum foil and connect it to the Microbit to explore how it conducts electricity. The extract below is from an end-of-class summing up session in which the pupils were invited by the teacher to present their projects (Table 4 and Fig. 4).

Table 4. Microbit as a burglar alarm.

Turn	Person	Utterance	Analytic concepts
3.1	Teacher	Ok, so what are you up to?	Scaffolding
3.2	David	Yeah, so, we, we have a more practical idea. We really just took the same program we made earlier and modified it, so when…	Example (code reuse)
3.3	Teacher	Can you show us?	Scaffolding
3.4	David	Yes, it is a very simple program. There, this is our program ((shares screen)). Very simple	Design unit (3)
3.5	Teacher	However, how… I am eager to hear how you stopped it from [ringing]…	Scaffolding
3.6	David	Since we have connected this buzzer, and sort of if both of the connectors to the buzzer are connected to the aluminum it will stop ringing. Therefore, what we did on my door was, I put the aluminum sort of right next to it [door end] so when you open [the door], it moves away from the aluminum and then it starts ringing	Rule

(continued)

Table 4. (*continued*)

Turn	Person	Utterance	Analytic concepts
3.7	Teacher	So the connection from the Microbit to the buzzer is cut in two, is that what you did?	Scaffolding
3.8	David	Sort of. We took ((looks at door))	
3.9	Teacher	Can you film it [with the webcam]?	
3.10	David	It is stuck to my door now. Umm, yes, I will just turn around the camera. I will stop sharing [the computer screen]. Here you see it—we've named it "TackyMech," and it starts ringing when it's not in contact with the aluminum ((buzzer sound))) and when it comes back again it stops ((buzzer stops ringing))	Design unit (3 software and 4 hardware); Rule; Group cognition

Technology Object: David volunteered to show the solution that he created with a peer when prompted by the teacher. He started with three code blocks from a previous exercise. The code worked by sending a ring-signal to the buzzer when the door was opened. David stated that when the buzzer was connected to the aluminum, the burglar alarm would stop ringing. This is one example of a rule in the design environment, that is, aluminum as electrical conductor. Based on the code alone (Fig. 4, left image), one may get the impression that the alarm will ring "forever." David said that the alarm would ring only when the door was opened as this would break the electrical circuit. In Fig. 4, we see David's code (left) and the set-up of the Microbit with the buzzer taped to the door (right). This extract is interesting as it is an example of how the pupil used the microbit as an integrated element of particle physics (electricity) by using aluminum as a conductor in a practical application.

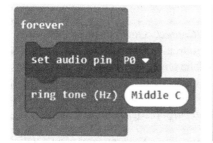

Fig. 4. Visual artefact table for Extract 3: The code to the left reads signals from the Microbit to the right (attached to the door), which triggers a buzzer when two aluminum cords are not in contact.

Discursive Object: The teacher prompted the knowledge building that occurred in this conversation four times, by asking questions and scaffolding the pupils' learning process [12]. In response, David explained what he and his peer did in steps that led to group cognition: sharing information about "a more practical idea" (Turn 3.2): with negotiation that led to a "very simple program," (Turn 3.4) and finally shared understanding of basic circuitry and program logic (understanding why buzzer "starts ringing when it's not in contact with the aluminum"). The latter (Turn 3.10) is an example of group cognition, as they named their hack "TackyMech." An essential element of group cognition is when multiple people build on each other's statements and participate in coherent interactions to achieve something beyond their individual efforts [25]. In Extract 3, the teacher scaffolded the interactions toward group cognition. The teacher asked questions about what the burglar alarm looked like and how it worked, and the pupil explained and reflected upon the process. These questions brought the technology objects into focus.

In sum, in the data we have shown, we identified two types of "objects" that increase in complexity: technology objects increase in the number of design units, that is, parts that can be combined in different ways [10], whereas discursive objects increase in level abstraction, from personal to shared perspectives [25, 26]. Both are important and interdependent.

6   Discussion and Conclusions

The research question asked in this study was what characterizes block-based programming as an explorative design space to learn STEM topics in an online collaborative setting? We have addressed the question by analyzing three examples in Sect. 5, using an analytical framework obtained from theories in EUD and CSCL. Application of the framework led to the following empirical results:

- Block-based programming in a collaborative context.
- Block-based programming as part of a domain-oriented design environment reduces the gap between the problem domain and the human-computer interface.
- Block-based programming can be integrated in school subjects.
- Block-based programming as explorative design method for solving domain specific tasks.

Block-Based Programming in a Collaborative Context. Our unit of analysis was the group. However, the programs created by the group members were made locally (each pupil had their own MakeCode environment and the physical components kit). To bridge the gap between individual artefacts and group work, we draw on CSCL. Collaborative learning is the discursive element of the analysis, including key collaborative processes such as "sharing information," "negotiation" and "group cognition" [25, 26].

Block-Based Programming to Reduce the Semantic Gap. The main aim of a DODE is to move the human-computer interface from resembling interaction with a programming language to interacting with higher-level abstractions, which ends with the problem domains [10]. Our empirical findings turn this model upside-down, starting with the problem domain as given by an assignment and ending with individual technology objects and collaboratively created knowledge (group cognition). For example, in data Extract 1, the domain-specific context was mathematics and the problem to be solved was basic understanding of probability (random numbers), which was materialized in the MakeCode/Microbit die.

Block-Based Programming Can Be Integrated in School Subjects. We found across the three examples that pupils could solve the tasks without advanced programming knowledge. We believe a reason for this is the intuitiveness of block-based programming and the automation of programming language syntax. Our findings indicate that pupils, if not explicitly taught programming knowledge, would choose blocks according to color, shape and parameters [8]. The use-modify-create model [16] suggested in the literature applied to the programming part in the three examples, but it did not apply to collaborative learning because it failed to consider domain orientation outside programming. To consider arbitrary (STEM) subject domains, the model could be prefixed with "concepts," whereby one or more domain specific concepts are introduced by a teacher before the pupils start programming with, for example, use-modify-create.

Block-Based Programming as an Exploratory Method for Solving Domain Specific Tasks. Our data illustrates how programming can be used as a method for collaborative learning of school subjects in math and science (STEM) topics. Our research indicates a method to learn STEM subjects. In Extract 3, we see how a pupil solved a physics task by combining knowledge of metal conductivity and programming physical objects. The programming serves as an intermediate stage between the mastery of a curricular goal in physics and the actual physical objects. This can be understood in two ways (bottom up and top down): 1) the physical objects served as stepping-stones to gradually understand the higher-level physics concepts through the medium of programming or 2) the concepts as first taught were then "lowered" to a more concrete level of abstraction by hands-on exploration to ground the concepts. In the creation of a burglar alarm, we observed both top-down and bottom-up understanding at work, which varied among the groups according to preferences in following teachers' instructions (top down) versus doing interesting things themselves (bottom up).

A *dilemma of integrating programming as part of the subjects* is that the teachers need to split their time in two, that is, teaching and scaffolding the subject and programming. We observed this phenomenon from the point of view of the pupils learning activities by identifying two types of artefacts that developed in parallel during the group work: 1) technical objects and 2) discursive objects. These objects developed in different directions, as one is concrete and the other abstract (design complexity in the number of building blocks vs. abstraction of knowledge in terms of the degree of shared understanding held by a group). The design complexity and abstraction of knowledge developed as the teachers gave the pupils tasks involving physical objects related to domain specific topics, and followed it up by scaffolding.

The usefulness of EUD can be assessed according to *access, flexibility* and *purpose*. Our empirical studies of block-based programming combine the three criteria. We have leveraged previous work in EUD by low-threshold interfaces supporting component-based design [21, 27] and previous research in high-ceiling block-based programming environments [23, 24]. We contributed by combining access and flexibility with a purpose beyond interest by connecting block-based programming with domain-specific learning activities [10]. Further work includes increasing the accessibility of computational tools and materials by defining them within the same programmable design environment, such as Minecraft, in which specific program constructs can be taught by practical problem solving in the immersive game environment. For educational applications, the use-modify-create model [16] can benefit an initial phase of setting a goal.

Finally, we have developed a new conceptual framework for analyzing collaborative learning in block-based programming by combining concepts from domain-oriented design environments (DODEs) and computer supported collaborative learning (CSCL) based on group cognition. We have named the new analytical framework design-based collaborative learning (DBCL), providing a set of analytic concepts to be used as an observation protocol in empirical research. Further research will harness the protocol.

Acknowledgments. This research is part of the research project "Programming and Making in School" funded by Regional Research Fund (RFF) in Norway. We thank Ellen Egeland Flø for helping in organization of the educational activities presented here.

References

1. Andersen, R.: Mutual development in online collaborative processes. Three case studies of artifact co-creation at different levels of participation. Ph.D. dissertation, Faculty of Educational Sciences, University of Oslo, Norway (2019)
2. Andersen, R., Mørch, A.: Mutual development: a case study in customer-initiated software product development. In: Pipek, V., Rosson, M.B., de Ruyter, B., Wulf, V. (eds.) IS-EUD 2009. LNCS, vol. 5435, pp. 31–49. Springer, Heidelberg (2009). https://doi.org/10.1007/978-3-642-00427-8_3
3. Bocconi, S., Chioccariello, A., Earp, J.: The Nordic approach to introducing computational thinking and programming in compulsory education. Report prepared for the Nordic@BETT2018 Steering Group, pp. 397–400 (2018)
4. Brennan, K., Resnick, M.: New frameworks for studying and assessing the development of computational thinking. In: Proceedings of the 2012 Annual Meeting of the American Educational Research Association, Vancouver, Canada, vol. 1, pp. 1–25 (2012)
5. Clarke, V., Braun, V.: Thematic analysis. In: Cooper, H. (ed.) APA Handbook of Research Methods in Psychology: Vol. 2 Research Designs, pp. 57–71. American Psychological Association, Washington, DC (2015)
6. Costabile, M.-F., Fogli, D., Letondal, C., Mussio, P., Piccinno, A.: Domain-expert users and their needs of software development. In: Proceedings of the HCI 2003 EUD Session, Crete (2003)
7. Dillenbourg, P.: Collaborative Learning: Cognitive and Computational Approaches. Advances in learning and instruction series. Elsevier Science, Inc., New York (1999)
8. Dwyer, H., Hill, C., Hansen, A., Iveland, A., Franklin, D., Harlow, D.: Fourth grade students reading block-based programs: predictions, visual cues, and affordances. In: Proceedings of the 11th Annual International Conference on International Computing Education Research (ICER 2015), pp. 111–119. ACM (2015)
9. Eisenberg, M.: Programmable applications: interpreter meets interface. SIGCHI Bull. **27**(2), 68–93 (1995)

10. Fischer, G.: Domain-oriented design environments. Autom. Softw. Eng. **1**(2), 177–203 (1994)
11. Fischer, G., Girgensohn, A.: End-user modifiability in design environments. In: Proceedings CHI 1990, pp. 183–192. ACM, New York (1990)
12. Hammond, J., Gibbons, P.: What is scaffolding? Teachers' Voices **8**, 8–16 (2005)
13. Hine, C.: Virtual Ethnography. Sage Publications, London (2000)
14. Hoadley, C.P.: Creating context: design-based research in creating and understanding. In: Proceedings of Computer Support for Cooperative Learning (CSCL), Boulder, USA (2002)
15. Jordan, B., Henderson, A.: Interaction analysis: foundations and practice. J. Learn. Sci. **4**(1), 39–103 (1995)
16. Lee, I., et al.: Computational thinking for youth in practice. ACM Inroads **2**(1), 32–37 (2011)
17. Lewis, C.M.: How programming environment shapes perception, learning and goals: logo vs. Scratch. In: Proceedings of the 41st ACM Technical Symposium on Computer Science Education (SIGCSE 2010), pp. 346–350. ACM, New York (2010)
18. Lieberman, H., Paternò, F., Klann, M., Wulf, V.: End-user development: an emerging paradigm. In: Lieberman, H., Paternò, F., Wulf, V. (eds.) End-User Development. HCIS, vol. 96, pp. 1–7. Springer, Heidelberg (2006). https://doi.org/10.1007/1-4020-5386-X_1
19. Lipponen, L., Hakkarainen, K., Paavola, S.: Practices and orientations of CSCL. In: Strijbos, J.W., Kirschner, P.A., Martens, R.L. (eds.) What We Know about CSCL. CULS, vol. 3, pp. 31–50. Springer, Dordrecht (2004). https://doi.org/10.1007/1-4020-7921-4_2
20. Mørch, A., Litherland, K., Andersen, R.: End-user development goes to school: collaborative learning with makerspaces in subject areas. In: Malizia, A., Valtolina, S., Morch, A., Serrano, A., Stratton, A. (eds.) IS-EUD 2019. LNCS, vol. 11553, pp. 200–208. Springer, Cham (2019). https://doi.org/10.1007/978-3-030-24781-2_16
21. Mørch, A., Zhu, L.: Component-based design and software readymades. In: Dittrich, Y., Burnett, M., Mørch, A., Redmiles, D. (eds.) IS-EUD 2013. LNCS, vol. 7897, pp. 278–283. Springer, Heidelberg (2013). https://doi.org/10.1007/978-3-642-38706-7_26
22. Reichertz, J.: Induction, deduction, abduction. In: Flick, U. (ed.) The SAGE Handbook of Qualitative Data Analysis, pp. 123–135. SAGE Publications, London (2014)
23. Repenning, A.: Agentsheets: a tool for building domain-oriented visual programming environments. In: Proceedings of the INTERACT 1993 and CHI 1993, pp. 142–143. Association for Computing Machinery, New York (1993)
24. Resnick, M., et al.: Scratch: programming for all. Commun. ACM **52**(11), 60–67 (2009)
25. Stahl, G.: From intersubjectivity to group cognition. Comput. Support. Coop. Work **25**(4), 355–384 (2016)
26. Stahl, G., Koschmann, T., Suthers, D.: Computer-supported collaborative learning: an historical perspective. In: Sawyer, R.K. (ed.) Cambridge Handbook of the Learning Sciences, pp. 409–426. Cambridge University Press, Cambridge (2006)
27. Won, M., Stiemerling, O., Wulf, V.: Component-based approaches to tailorable systems. In: Lieberman, H., et al. (eds.) End-User Development. HCIS, vol. 9, pp. 115–141. Springer, Dordrecht (2006). https://doi.org/10.1007/1-4020-5386-X_6
28. Wulf, V., Golombek, B.: Direct activation. A concept to encourage tailoring activities. Behav. Inf. Technol. **20**(4), 249–263 (2001)

Lessons Learned from Using Reprogrammable Prototypes with End-User Developers

Marcel Borowski$^{(\boxtimes)}$ and Ida Larsen-Ledet ⓘ

Department of Computer Science, Aarhus University, Aarhus N, Denmark
{marcel.borowski,ida.ll}@cs.au.dk

Abstract. Involving end-users in the development of a product before it is deployed has great potential to increase the fit between a product and individual users' needs. While end-users can be directly involved in modifying low-fidelity prototypes, they are left out when it comes to high-fidelity interactive prototypes—in part because these cannot be modified directly or require time-consuming edit-compile-run cycles. High-fidelity prototypes, however, are more engaging for users. We created a reprogrammable high-fidelity prototype and explored its use in short-term prototyping workshops with end-user developers, i.e. end-users with programming experience, in the domain of collaborative writing. We report observations and pitfalls, and distill four lessons learned into guidelines on how to use reprogrammable high-fidelity prototypes with end-users in contexts with limited resources. Our experiences demonstrate, among other things, that reprogrammable high-fidelity prototypes are difficult to work with—even for experienced programmers—and emphasize the need for careful attention to guiding participants, time for familiarization, and catering to multiple levels of programming experience.

Keywords: Malleable software · Reprogrammable software · Tailoring · Prototyping · Co-design · End-user development

1 Introduction

Prototyping plays an essential part in the design and development of software. Approaches like, for instance, co-design and participatory design recommend involving users as experts of their own experience [3,23]. Prototypes can be either low-fidelity (e.g., mock-ups or storyboards) or high-fidelity (e.g., interactive applications). Colombo and Landoni's study [8] on co-designing with children found that high-fidelity prototypes are more engaging and allow immediate feedback on and evaluation of designs. This immediacy is important as it allows end-users to reflect on the interactive design and provide valuable input while it is still possible to make changes [4]. In contrast to highly flexible paper mock-ups that can be

---

M. Borowski and I. Larsen-Ledet—Both authors contributed equally to this research.

© Springer Nature Switzerland AG 2021
D. Fogli et al. (Eds.): IS-EUD 2021, LNCS 12724, pp. 136–152, 2021.
https://doi.org/10.1007/978-3-030-79840-6_9

quickly manipulated but only offer limited engagement with the details of interactive behavior, high-fidelity prototypes are resource-intensive and usually need to be prepared by the researchers or designers in-between sessions with users [4,5], or require edit-compile-run cycles that result in waiting time and can cause participants to become disengaged [4]. This can be especially challenging in explorative research, where resources for implementing prototypes are limited and where there are often harsh constraints on how much time volunteer participants have for co-design and evaluation.

Making software more malleable, i.e. enabling users to modify and reprogram it at run-time, is one step towards mitigating this and allows for prototypes that are simultaneously high-fidelity *and* highly flexible. While approaches have been taken, in which reprogrammable prototypes are utilized in the design process (e.g., [2,16,24]), guidelines on what to consider when using reprogrammable prototypes, in particular in situations with limited resources, are lacking.

As part of a longer project on co-designing for collaborative academic writing [15], we created a prototype that was extensible and reprogrammable at run-time and deployed it in two short-term prototyping workshops. A total of 13 participants worked on collaboratively tailoring and reprogramming the functionality of their prototypes as end-user developers [10]—end-users with some level of technical and/or programming knowledge.

This paper documents successes and breakdowns in our use of reprogrammable prototypes in short-term prototyping workshops in experimental research design processes. We report observations of participants' work with the prototype during the workshops and provide an overview of breakdowns and lessons learned divided into four themes. By collecting and framing our insights as lessons, we aim to help others get off to a good start when conducting prototyping workshops involving reprogrammable prototypes. Each theme presents recommendations and suggestions for conducting similar prototyping workshops: (1) Ensuring participants' familiarization with the prototype, (2) avoiding conflation of platform and prototype, (3) aligning expectations with participants and guiding their exploration, and (4) supporting participants with different levels of programming experience. Further, we found that while the short time frame of our workshops was enough to identify the aforementioned themes, it was too short for participants to engage deeply with reprogramming. Still, our results affirm findings that working on high-fidelity prototypes inspires end-users to propose modifications [4], and inform researchers with limited resources and time with participants about how to facilitate engaging short-term reprogramming workshops.

2   Related Work

Our work is situated in the intersection of malleable and reprogrammable software, as well as cooperative prototyping and malleable prototypes. We describe the two domains and how they relate to our project.

Malleable Software and Tailoring. Malleable and tailorable software has been explored in a variety of directions in the past: Cabitza et al. [7] offered an extensive deconstruction of the term *malleability* and classified features of it such as versatility, interoperability, and extensibility. While malleability describes the properties of a system, *tailoring* describes the act of modifying malleable software. Tailoring can happen at different levels (e.g., [20]), each requiring different levels of technical skill—from customizing parameters to reprogramming existing software to writing code for new functionality. MacLean et al. [19] called this "tailoring power" and identified different roles of users that "live" at these different skill levels. Moving from one level of tailoring, e.g. using configuration menus, to the next, e.g. reprogramming the behavior of the system, usually involves a steep learning curve and makes it difficult to transition from one level to the next. MacLean et al. flattened this curve in their malleable system *Buttons* by providing a wider variety of intermediate-level tailoring techniques. They, further, stress the need for creating a "tailoring culture" besides having a tailorable artifact, as only this would shift expectations of users towards changing their software. They did this by employing a designer as a *handyman*, that works with end-users and takes "careful account of the users' real requirements" [19]. Other researchers have similarly noted that customization is not an individual activity [18], and yet others have explored how particular users can mediate between end-users and designers and developers as so-called *gardeners* [11] or *end-user developers* [10].

Cooperative Prototyping and Malleable Prototypes. In their work about cooperative prototyping, Bødker and Grønbæk [4] argue that users need to experience prototypes hands-on in order to envision and shape future use. They emphasize that interactive high-fidelity prototypes—to a greater extent than mock-ups—allow users to experience dynamic properties. With similar reasoning, Bellucci et al. [2] call for "repurposing malleable technologies" for prototyping in their *Extreme Co-Design* approach, and Maceli and Atwood [17] emphasize that as "our technologies have evolved to begin to support the creation of personalized environments", so our "co-design methodologies must evolve as well, to support today's designers and end users to work together in creating tools for future end-user crafters." Zhu and Herrmann [24] demonstrate how co-located prototyping in their web-based *MikiWiki* environment can support collaboration between designers and end-users.

In our work, we focus on end-user developers and on the tailoring dimensions *extension* (adding and removing pre-made extensions) and *reprogramming* (modifying extension code). Our notion of reprogramming is similar to "incremental programming" [9] and, like in cooperative prototyping, the prototype is modified during the workshop.

3   Case

3.1   Summary of the Preceding Work

The reflections presented in this paper stem from a project on collaborative writing in academia [15]. The reprogrammable prototype discussed here was implemented based on ideation activities with present and former students as well as academic employees from our local university. The needs and preferences identified in collaboration with the workshop participants were characterized by contrasts among individuals and contexts. These contrasting requirements made a reprogrammable prototype appealing, not only with regard to the prototyping situation but also potentially in an end product where it could enable users to tailor their writing tool to particular situations. For example, one contrast was between desiring a high degree of responsivity among writers or prioritizing writers' ability to immerse themselves in their individual writing tasks without being disrupted.

The design material we drew on when preparing the prototyping workshop was all made by the participants during preceding workshops and consisted of descriptions of issues and themes they experienced in collaborative writing, as well as notes and sketches describing envisioned solutions.

3.2   Prototype

The prototype was implemented using the Codestrates [22] platform that in turn builds on Webstrates [12]. *Webstrates* [12] is an experimental environment that explores the notion of *shareable dynamic media*. Its implementation synchronizes the DOM (Document Object Model) of web pages across all clients that are visiting a page with a server. The synchronization allows for real-time sharing, editing, and reprogramming of web pages among multiple users using web technologies such as HTML, CSS, and JavaScript. Thus, Webstrates turns web pages into *substrates*, i.e. "software entities that act as applications or documents depending upon use" [12]. *Codestrates* [22] adds an authoring environment on top of Webstrates, allowing both development and use of applications to happen within one environment. The authoring environment is inspired by computational notebooks (e.g., [13]), where regular text and executable blocks of code are placed within the same environment, and allows live computation within the document—at most requiring a page refresh for code changes to take effect.

Our primary reason for using a Webstrates-based system was the inherent support for real-time multi-user collaborative editing. We made use of this to provide participants with a barebones text editor to build on. By using Codestrates, we were furthermore able to make runtime changes easily accessible. This was a highly desirable property as we aimed to create a prototype that was both stable and "flexible enough to allow in-session modification" [4] to mitigate the otherwise known problem of participant disengagement (see Sect. 1).

The Prototype Writing Tool. The prototype consisted of a basic collaborative writing tool with the possibility of adding a number of extensions. Although the participants could implement their own extensions, this was not realistic with the time allotted for the workshops. Before the first prototyping workshop, we had therefore implemented a set of extensions based on the preceding ideation activities (cf. Subsect. 3.1). In addition to allowing the prototype to be reprogrammed directly in the browser, Codestrates has a built-in package manager [6] which provided facilities for handling extensions.

Table 1. Extensions available for participants to add to their prototypes.

Inspiration Prompt Provides suggestions for phrases in order to combat writer's block	**Comments** Lets notes/comments be attached to pieces of text. Anyone can view and delete comments
Meta Notes Attaches a note to a whole paragraph. Three categories of such notes are available: overview, general notes, and revisions	**Paragraph Voting** Lets writers approve paragraphs as "finished" by voting. A paragraph with an approval vote from all writers is framed by a golden border
Paragraph State A button that toggles through different appearances of a paragraph to express its state: not set, draft (typewriter font), review (serif font), or finished (serif font and golden frame)	**Where am I needed?** Shows a list of paragraphs with few revisions or no recent revisions. Clicking on an entry takes the writer to the given paragraph
Revision Overview Overview of the revision history in a stylized miniature of the document, that can be color-coded according to four criteria: number of edits, last edit time, first edit time, or whether or not a particular user has edited the paragraph	**Revision Overlay** Visualizes revision information as lines of varying thickness and color next to each paragraph, showing either: whether a particular user has edited the paragraph or not; relative total edit count; or relative time of editing
Revision Display A display next to each paragraph, showing the number of edits made to that paragraph. Clicking the display shows number of edits per user, with timestamps of their first and last edits	**Paragraph Locking** Lets writers block co-writers from editing a paragraph and partly or fully obscure the contents of it

The basic writing tool only supported simultaneous writing and simple text formatting. Each extension introduced what may be understood as a "feature"— e.g. a button for changing the appearance of a paragraph or a tool that would suggest phrases (see Table 1). The prototype was self-contained and each group worked on their own copy of it, which could be immediately used and modified. Reprogramming was possible at the level of appearance (HTML and CSS) and behavior (JavaScript). While extensions could be reprogrammed just like the barebones writing tool, they were additionally intended to allow participants to easily add and remove features in order to build up a custom writing tool in a plug-and-play fashion that did not require programming. We had implemented a total of ten extensions that were all available to the participants (see Table 1).

Modifying the Prototype Substrate. In addition to each substrate being reprogrammable, it is also possible to extend Codestrates' own functionality from within itself (see [22]). This blurs the boundary between Codestrates, as a platform on which the prototype is implemented, and the prototype as a substrate that relies on the Codestrates platform. For this study, we understand *Codestrates* as the architecture providing extensibility through its package management and reprogramming capabilities. By *prototype* we refer to the writing tool, including any modifications or extensions added to augment it.

Since Codestrates follows the structure of computational notebooks, it contains input areas for regular text as well as for blocks of program code. We utilized this in the prototype by letting the Codestrates text editing fields make

(a) The writing view with only writing tools visible. The vertical bars on the left are the Revision Overlay extension.

(b) The regular Codestrates view that is focused on programming. Code is accessible in a computational notebook like fashion.

Fig. 1. Screenshots of the prototype's two views. The views can be switched with the "Switch Theme" menu entry on the left.

up the text area of the writing tool. This meant that the text editing facilities that were part of the prototype's design were placed adjacent to (and potentially intermingled with) the implementation code for the prototype and any included extensions. Both the content in the regular text areas and the implementation code could be edited collaboratively in real-time. To aid participants in distinguishing the activity of implementing functionality from that of trying out the prototype, we had implemented two views: One for programming, which included features such as disabling packages or running code, and one intended for writing in which the only UI elements visible were the ones that were part of the prototype's user interface, e.g. text formatting (see Fig. 1 and the accompanying video).

3.3   Workshop Procedure

These prototyping workshops were intended (1) for participants to see their design ideas come to life in a high-fidelity prototype that still permitted further ideation and refinement during the workshop, and (2) for us to identify potentials and breakdowns of using reprogrammable prototypes in short-term workshops. The participants were divided across two identically structured workshops in order for us to accommodate a large number of participants (N = 13) and still be able to interact with each group and help them out when needed. Both workshops lasted two hours and were facilitated by the authors. The short time frame was due to limited project resources, which meant that participants were uncompensated volunteers. While the time frame was only enough for a small amount of reprogramming, it was enough for us to identify a number of lessons that others with similarly limited resources can learn from.

The workshops were both structured as follows: First, the Codestrates platform and its package management were briefly explained to participants.

Next, we presented the prototype and demonstrated how to add and modify extensions. We, further, showcased all ten extensions and outlined their functionality. The whole introduction lasted 20 min and took place in plenary using a large display to do a live demo. To supplement the introduction, and for reference throughout the workshop, participants were each given a pamphlet containing a description of each extension as well as instructions on how to access, use, and modify the prototype. After the introduction, we divided the participants into groups: three groups per workshop, six groups in total (see Table 2). The participants used their personal laptops to access and work on their group's copy of the prototype.

First, groups were instructed to explore the prototype and try out the extensions they found most interesting. Following a few minutes of exploration, the groups were instructed to each select one of three writing scenarios: (a) jointly writing a master's thesis, (b) remotely authoring a book, and (c) co-authoring a scientific paper. They were tasked with tailoring the prototype to fit their scenario. The scenarios were meant to guide participants' work with the prototype by providing them with a focus. While using and modifying the prototype, each group also created storyboards on paper to document ideas for features and modifications. This was intended to avoid ideation being hindered by technical obstacles, such as not knowing how to implement an idea. Each group was also given and encouraged to continuously fill out, a free-text questionnaire about the prototyping workshop and the project as a whole (see also Subsect. 3.5).

The prototype exploration and modification activity lasted one hour. 30 min into it, we introduced a set of changes to the scenarios. These disruptions were meant to push participants to reconsider assumptions at play in the modifications they were making. After working with the prototype for one hour, the groups took turns presenting what they had worked on. This was followed by a plenary discussion about reflections spurred by the questionnaire.

3.4   Participants

13 people participated in the workshops. We recruited participants from our local university. The only requirement for participation was current or recent experience with collaborative academic writing. Experience with programming was not a requirement. Participants were between 18 and 55 years old, three described their gender as female and ten as male. All but one participant were studying or working in a technology- and/or design-focused field.

Each participant filled in an anonymized demographic questionnaire when they entered the project. This information was used for providing the overview of participants' backgrounds in Table 2. The table also contains a categorization of how often the participants did programming in their daily life at the time of the prototyping workshop (similar to [21]). This is based on short meetings we had with each participant prior to the prototyping workshop in order to group them based on programming experience (both frequency and kind of experience, e.g., web development vs. hardware). This was done with the expectation that grouping participants with similar skill sets would ensure that all group members felt like they were able to contribute. The categorization has been confirmed with participants for the reporting in this paper, resulting in a few minor adjustments; however, none that would have impacted the groupings.

3.5 Data Collection and Analysis

We collected the following artifacts that participants worked on during the workshops: storyboards, their modified copies of the prototype, the mock documents used during prototyping, i.e. the text being edited when trying out the prototype, and the free-text questionnaire. The data obtained from the free-text questionnaire comprised answers to ten questions, of which the ones relevant to the present paper asked about the prototyping process: In particular, whether participants experienced any confusion or surprises and if they could think of any customization options that were missing. We additionally took photos throughout the workshops, and video and audio recorded the plenary activities and the dialogues of each group (using one stationary camera per group). The recommendations in this article are based on observations we made during the workshop, supplemented with the data mentioned above. The photos have primarily been used for dissemination about the workshops.

We conducted a qualitative analysis with the recordings as our primary source. Using the video material, incidents in the group work were categorized according to the type of episode (with the five labels: discussion, coordination, prototype work, problem, something unclear) through meaning condensation [14]. The plenary discussions were transcribed as part of the overall project, presented elsewhere [15]. Our analysis was further informed by the questionnaire and the transcripts of the plenary discussions.

4   Observations

In this section, we describe for each group, first: what modifications participants made to their prototype instances, and second: what their process was like during the workshop. We refer to participants as P1 – P13 and to groups as G1 – G6. During the two workshops, five out of the six groups reprogrammed the prototype. Three of these groups did so by changing functionality using JavaScript (G2, G3, G6), one group focused on modifying appearance using CSS (G5), and one group attempted to modify the prototype but did not succeed (G1).

G1 (Thesis Scenario). G1 attempted to create an extension for planning the content of paragraphs, a *"planning state"* (G1). Their idea circled around initial phases of writing, where this extension would prompt authors to plan each paragraph's content using a list of bullet points.

G1 began by looking through the pamphlet and discussing which extensions they liked, before installing a couple (Paragraph Locking and Meta Notes) and playing around with them while discussing ideas based on them. Most of the exploration was done separately, with occasional verbal exchanges and use of the pamphlet. They spent quite some time trying to figure out how to get started with

Table 2. Overview of the the groups participating in the prototyping workshops. G1 – G3 participated in the first workshop, G4 – G6 in the second.

Group	Part.	Occupation	Background	Programming Freq.
G1	P1	Software Engineer	IT Product Development	Regularly
	P2	Software Engineer	IT Product Development	Daily
G2	P3	Software Engineer	Computer Science	Daily
	P4	Software Engineer	IT Product Development	Daily
G3	P5	Assistant Professor	Computer Science	Occasionally
	P6	Postdoc	Molecular Biology	Daily
	P7	Postdoc	Computer Science	Occasionally
G4	P8	Associate Professor	Interaction Design	Rarely
	P9	Associate Professor	Digital design	Rarely
G5	P10	Ph.D. Student	Design	Regularly
	P11	Master's Student	Digital Design	Occasionally
G6	P12	Master's Student	IT Product Development	Regularly
	P13	Ph.D. Student	Computer Science	Daily

programming, mainly talking about how to do it rather than actually doing any programming. It took a while for them to figure out how to access the code for the different extensions, and they generally struggled with a lack of overview of the implementation, having trouble locating things in the code or being surprised that making changes to the rich-text implementation would affect all running instances of it. Another problem seemed to be that Codestrates violated their expectations from previous programming experience, such as when P1 made a remark about not knowing how to do something "in onCreate", i.e. when the prototype is loaded. A couple of times, they remarked on not having enough time to do what they wanted, and they ended up deciding to mock up their desired feature instead of fully implementing it. In the plenary session, they explained that they had missed the Paragraph States extension as an obvious starting point *"due to the fact that there are so many packages"* (referring to the extensions).

G2 (Thesis Scenario). The participants in G2 mostly worked individually. While P4 (unsuccessfully) attempted to modify the Revision Display to show the number of edits contributed by each individual author, P3 modified the "Where am I needed?" extension to make it possible to tag co-authors in a paragraph: Authors could then be tagged using the notation @username within a paragraph, upon which the paragraph would be listed in the "Where am I needed?" dialog box (see Fig. 2a).

G2 began their work by individually reading the pamphlet. Early on, they clarified with a facilitator what was "allowed"—getting confirmation that "ridiculous" ideas were also allowed. G2 quickly turned their focus to the code, individually trying to understand it. P4 seemed to struggle with this, making

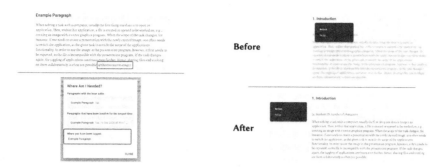

(a) G2's modification, a tagging feature that was integrated into the "Where am I needed?" extension.

(b) G5's modification, an updated style of the Meta Notes extension. The blur was removed and the notes box moved.

Fig. 2. Screenshots of examples of the groups' modifications. Text content and user names in the screenshots were modified to ensure anonymity.

use of the browser's developer tools and console to explore it: "*There is a lot to figure out; where to start and what to do.*" After some time of trying out an extension, they drew a storyboard about an idea for a tagging feature. While P3 started working on that feature, P4 continued to explore the prototype and try to understand the code. G2 began modifying code within 20 min, unlike the other groups who all spent around half of the allotted hour before starting to do any programming. P3 switched to using the external code editor Atom and copied code back and forth from Codestrates because he found the Codestrates editor to lack essential features, such as advanced find and replace. Finally, the naming of extensions caused some misunderstandings, as P4, e.g., mistook the background service for tracking changes (Revision Tracker) to be the Revision Display extension. As understanding the code in the given time was too complex, P4 ended up creating a storyboard about his idea instead.

G3 (Book Scenario). G3 modified the Revision Overlay extension to not only indicate *when* the last edit of a paragraph happened, but also by which co-author. G3 began by trying to become familiar with the system and looking through the pamphlet. G3's ideas for modifications took outset in the extensions, such as when they discussed how the "Where am I needed?" extension could be modified to allow writers to indicate that they need help from co-writers. When asking a facilitator whether their intended modification would be feasible within the time frame of the workshop revealed their ambitions to be unrealistic, they instead described their idea in a storyboard. While trying to reprogram an extension, G3 struggled to understand the underlying architecture of the prototype—the lack of an inspection feature for the system state was another hurdle. Help from the facilitator was crucial for the group to succeed in creating their modification.

Although programming collaboratively, each group member primarily used their own laptop and occasionally looked at the screen of the other members to see what they were doing. P7 commented on this collaborative coding as being "*a completely new experience*" and that "*it's kind of weird to be typing around in the same code at the same time.*"

G4 (Book Scenario). G4 did not attempt to modify the prototype beyond adding existing extensions.

G4 started by exploring the prototype, including switching between the writing and programming themes. In doing so, both participants faced minor technical problems such as toggling full screen mode and not knowing how to exit it. P8 also struggled with her laptop running slow, resulting in the prototype becoming unresponsive and requiring P8 to reload the page multiple times during the second half of the workshop. The facilitators lent P8 one of their laptops for the last third of the workshop. Besides experimenting with the provided extensions, the group also inquired about the potential to create images in a document. A facilitator provided this by helping them install a drawing extension from another project. Consisting of two participants that rarely program, G4 focused on exploring existing extensions and making storyboards.

G5 (Thesis Scenario). G5 modified the Meta Notes extension. Initially, the extension displayed notes on top of the text and blurred the text underneath. G5 changed the styling of the extension, so that the notes were placed besides the text and the text was not blurred anymore (see Fig. 2b).

G5 started by skimming the pamphlet to get an overview of the available extensions. Initially, they had some problems with basic functions of the prototype, such as creating new code blocks. They also required help from a facilitator to find the CSS code to modify. After making their modification, G5 discussed possible ways of using other extensions in their scenario. Because of the limited time, they sketched their ideas on paper and using the drawing extension within the prototype (inspired by G4). In the second half, one participant experienced a bug that caused the prototype to freeze, but this was resolved by a facilitator.

G6 (Thesis Scenario). G6 updated the Paragraph State extension to display what state a paragraph is in (draft, review, or finished) with a text label instead of only indicating it through styling.

G6 began by discussing which extensions to install, looking through the package manager and the pamphlet. From early on, they anchored this discussion in their chosen scenario. They decided to work towards their idea by modifying Paragraph States. This spurred further elaboration, in the form of improvements they wanted to make to Paragraph States. When it came to exploring implementation details, P13 was quick to get a grasp of both the Codestrates user interface (such as how to access the implementation code) and its inner workings, and on a number of occasions would explain things to P12 when he expressed confusion. They were both slowed down by being restricted to JavaScript and CSS, since they were familiar with other languages and programming libraries that they would have liked to draw on. They interacted with a facilitator on multiple occasions, to discuss how to accomplish particular things. Along the way, they sometimes used a storyboard to communicate about their ideas. Making a storyboard later became a way for P12 to contribute when P13 wanted to focus on programming while P12 was not sure what to do. For the majority of the time, they worked separately on each their laptop. The real-time shared editing caused some trouble, with P13 asking P12 to refrain from writing anything until P13 was done making some edits to the code *"because my [caret] is flying around when you do it."*

5   Lessons Learned

We now report on four lessons learned from using a reprogrammable prototype during short-term prototyping workshops. Based on our experiences, we provide suggestions and recommendations in the gray boxes at the end of each subsection to guide the design of studies and prototypes. As mentioned, while the time frame we had available was not enough for substantial reprogramming, it was sufficiently long for us to identify a number of breakdowns. These recommendations will not—and are not intended to—overcome this issue or the lack of a tailoring culture [19]. Rather, they aim to inform about what breakdowns can occur and how to mitigate them in similar workshops.

5.1   Familiarization

Many of the problems that participants faced originated in confusion about the underlying Codestrates platform. G6, for instance, had trouble finding the implementation code they wanted to change, and G4 initially struggled with adding extensions. The real-time collaborative editing, further, meant that modifications were instantly shared within the groups, which presented participants with both advantages and challenges. For example, many groups would switch quite fluently between focusing on individual activities and asking questions regarding things other group members were currently doing. But we also saw several instances in which the real-time sharing caused visual disruption or broken code.

After some time familiarizing themselves with the prototype, the participants could largely overcome these issues. However, the fact that most groups spent so much of the time allotted for modifications on getting familiar with the prototyping environment indicates that we underestimated the necessary scope of familiarization. Although participants did explore the extensions while getting familiar with the environment, the level of *extension* resulting from this was minimal due to the overhead of figuring out how to add and use extensions, and only G2 spent the majority of the time *reprogramming*. Letting participants interact with the prototype during the demo (see Sect. 3), could likely have revealed confusion and helped facilitators resolve it earlier in the process. Providing a pamphlet as written documentation did support familiarization and allowed participants to read up on things later but could not stand on its own.

- Ensure that participants understand central principles of the prototyping platform, e.g. through hands-on tasks.
- Engage participants actively when introducing the prototype, e.g. through a tutorial.
- Provide simple written and illustrated documentation for participants.

5.2 Conflation of the Platform and the Prototype

Switching back and forth between development and use led participants to focus on Codestrates and technical issues rather than on the prototype—an issue also found in earlier studies where "discussions quite easily get focused on the current prototype and rather technical issues" [4]. As described in Subsect. 3.2, reprogramming took place directly in the prototype's user interface. While this is beneficial in that there is no need for external applications like an IDE, this paradigm is rather different from conventional development paradigms and is hence unfamiliar even to many experienced programmers. We suspect this was the reason for participants' conflated understanding of the underlying Codestrates platform and the actual prototype. This conflation also surfaced in the plenary discussions, where participants would not distinguish between their experience of using Codestrates and discussing ideas for prototype designs. There is a trade-off in using a novel development paradigm that allows new and possibly better ways of reprogramming, but which may also prevent participants from reusing previous experience and cause the platform to become the focus of discussion instead of the prototype design. If quick engagement with reprogramming is desirable, using familiar development paradigms should be considered. Otherwise, more time for familiarization (see also above) may be required.

- Consider whether the development environment should be separate from the prototype.
- If relevant, explain the interwovenness of using and developing the prototype in the same environment.
- Demonstrate the borders between the platform and the prototype and facilitate exploration of them before participants start developing.

5.3 Aligning Expectations and Facilitating Exploration

We experienced a number of situations in which we had not managed to adequately guide participants' expectations for what would be achieved in the workshop. For one, most groups struggled with implementing desired changes within the allotted time frame, among other things because they jumped straight to plans for major changes instead of starting by exploring minor adjustments. Some participants downplayed what they had accomplished, such as when P3 presented what

we saw as a successful modification as *"a half-assed implementation of something."*
In addition to frustrations caused by the short time frame, we suspect that participants' expectations for themselves are connected with assumptions about the facilitators' expectations and how to live up to those. P4 asking what was "allowed" exemplifies how participants' work is guided by trying to fulfill facilitators' expectations. We do not see it as problematic that participants wanted to align their goals with our expectations but include it as an example of the importance of clear communication about expectations. The scenarios seemed to provide guidance for some participants, but our experiences show that they may need supplementing with more explicit communication about expectations.

- Make clear to participants what *kinds of modifications* are possible, what will be *feasible in the allotted time*, and what would be a *satisfactory outcome*. Note that the purpose is not to set a standard but to make participants understand that small contributions are fine.
- Walk participants through different levels of what is possible, e.g. progressing from changing styling to changing the behavior of an extension.
- Provide concrete tasks or scenarios to solve and/or discuss.
- Provide clearly available options for exploring the prototype, e.g. through configuration options or highlighted parts of the code.

5.4 Catering to Different Levels of Programming Experience

How frequently participants programmed in their day-to-day life varied from programming daily, e.g. as a software engineer, to only programming rarely. From the provided extensibility through the package management and reprogrammability of code, all groups used the package management while exploring different features, but use of reprogrammability was dependent on the participants' programming skills. All groups except G4—the only group without a participant who programs regularly or daily—engaged in reprogramming extensions. While G5 focused on style changes, the remaining groups changed the functionality of extensions. The provided extensions supported participants in coming up with ideas and supported dialogue—e.g., G3 discussed improving the Revision Overlay extension: *"So what can we do with this overlay, how can we make it more interesting?"* (P5). Our observations additionally confirm that providing pre-implemented extensions was necessary, given the limited time frame.

We see both opportunities and difficulties with our approach: For participants with programming experience, reprogrammability can be motivating and spark creativity. For participants without much programming experience, however, the learning curve was too steep and did not allow them to engage in modifying extensions—this echoes the results of [19]. Those participants need additional tools that support reprogrammability in a more accessible way, for instance by having a GUI for configuration of, e.g., styling and parameters, or by enabling direct manipulation for configuring the prototype [4]. Such directly available options could also be useful for spurring exploration (cf. Subsect. 5.3).

- Provide different levels of tailorability suitable for the participants, e.g. by supplementing scripting with a GUI for configuration.
- Create a starting point, such as extensions that participants can build on instead of starting from scratch.

6   Limitations and Future Work

This project had a number of limitations. First, only 3 of the 13 participants were women. Research indicates that gender can impact the way people approach end-user programming environments (e.g., [1]). With a different gender distribution, and perhaps all-women groups, we may have uncovered more or different issues and seen more diverse examples of resourcefulness from participants. Second, the short duration of the workshops meant limited time for both familiarization and modification. Some of the presented issues can likely be alleviated with longer workshops and/or several workshops with the same participants. Third, (real-time) collaborative writing as a use case is relatively close to real-time collaborative programming, which likely added to the conflation of prototype and platform observed in participants' discussions. Our suggestions for guided familiarization may reduce this, but it may also be that the mode of collaboration needs to be considered more carefully against the use case. Finally, preparing the prototype in advance of the workshop involved a trade-off: While it reduced downtime for debugging or larger implementation changes, in which participants could become disengaged, it also excluded participants from an implementation step that could have given them a greater sense of agency and ownership in the process. In addition, we note that our guidelines are aimed at research on the use of reprogramming. Product-oriented user-involvement likely requires other steps.

7   Conclusion

This paper illustrates breakdowns and pitfalls of using reprogrammable prototypes in prototyping workshops with limited resources and offers guidelines on how to mitigate them. Based on two prototyping workshops, we have compiled suggestions under four themes: (1) Ensuring participants' familiarization with the prototype, (2) avoiding conflation of platform and prototype, (3) aligning expectations with participants and guiding their exploration, and (4) supporting participants with different levels of programming experience. We believe some of the suggestions are also applicable for other user groups than end-user developers and encourage more research to explore such workshops with different user groups. We also generally encourage the employment of reprogrammable software in prototyping processes to engage end-users more deeply with the interactive behavior of prototypes, while keeping in mind the limitations of short-term workshops like ours.

Acknowledgments. We are grateful to the people who took the time to participate and share their thoughts and ideas with us, both during and after the workshops— this work would not have been possible without them. We also thank our colleagues for feedback and insightful discussions: Peter Lyle, Philip Tchernavskij, Carla Griggio, Tiare Feuchtner, and Wenkai Han, as well as Susanne Bødker and Clemens N. Klokmose, who have provided guidance throughout the writing of this paper. Finally, we appreciate the feedback and suggestions from the anonymous reviewers.

This project has received funding from the European Research Council (ERC) under the European Union's Horizon 2020 research and innovation programme (grant agreement No 740548).

References

1. Beckwith, L., Burnett, M., Wiedenbeck, S., Cook, C., Sorte, S., Hastings, M.: Effectiveness of end-user debugging software features: are there gender issues? In: Proceedings of ACM CHI 2005 (2005). https://doi.org/10.1145/1054972.1055094

2. Bellucci, A., Jacucci, G., Kotkavuori, V., Serim, B., Ahmed, I., Ylirisku, S.: Extreme co-design: prototyping with and by the user for appropriation of web-connected tags. In: Díaz, P., Pipek, V., Ardito, C., Jensen, C., Aedo, I., Boden, A. (eds.) IS-EUD 2015. LNCS, vol. 9083, pp. 109–124. Springer, Cham (2015). https://doi.org/10.1007/978-3-319-18425-8_8

3. Bødker, S.: Through the Interface - a Human Activity Approach to User Interface Design. DAIMI Report Series (1987)

4. Bødker, S., Grønbæk, K.: Design in Action: From Prototyping by Demonstration to Cooperative Prototyping (1992)

5. Bødker, S., Grønbæk, K., Kyng, M.: Cooperative design: techniques and experiences from the Scandinavian scene. In: Readings in HCI (1995). https://doi.org/10.1016/B978-0-08-051574-8.50025-X

6. Borowski, M., Rädle, R., Klokmose, C.N.: Codestrate packages: an alternative to "one-size-fits-all" software. In: Proceedings of the ACM CHI EA 2018 (2018). https://doi.org/10.1145/3170427.3188563

7. Cabitza, F., Simone, C.: Malleability in the hands of end-users. In: Paternò, F., Wulf, V. (eds.) New Perspectives in End-User Development, pp. 137–163. Springer, Cham (2017). https://doi.org/10.1007/978-3-319-60291-2_7

8. Colombo, L., Landoni, M.: Low-tech and high-tech prototyping for eBook co-design with children. In: Proceedings of the ACM IDC 2013 (2013). https://doi.org/10.1145/2485760.2485824

9. Costabile, M.F., Fogli, D., Mussio, P., Piccinno, A.: End-User Development: The Software Shaping Workshop Approach (2006). https://doi.org/10.1007/1-4020-5386-X_9

10. Fogli, D., Piccinno, A.: Co-evolution of end-user developers and systems in multi-tiered proxy design problems. In: Dittrich, Y., Burnett, M., Mørch, A., Redmiles, D. (eds.) IS-EUD 2013. LNCS, vol. 7897, pp. 153–168. Springer, Heidelberg (2013). https://doi.org/10.1007/978-3-642-38706-7_12

11. Gantt, M., Nardi, B.A.: Gardeners and gurus: patterns of cooperation among CAD users. In: Proceedings of the ACM CHI 1992 (1992). https://doi.org/10.1145/142750.142767

12. Klokmose, C.N., Eagan, J.R., Baader, S., Mackay, W.E., Beaudouin-Lafon, M.: Webstrates: shareable dynamic media. In: Proceedings of the ACM UIST 2015 (2015). https://doi.org/10.1145/2807442.2807446

13. Kluyver, T., et al.: Jupyter notebooks–a publishing format for reproducible computational workflows (2016)

14. Kvale, S.: Doing Interviews. Sage, London (2007)

15. Larsen-Ledet, I., Borowski, M.: "It looks like you don't agree": idiosyncratic practices and preferences in collaborative writing. In: Proceedings of the ACM OzCHI 2020 (2020). https://doi.org/10.1145/3441000.3441032

16. Letondal, C.C.: Participatory programming: developing programmable bioinformatics tools for end-users. In: Lieberman, H., Paternó, F., Wulf, V. (eds.) End User Development. Human-Computer Interaction Series, vol. 9, pp. 207–242. Springer, Dordrecht (2006). https://doi.org/10.1007/1-4020-5386-X_10

17. Maceli, M., Atwood, M.E.: "Human Crafters" once again: supporting users as designers in continuous co-design. In: Dittrich, Y., Burnett, M., Mørch, A., Redmiles, D. (eds.) IS-EUD 2013. LNCS, vol. 7897, pp. 9–24. Springer, Heidelberg (2013). https://doi.org/10.1007/978-3-642-38706-7_3

18. Mackay, W.E.: Patterns of sharing customizable software. In: Proceedings of the ACM CSCW 1990 (1990). https://doi.org/10.1145/99332.99356

19. MacLean, A., Carter, K., Lövstrand, L., Moran, T.: User-tailorable systems: pressing the issues with buttons. In: Proceedings of the ACM CHI 1990 (1990). https://doi.org/10.1145/97243.97271

20. Mørch, A.: Three levels of end-user tailoring: customization, integration, and extension. Comput. Des. Context **1**, 51–76 (1997). https://mitpress.mit.edu/books/computers-and-design-context

21. Perera, C., Aghaee, S., Blackwell, A.: Natural notation for the domestic internet of things. In: Díaz, P., Pipek, V., Ardito, C., Jensen, C., Aedo, I., Boden, A. (eds.) IS-EUD 2015. LNCS, vol. 9083, pp. 25–41. Springer, Cham (2015). https://doi.org/10.1007/978-3-319-18425-8_3

22. Rädle, R., Nouwens, M., Antonsen, K., Eagan, J.R., Klokmose, C.N.: Codestrates: literate computing with webstrates. In: Proceedings of the ACM UIST 2017 (2017). https://doi.org/10.1145/3126594.3126642

23. Sanders, E.B.N., Stappers, P.J.: Co-creation and the new landscapes of design. CoDesign (2008). https://doi.org/10.1080/15710880701875068

24. Zhu, L., Herrmann, T.: Meta-design in co-located meetings. In: Dittrich, Y., Burnett, M., Mørch, A., Redmiles, D. (eds.) IS-EUD 2013. LNCS, vol. 7897, pp. 169–184. Springer, Heidelberg (2013). https://doi.org/10.1007/978-3-642-38706-7_13

Design of a Chatbot to Assist the Elderly

Stefano Valtolina(✉) ⓘ and Mattia Marchionna

Department of Computer Science, Università degli Studi di Milano, Milan, Italy
stefano.valtolina@unimi.it, mattia.marchionna@studenti.unimi.it

Abstract. Nowadays, conversational agents are solutions that can provide a highly valuable addition to the existing healthcare services to assist the elderly in following their care plans and gradually changing adverse patterns of behaviour. Nevertheless, the development of a conversation agent in the healthcare domain presents several technical, design and linguistic challenges. In our paper, we describe a chatbot conversing with elderly persons, with age-related problems. Charlie, the name of our chatbot, has been designed to provide the elderly with companionship through innovative strategies based on gamification, active notifications, and promotion of self-compassion that can be explored for preventive mental healthcare. Moreover, Charlie can be used to monitor meaningful or anomalous situations that can affect aged people. To specify these situations in the paper we describe a web application that enables medical assistants and relatives to create rules that depend on data gathered by Charlie such as the number of required news, followed tips, completed games, but also biometrical data such as the number of steps made during the day, burned calories or the number of hours of sleep. To help caregivers in creating these rules, we are studying how to endow our web app with a recommendation service for predicting recurring anomalous situations and, accordingly, provide suggestions on which characteristics the elderly will have to change to improve their lifestyle.

Keywords: End-user development · Virtual assistants · CUI – conversational interface in healthcare · AI for HCI

1 Introduction

Since the COVID-19 pandemic outbreak, healthcare systems have been subjected to enormous stress and people all across the sector are looking for digital solutions to help ease the pressure. Specifically, due to this pandemic, the elderly are increasingly alone and many are beginning to establish empathic relationships with human and virtual telephone operators. Loneliness, especially in old age, begins to become a serious problem. A research study commissioned by Ipsos, Comieco and Symbola [1] claims as 60% of those who suffer from it today are in a particularly fragile age range. The result is confirmed by another study [2] carried out by the Enuan, a startup that deals with artificial intelligence applied to voice and chat channels. This study states how from March 2020 onwards, especially during the months of lockdown and forced smart working, the most empathic interactions have increased by over 30%. For supporting health facilities

D. Fogli et al. (Eds.): IS-EUD 2021, LNCS 12724, pp. 153–168, 2021.
https://doi.org/10.1007/978-3-030-79840-6_10

that are overburdened by the task of assisting a lot of patients in complying with their care plans, and for helping the elderly to deal with this lockdown and isolation that are disrupting their social life, this paper aims at studying a personal chatbot for elderly able to act as a medical consultant, friend, assistant and entertainer.

In detail, the first research question that this paper wants to answer concerns the value of involving a virtual assistant in helping older people not to feel alone, to be engaged in entertaining activities, to manage their medicines and to establish remote connections with their relatives. To this aim, in Sect. 2 we present several works that motivated us to use a conversation agent in our context of the study. Nevertheless, we identified how some works propose solutions that miss in addressing pre-emptive care for strengthening mental health or improving the quality of life, without necessarily assuming diagnosed disorders, as happening for the elderly.

For this reason, Sect. 3 describes our study that starts by investigating the problems relating to the elderly, their needs and the existing technological solutions and then proposes a conversational user interface (CUI) that is software that runs simple and structurally repetitive tasks inside a messaging application. Our idea is to design a conversation to share knowledge and emotion that can be affordable for non-technical people. The challenge is to understand which communication characteristics and interaction strategies encourage their use, specifically for the elderly. Specifically, we want to investigate the level of acceptability by senior users of a combination of assistance, entertainment, gamification and self-compassion strategies to evaluate the better solutions that can support the elderly in their daily routines.

A second research question we try to answer in Sect. 4 is how to train our chatbot to monitor relevant and critical situations that can affect the lives of our dear seniors. After observing the elderly's daily activities, caregivers, that is health assistants or family members need to identify critical behaviours that need to be avoided or regulated. For doing this, we designed a web application that allows us to define some rules that are automatically triggered when specific situations take place. This web app aims at providing non-professional users (health assistants or relatives) with an environment for creating rules using an easy and visual language, familiar to them. Those rules are used for monitoring events related to the elderly's habits and are automatically triggered to notify behaviour that needs to be corrected. To provide help to the health assistants and relatives in their rules creation task, we provided the web app with an Artificial Intelligence (AI) module to make predictions and to compute suggestions helpful to monitor the elderly's behaviours. The main feature of this AI module is its capability of describing the reasons for the computed predictions, by computing the smallest change to the feature values that increases the prediction. Such explanations are important since they not only allow us to understand our dear seniors' conditions but also shall ensure that caregivers can trust the output of the automatic learner, which would be otherwise viewed as a "black-box". Finally, Sect. 5 reports conclusions and future works.

2   Elderly Assistance with a Virtual Agent

Chatbots [3] are commonplace in the online retail space, but they are also emerging in the healthcare sector [4]. In this area, well-designed chatbots can help to communicate more efficiently with a non-expert target audience [5, 6]. Several studies [3, 7–10] and commercial systems [11–13] highlight how virtual agents can help patients to deal with common issues, such as remembering to take medicines, doing some exercises, following a specific diet. Other works [14, 15] focused on how hospitalized medical patients would respond to a conversational agent that would provide empathic support. Similarly, King et al. in [16] describe an agent that aims at delivering personalized physical activity advice to older adults which the goal of increasing their brisk walking. Finally, a last important study presented in [17] reviews existing substantial scientific works concerning medical chatbots from a behaviour change perspective. Specifically, the authors identify problems of acceptance of medical chatbots in society and the use of chatbots to change harmful behaviour. They mainly suggest how, to design an effective medical chatbot, is useful to insert chatbots in messaging apps, establish an understandable agreement process between the user and the chatbot and implement emotionality of the chatbot's responses. Likewise, [6] investigates which functionalities text-based chatbots can provide to benefit human interactions and what are the challenges and strategies associated with them not only in the medical domain.

In general, these works focus is on what should be "fixed", e.g. they suggest moving more, changing diet habits, and how to mitigate depressive symptoms, and suicidal tendencies and the target is the person with these problems [18]. They miss in addressing preemptive care for strengthening mental health or improving the quality of life, without necessarily assuming diagnosed disorders, as happening for the elderly.

The main research question we try to answer in this paper aims at studying how to design a chatbot able to adapt its functionality, interface, personality, information access, and content to increase its communication skills to an individual or a category of individuals. Moreover, we want to investigate the efficacy of a combination of assistance, entertainment, gamification and self-compassion strategies to evaluate the better solutions that can support the elderly in their daily routines. In summary, we aim to understand if it is possible to use chatbots not only to fill a void for lonely pensioners but to help them for increasing the perception of their quality of life as well.

3   Design Strategies to Develop a Chatbot for Assisting the Elderly

Understanding users' background and collecting as many features about them as possible helps narrow the bot focus and provide personalized services. For this reason, we focused our study on the design of a virtual agent, named Charlie, able to act as a caregiver but also as a friend of people aged 60 years and above. Taking into account the results presented in the literature [19–23] we designed a set of functionalities to bring alive our chatbot. A chatbot able to develop easy connections with older users, and for this, we developed it as an empathetic, sensitive, sociable and friendly robot.

Some studies (e.g. [24]) suggest avoiding defining a chatbot default gender. Indeed overly humanized agents could create a higher expectation on users, which eventually leads to more frustration when the chatbot fails [6]. Despite the name borrowed from nice characters of films and comics, we designed Charlie as a bot (as shown in Charlie's icons in Figs. 1, 2 and 4).

About Charlie's choice of age, we decided to give it child traits. This because children and the elderly can in some ways be very similar. They both need to be looked after, taken by the hand, helped to cheer up or relax. Such context of use should feel friendly since Charlie invites the elderly into an intimate one-on-one chat space [23]. Moreover, Charlie talks a lot about himself but he also needs to be very good at listening to what others have to say. Charlie is so used as a sort of psychiatric counselling to change aspects of user habits and lifestyle, such as the habit of taking medicine or drinking waters more often [25, 26].

From a technical point of view, the chatbot agent is designed and developed by using Dialogflow [27]. DialogFlow is a natural language processing (NLP) platform provided by Google Corporation that can be used to build conversational applications and experiences on multiple platforms (e.g. Facebook, Messenger) or devices (e.g. Google Home. To create a customized web interface for Charlie, the interactions are carried out through a service built in *node.js* [28]. Charlie's functionalities have been designed to allow him to know the user's preferences. To do it, Charlie triggers specific Google Cloud functions [29] that are used to save the user's preferences, intentions and actions in a database of the Firebase platform [30].

For example, Charlie can trigger small talks about sports or the world of celebrities (Fig. 1). Since the user expresses the intention to find in-depth this argument, Charlie will save the preference in the internal database so that the subsequent interactions will comply with it. Moreover, as depicted in Fig. 2, Charlie can also send healthy tips to the user every day and suggests to her/him how to follow them. Adopting a gamification strategy, in the evening Charlie will ask the user if she/he has followed the advice or not and if yes, she/he will receive a "bot-coin" (a sort of recognition/prize). In exchange for recognition and rewards, this approach aims at helping users to follow a healthy life.

Charlie can also help if the user is subject to cognitive impairment and memory reduction. To do it, he can also ask the user if she/he needs help to remember something and helps her/him to fix a timetable (Fig. 2 – Second screenshot).

Another Charlie's functionality is used to provide the user with short quizzes on preferred topics to stimulate her/him and to satisfy her/his need for entertainment. When a quiz is activated, the user can select the number and difficulty of the questions (Fig. 3). Once the quiz is finished, Charlie will display the result obtained, with the correct and wrong answers (Fig. 3 – Second screenshot). In this way, Charlie can save the number of quizzes carried out during the day and statistics on wrong and correct answers in the Firebase database.

Finally, Charlie can ask the user for helping him in solving some riddles (Fig. 4 – First screenshot) or he can talk about an anecdote about his life that can generate self-compassion in the user (Fig. 4 – Second screenshot). These anecdotes see him as the protagonist and they are unfortunate or unpleasant events. According to some studies [12], this would lead to self-compassion in the user, a stimulus to reflect on one's life and a sense of identification. First of all, Charlie involves the user by asking her/him for an opinion on the matter and, if the user wishes, she/he can also share a similar episode. This would then help develop self-compassion and fill the need to be heard and understood.

Fig. 1. Example of engagement interaction strategy provided by Charlie.

Fig. 2. Example of a healthy tip that Charlie can give to the user. In the second screenshot, Charlie asks the user if she/he needs help to remember something and helps her/him to fix a timetable.

3.1 A Preliminary Evaluation of Charlie's Functionalities

To evaluate Charlie's personality and the level of acceptability by senior users, we conducted a test involving four students of the bachelor degree in Computer Science for New Media communications and two students of master degree in Computer Science at the University of Milano. Each student contacted a couple of aged relatives, who after signed an informed consent, have been involved in the evaluation of Charlie's personality and acceptance.

All participants (12 in total, aged 60 through 70 years old) live in pairs or alone, and have a quite good skill and inclination in using technology (all have a smartphone and use it to chat, see videos on YouTube, browse the Web). We asked testers to interact with the agents daily in their homes for a week. After that, students carried a set of interviews and accordingly defined an affinity diagram [31] (Fig. 5) to group keywords and recurring themes that have meanings considering the experimented interactions.

The adopted structured interview is based on the Unified Theory of Acceptance and Use of Technology (UTAUT) model, a model based on TAM [32], that has been tested extensively in various fields and promises to be a great tool for analyzing users acceptance of health technology [33–35]. In [36] authors demonstrate how this model can effectively measure older users' perceptions and their level of acceptance in using healthcare applications. According to this study, we designed specific questions to measure the strength of one's intention to perform a specified behaviour [37] and questions to investigate how much users considered easy to use Charlie.

Specifically, we provided senior users with questions for measuring the evoking anxious or emotional reactions they experimented with when they used our chatbot, for measuring their trust in Charlie in terms of safety and reliability, and for measuring how much physicians' opinions can influence their perception of technology as useful.

Although the number of interviews makes it impossible to present a statistically significant analysis, we carried out a qualitative study that allowed us to define a set of keywords or themes that are used to assess the perception of Charlie's personality and his level of acceptability by users. In details, when it comes to Charlie's personality, testers described him as a young, cheerful, active, friendly and smart assist (Fig. 6). The perceived age of Charlie varied, but most of the participants agreed that he had the innocence of childhood regardless of age.

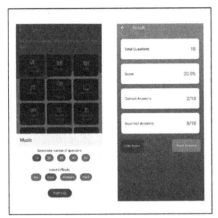 

Fig. 3. By using this screenshot, the user can select the number of questions and the difficulties of the quiz. The second final screenshot is used by Charlie to visualize correct and wrong answers.

Fig. 4. In the first screenshot, Charlie presents a riddle and in the second, he presents an example of a self-compassion strategy.

In the evaluation of the core of Charlie's personality, more people mentioned that the chatbot was efficient and helpful, while fewer people described the chatbot as imaginative or creative. Moreover, in some cases, people perceived Charlie's chatbot to be a robot rather than a human. Participants reported that how the chatbot used words and phrases contributed to their impression of the chatbot's personality. They reported that they felt the chatbot was warm-hearted, energetic, or cheerful. Meanwhile, a few participants mentioned that the number of words per message and the number of messages that the chatbot sent at a time led to perceptions that the chatbot was pushy and compulsive. Another important cue upon which the research participants when judging the chatbot's personality was the visual cues. In particular, emojis played a crucial role in affecting participants' judgment of the chatbot's gender and characteristics. Several interviewees mentioned that the emojis made them feel that the chatbot was cheerful, friendly, and approachable. Meanwhile, the emojis also affected interviewees' perceptions of the chatbot's gender. Two participants mentioned that the emojis that Charlie used remembered them that Charlie is a robot. In general, the affinity diagram (Fig. 5) highlight how Charlie is considered polite, smart, charming, helpful and reliable.

The results of the performed analysis have shown very comforting outcomes even if it is necessary to carry out more detailed tests with real users to be able to give clearer and more truthful information in the middle and long period. Unfortunately, due to the current situation linked to the COVID 19 pandemic, these tests are still to be carried out.

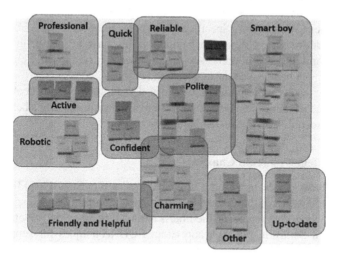

Fig. 5. Affinity diagram to sort cues that shape Charlie's personality.

"Boy, 6 years old, playful, enterprising kid." (tester n. 4)

"Constructive and cheerful, outgoing and[has] child-like attitude towards daily routines." (tester n. 2)

"He would be a playful boy" (tester n.5)

Fig. 6. Examples of answers about Charlie's personality of participants at the test.

4   A EUD Solution for Training the Virtual Agent

4.1   EUD Strategies for Designing Chatbots

Charlie's functionalities described in the previous section allow him to act as a friend and a caregiver for the elderly. In addition to supporting the dear seniors in their daily activities, Charlie has the task to monitor her/his behaviours to detect eventually anomaly situations and warn the health assistant or relatives accordingly. To define what to monitor we designed a web application that can be used by health assistants or relatives themselves. The idea is to adopt an end-user development (EUD [38]) strategy to involve them in the specification of rules that best fit their dear seniors [39, 40]. EUD represents the ideal approach for empowering non-technical users making them developers of rules [41, 42] that will be at the base of the chatbot design. In the EUD approach, this problem can be faced through a design environment where visual entities representing the conditions that need to be connected graphically to define the sequence of operations for monitoring specific situations. Visual strategies typically used for modelling Event-Condition-Action rules can be described through the most famous systems that apply them: IFTTT, Atooma, and Yahoo's Pipes. In [43–45] authors discuss how the first two design strategies support users without programming knowledge to define their context-dependent applications. Specifically [46] describes how these EUD strategies allow users to define sets of desired behaviours in response to specific events. This is made mainly through rules definition-wizards. Rules can be typically chosen among existing ones or can be tweaked through customization.

Based on the results of these studies, we devised a new solution specifically addressed to enable non-technical users in designing rules to monitor the elderly's behaviours and gathering data according to spatio-temporal dimensions.

4.2   EUD Strategies to Train Charlie

The web app has been designed on a previous application, SmartFit [43] specifically developed for allowing coaches and athletic trainers of non-professional sports teams to monitor and analyze data regarding the fitness and well-being of the athletes.

Designed on SmartFit, our web app adopt EUD techniques for supporting non-experts in computer science in designing rules. In detail, it enables caregivers and relatives in capturing a set of measurements describing their dear's behaviour over a period, typically a day. Such measurements concern activities carried out by the elderly such as the number of solved quizzes or riddles, how many she/he retrieved news on her/his favourite topics, how many Charlie's suggestions or stories she/he have followed and listened to. We are also endowing the elderly with an electronic bracelet for gathering biometric data such as the heartbeat, the quality of sleep (hours of sleep, number of awakenings for the night, and minutes of restless sleep), the burned calories and physical activities (number of steps or kilometres walked).

Based on these gathered data, the web app aims at supporting non-expert users in the composition of rules based on an ECA (Event-Condition-Action) paradigm. Adopting this paradigm, users can specify conditions and temporal operations for implementing the rules. For example, Fig. 7 presents a dashboard on which the caregivers can visualize the set of defined rules to monitor her/his dear senior's behaviour. The conditions can be composed by using simple drop-down menus to combine groups of statements connected through AND/OR operators. The order of the conditions can be changed just by dragging and dropping the statements into the right position.

The strategy used to create rules extends the IF-THIS-THEN-THAT approach and supports the definition of time dimensions that are exploited for expressing more articulated rules. The time dimension is used for creating rules by using temporal operators that point out temporal correlations among relevant events. In detail, users can use a set of temporal operators such as $opt \in \{before, after, when\}$ to specify if she/he wants to monitor events that happen according to specific time constraints. For example, as depicted in Fig. 8 the user can specify to monitor if her/her dear has had a difficult night (e.g. less than 5 h of sleep with at least 3 awakenings) when she/he did not take all the medicines the day before.

Fig. 7. Screenshot of the dashboard used to visualize the defined rules to monitor the elderly's behaviour

In Sect. 1 of this Fig. 8, the user indicates the name of the rule and the message that will arise when the conditions will be met. In Sect. 2, the user specifies a rule that is used to check if the aged person has slept less than 5 h AND that the number of awakenings for the night has been more than 3 AND that the day before the monitored senior has not taken her/his medicines; or she/he has taken less than a given number of medicines (e.g. 5) that the user can specify using the proper label. Finally, in Sect. 3 the user indicates the temporal correlation that exists between the conditions expressed in Sect. 2.

As soon as a rule is defined, it is implemented as a new Google Cloud function that by accessing the data stored in the database of the Firebase platform allows Charlie to check if the rules will be verified. When the conditions of the rule will be met, a notification (expressed in Sect. 1 of Fig. 8) will be raised both in the web app to warn caregivers and in the bot to alarm the user.

4.3   Intelligent Suggestions of Rules

By using specific rules, caregivers can detect relevant and significant events that may affect their dears' life and that depend on data gathered by Charlie.

Unfortunately, the problem with this system is that the caregiver is often "lost in the data sea" and does not know which parameters she/he has to check for monitoring the senior's behaviour. To help caregivers in the monitoring task, we are extending our web app with machine learning techniques that enable predictions based on counterfactual explanations [47, 48], to compute suggestions about the better rules to adopt.

Essentially, suggestions are provided as rules, which describe a change in the behaviours. The idea is to endow the web app with functionality to compute predictions and the consequent rules, by extracting knowledge from the data describing the elderly's behaviours. In particular, we are investigating a machine learning approach that produces a set of readable and understandable IF-THEN rules, which are easily interpretable and follow a similar pattern to human thinking.

To a first approximation, an initial step is to identify recurrent behaviours that can be used to classify the elderly's lifestyle through a set of labels, such as "depression", "sense of loneliness", "mood disorders", "anxiety", "normal" according to Geriatric Depression Scale [49–51]. To do it, we need to choose the so-called "right data" [52] by selecting the most informative (discriminating) features while discarding redundant information. To identify the most informative features, we are analysing the data collected during the tests performed with aged relatives of our university students (as described in Sect. 3.1). During the monitoring weeks involving 12 elderly, the collected data daily by Charlie

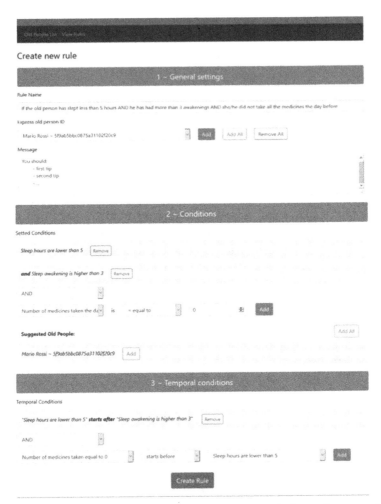

Fig. 8. Workflow used to specify a new rule. In Sect. 1, the user indicates the name of the rule and the message that will arise when the conditions will be met. In Sect. 2, by using AND OR operators, the user specifies the condition to monitor. Finally, in Sect. 3 the user indicates the temporal correlation that exists between the conditions expressed in Sect. 2. In the depicted case, the user adds a new temporal condition specifying to check if the monitored senior has slept less than 5 h **after** that she/he has had more than 3 awakenings AND that **the day before** she/he has taken less than 5 medicines.

were: The number of completed quizzes, statistics on wrong and correct answers, the number of news and stories requested or told by the user, the number of times the user forgot the take medicines or to call her/his relatives (in case she/he scheduled a reminder about it). With the caregivers' help, we are working for recruiting other seniors whose behaviours can fit the labels used to define the lifestyles. In this way, we can train our recommendation service and evaluate better prediction models.

The statistical analyses that we are carrying out by using ANOVA [53] aim at computing the p-values to check if the feature distribution in different classes have the same mean, against the alternative hypothesis that they have different means. The final goal is to keep only features for which the feature distribution in different classes have different means, that is, we want to keep the features for which the p-value allows us to discard the null hypothesis at 5% significance level, that is $p < 0.05$ (95% confidence). Of course, to obtain more meaningful results we need to complete the current data collection to monitor the elderly's behaviour. Moreover, to increase the number of features from which to select more discriminative ones, our idea is also to endow the elderly with an electronic bracelet for gathering biometric data such as the heartbeat, the quality of sleep, burned calories and physical activities. Unfortunately, gathering these data is experiencing considerable delays for reasons due to the CODIV pandemic. Anyway, we designed an analysis protocol as described below.

4.4 Protocol for Counterfactual Explanations

Once the ANOVA test will be completed, a second step will aim at calculating the inter-features relationships to check if discriminative features are highly correlated that is if the redundant information is included in the selected feature set. To remove such redundant information, we will compute the pairwise Pearson linear correlation coefficient between each pair of feature vectors. For each couple of features, of which we obtain an absolute Pearson correlation coefficient ≥ 0.5, we will remove the less discriminative feature that is the feature for which the corresponding p-value is higher.

At this point, the next step of our protocol of analysis will deal with the multiclass classification problem by using an internal Leave-One-Out cross-validation (LOOCV) procedure based on ECOC models, which have been shown to improve the performance of multiclass classifiers. Rather than limiting the choice of algorithms or adapting the algorithms for multi-class problems, ECOC approach is to reframe the multi-class classification problem as multiple binary classification problems. Two common methods that can be used to achieve this include a KNN, and an SVM classifier. Our idea is to employ a greedy method that will sort the selected features according to their *p-values* (from the smallest to the highest), and, for each classifier, chooses the first features which allow minimizing the classification error computed through LOOCV.

Once the best predictive model will be detected, the data that Charlie is collecting will be used to compute prescriptive suggestions for improving the elderly's behaviour, based on the computation of the so-called counterfactual explanations. One of the main goals of our study is the ability to explain the computed predictions. To open the so-called "black-boxes", a great deal of research work have been recently devoted to the development of automatic techniques for explaining the predictions computed by machine learning methods, and the growing literature about this subject has indeed generated a novel field of research called "interpretable machine learning" [47, 48]. Among the different techniques for explaining the classifiers' decision, counterfactual explanations are sometimes preferred because they explain the output of the classifier for the specific input point.

Counterfactual Explanations are defined as statements taking the form [48]: "*Score p was returned because variables V had values (v1, v2, ...) associated with them. If V instead had values (v1', v2', ...), and all other variables had remained constant, score p' would have been returned*". In the field of pattern classification, counterfactual explanations explain how to change the values of the input data to obtain the desired classification result. Therefore, by computing counterfactual explanations we may provide prescriptive suggestions. In our context of use, thinking in counterfactuals terms requires imagining how the elderly's acceptable behaviour (labelled as "normal") contradicts the observed undesired situations such as "depression", "sense of loneliness", "mood disorders", "anxiety". To do it we have to compute the smallest changes to the feature values of the current prevision to transform them into values that characterize the "normal" status. For example for a person labelled as "anxious", we need to understand how to mitigate this situation. A possible suggestion could be: If you want to avoid anxiety attacks you will have to increase your physical activity (the number of steps taken during the day has to be more than 1000 units and the calories burned more than 200 kilocalories), to have daily social interaction with your relatives (ask Charlie to schedule a daily reminder to call your children), and to solve more than 3 quizzes that Charlie will be glad to offer you.

Based on these counterfactual explanations, we are working to endow our web application with functionality to suggest to caregivers new rules able to check anomalous situations and to provide suggestions on how to remedy them.

5   Conclusions

In this paper, we have presented Charlie as an empathetic, sensitive, sociable and friendly child robot that provides the elderly with interactive activities based on s gamification, active notifications, and promotion of self-compassion. According to the analysis of discussions carried out with the elderly involved in the preliminary test, we can conclude that Charlie is considered by users polite, smart, charming, helpful and reliable. This solution can offer a pool of interactive strategies that can relieve the state of loneliness the aged people live. The final goal is to support pre-emptive care for improving the elderly's quality of life, avoiding necessarily "fixing" something but offering assistance and companionship without assuming diagnosed disorders. The chatbot has been also presented during a hackathon organized by Facebook and Funka aimed at encouraging students from Europe to create innovative digital solutions to increase social inclusion. Charlie, after being submitted to a jury made up of representatives of organizations for disabled people, policymakers and industries, was among the top three finalists.[1]

Then the paper describes our studies on how to allow caregivers, such as medical assistants or relatives, to implement in Charlie the possibility to monitor their dear seniors' behaviours. To this aim, we designed a web application that enables caregivers to create rules for detect relevant and significant events that depend on data such as the number of required news, followed tips, completed games, suggestions to Charlie on how to solve his problems, but also biometrical data that can be achieved by using

---

[1] http://www.euroblind.org/events/facebook-funka-accessibility-hackathon   https://www.funka.com/en/about-funka2/news/en/facebook-funka-accessibility-hackathon-winner/.

smart wristbands such as the number of steps made during the day, burned calories or the number of hours of sleep.

In the design of the web app, we dealt with the problem that rarely users know which parameters to follow for better assisting their dear seniors. To help them in the monitoring task, we need to use machine-learning techniques that enable predictions and to do it, we are studying a method, based on counterfactual explanations, to compute suggestions for improving the elderly's quality of life. Suggestions that are then transformed into rules integrated into the chatbot intents for extracting knowledge from the collected measurements describing the elderly's behaviour. While creating these rules, users must specify what happens when a particular set of conditions is met/not met by defining a list of actions to be performed, such as by specifying that a warning needs to be sent via direct messages. In this way, we hope to help caregivers and relatives in the definition of what Charlie needs to monitor for taking under control their dear's behaviours and attitudes.

Despite the limitations due to the pandemic situation, at the moment we are planning several user tests to, on the one hand, gather data for training our machine learning model and on the other hand to test the of use Charlie and our web application in real contexts of use. In this way, we will have the possibility to investigate the outcomes of the application of our method based on counterfactual explanations.

References

1. https://agcult.it/a/22645/2020-07-23/italiani-e-solitudine-symbola-nuove-tecnologie-ma-anche-lettura-e-impegno-civico-gli-antidoti-piu-diffusi. Accessed Apr 2021
2. https://www.enuan.com/. Accessed Apr 2021
3. Chakrabarti, C., Luger, G.F.: A semantic architecture for artificial conversations. In: The 6th International Conference on Soft Computing and Intelligent Systems, and the 13th International Symposium on Advanced Intelligence Systems, pp. 21–26. IEEE (2012)
4. Jain, A.M.D., Daniel, D., Fraser, H., Saravanakumar, S., Nair-Hartman, A.: The emergence of value-based health: how healthcare is using technology to create insights, enhance efficiency, and improve patient outcomes. IBM Institute for Business Value (2019). http://ibm.co/value-based-health
5. Rapp, A., Curti, L., Boldi, A.: The human side of human-chatbot interaction: a systematic literature review of ten years of research on text-based chatbots. Int. J. Hum. Comput. Stud. **151**, 102630 (2021)
6. Chaves, A.P., Gerosa, M.A.: How should my chatbot interact? A survey on social characteristics in human–chatbot interaction design. Int. J. Hum. Comput. Interact., 1–30 (2020)
7. Muppirishetty, P., Lee, M.: Voice user interfaces for mental healthcare: leveraging technology to help our inner voice. In: 3rd ACM Conference on Computer-Supported Cooperative Work and Social Computing, CSCW (2020)
8. Valério, F.A.M., Guimarães, T.G., Prates, R.O., Candello, H.: Chatbots explain themselves: designers' strategies for conveying chatbot features to users. SBC J. Interact. Syst. **9**(3), 61–79 (2018)
9. Valério, F.A., Guimarães, T.G., Prates, R.O., Candello, H.: Here's what i can do: chatbots' strategies to convey their features to users. In: Proceedings of the Xvi Brazilian Symposium on Human Factors in Computing Systems, pp. 1–10 (2017)

10. Bickmore, T.W., Caruso, L., Clough-Gorr, K.: Acceptance and usability of a relational agent interface by urban older adults. In: CHI 2005 Extended Abstracts on Human Factors in Computing Systems, pp. 1212–1215 (2005)

11. Bickmore, T.W., Picard, R.W.: Establishing and maintaining long-term human-computer relationships. ACM Trans. Comput. Hum. Interact. (TOCHI) **12**(2), 293–327 (2005)

12. Lee, M., Ackermans, S., van As, N., Chang, H., Lucas, E., IJsselsteijn, W.: Caring for Vincent: a chatbot for self-compassion. In: Proceedings of the 2019 CHI Conference on Human Factors in Computing Systems, pp. 1–13 (2019)

13. Smith, J.: GrandChair: conversational collection of grandparents' stories. Doctoral dissertation, Massachusetts Institute of Technology (2000)

14. Bickmore, T.W., Mitchell, S.E., Jack, B.W., Paasche-Orlow, M.K., Pfeifer, L.M., O'Donnell, J.: Response to a relational agent by hospital patients with depressive symptoms. Interact. Comput. **22**(4), 289–298 (2010)

15. Bickmore, T.W., Schulman, D., Sidner, C.L.: A reusable framework for health counseling dialogue systems based on a behavioral medicine ontology. J. Biomed. Inform. **44**(2), 183–197 (2011)

16. King, A., Bickmore, T., Campero, I., Pruitt, L., Yin, L.X.: Employing "virtual advisors" to promote physical activity in underserved communities: results from the COMPASS study. Ann. Behav. Med. **41**, S58 (2011)

17. Gentner, T., Neitzel, T., Schulze, J., Buettner, R.: A Systematic literature review of medical chatbot research from a behavior change perspective. In: 2020 IEEE 44th Annual Computers, Software, and Applications Conference (COMPSAC), pp. 735–740. IEEE (2020)

18. Melia, R., et al.: Mobile health technology interventions for suicide prevention: systematic review. JMIR mHealth uHealth **8**(1), e12516 (2020)

19. Nass, C., Moon, Y.: Machines and mindlessness: Social responses to computers. J. Soc. Issues **56**(1), 81–103 (2000)

20. Reeves, B., Nass, C.: The Media Equation: How People Treat Computers, Television, and New Media Like Real People. Cambridge University Press, Cambridge (1996)

21. De Angeli, A., Johnson, G.I., Coventry, L.: The unfriendly user: exploring social reactions to chatterbots. In: Proceedings of The International Conference on Affective Human Factors Design, London, pp. 467–474 (2001)

22. Brahnam, S., De Angeli, A.: Gender affordances of conversational agents. Interact. Comput. **24**(3), 139–153 (2012)

23. Lee, S., Choi, J.: Enhancing user experience with conversational agent for movie recommendation: effects of self-disclosure and reciprocity. Int. J. Hum. Comput. Stud. **103**, 95–105 (2017)

24. Neff, G., Nagy, P.: Automation, algorithms, and politicsl talking to bots: symbiotic agency and the case of tay. Int. J. Commun. **10**, 17 (2016)

25. Oh, K.J., Lee, D., Ko, B., Choi, H.J.: A chatbot for psychiatric counseling in mental healthcare service based on emotional dialogue analysis and sentence generation. In: 2017 18th IEEE International Conference on Mobile Data Management (MDM), pp. 371–375. IEEE (2017)

26. Lee, D., Oh, K.J., Choi, H.J.: The chatbot feels you-a counseling service using emotional response generation. In: 2017 IEEE International Conference on Big Data and Smart Computing (BigComp), pp. 437–440. IEEE (2017)

27. Dialogflow API. https://cloud.google.com/dialogflow/es/docs/reference/rest/v2-overview. Accessed Apr 2021

28. OpenJS Foundation: About Node.js. https://nodejs.org/en/about/. Accessed Apr 2021

29. https://cloud.google.com/functions. Accessed Apr 2021

30. https://firebase.google.com/. Accessed Apr 2021

31. Lucero, A.: Using affinity diagrams to evaluate interactive prototypes. In: Abascal, J., Barbosa, S., Fetter, M., Gross, T., Palanque, P., Winckler, M. (eds.) INTERACT 2015. LNCS, vol. 9297, pp. 231–248. Springer, Cham (2015). https://doi.org/10.1007/978-3-319-22668-2_19

32. Venkatesh, V., Morris, M.G., Davis, G.B., Davis, F.D.: User acceptance of information technology: toward a unified view. MIS Q. **27**, 425–478 (2003)

33. De Veer, A.J., Peeters, J.M., Brabers, A.E., Schellevis, F.G., Rademakers, J.J.J., Francke, A.L.: Determinants of the intention to use e-Health by community dwelling older people. BMC Health Serv. Res. **15**(1), 1–9 (2015)

34. Liu, C.F., Tsai, Y.C., Jang, F.L.: Patients' acceptance towards a web-based personal health record system: an empirical study in Taiwan. Int. J. Environ. Res. Public Health **10**(10), 5191–5208 (2013)

35. Kohnke, A., Cole, M.L., Bush, R.: Incorporating UTAUT predictors for understanding home care patients' and clinician's acceptance of healthcare telemedicine equipment. J. Technol. Manag. Innov. **9**(2), 29–41 (2014)

36. Cimperman, M., Brenčič, M.M., Trkman, P.: Analyzing older users' home telehealth services acceptance behavior—applying an extended UTAUT model. Int. J. Med. Inform. **90**, 22–31 (2016)

37. Davis, F.D., Bagozzi, R.P., Warshaw, P.R.: Extrinsic and intrinsic motivation to use computers in the workplace 1. J. Appl. Soc. Psychol. **22**(14), 1111–1132 (1992)

38. Koch, M.: End-user development. Wirtschaftsinformatik **48**(6), 455 (2006). https://doi.org/10.1007/s11576-006-0107-x

39. Petre, M., Blackwell, A.F.: Children as unwitting end-user programmers. In: Proceeding of the IEEE Symposium on Visual Languages and Human-Centric Computing (VL/HCC 2007), pp. 239–242 (2007)

40. Fischer, G., Giaccardi, E., Ye, Y., Sutcliffe, A., Mehandjiev, N.: Meta-design: a manifesto for end-user development. Commun. ACM **47**(9), 33–37 (2004)

41. Costabile, M.F., Mussio, P., Parasiliti Provenza, L., Piccinno, A.: End users as unwitting software developers. In: Proceedings of the 4th International Workshop on End-User Software Engineering, pp. 6–10. ACM, New York (2008)

42. Barricelli, B.R., Valtolina, S.: A visual language and interactive system for end-user development of internet of things ecosystems. J. Vis. Lang. Comput. **40**, 1–19 (2017)

43. Valtolina, S., Barricelli, B.R.: An end-user development framework to support quantified self in sport teams. In: Paternò, F., Wulf, V. (eds.) New Perspectives in End-User Development, pp. 413–432. Springer, Cham (2017). https://doi.org/10.1007/978-3-319-60291-2_16. ISBN 9783319602905

44. Ghiani, G., Manca, M., Paternò, F., Santoro, C.: Personalization of context-dependent applications through trigger-action rules. ACM Trans. Comput. Hum. Interact. **24**(2), 33 (2017)

45. Desolda, G., Ardito, C., Matera, M.: Empowering end users to customize their smart environments: model, composition paradigms and domain-specific tools. ACM Trans. Comput. Hum. Interact. **24**(2), 52 (2017)

46. Caivano, D., Fogli, D., Lanzilotti, R., Piccinno, A., Cassano, F.: Supporting end users to control their smart home: design implications from a literature review and an empirical investigation. J. Syst. Softw. **144**(2018), 295–313 (2018)

47. Molnar, C.: Interpretable machine learning. Lulu.com (2020). https://christophm.github.io/interpretable-ml-book/

48. Wachter, S., Mittelstadt, B., Russell, C.: Counterfactual explanations without opening the black box: automated decisions and the GDPR. Harv. JL & Tech. **31**, 841 (2017)

49. http://www.minddisorders.com/Flu-Inv/Geriatric-Depression-Scale.html. Accessed Apr 2021

50. Holmén, K., Ericsson, K., Winblad, B.: Quality of life among the elderly: state of mood and loneliness in two selected groups. Scand. J. Caring Sci. **13**(2), 91–95 (1999)

51. Gerino, E., Rollè, L., Sechi, C., Brustia, P.: Loneliness, resilience, mental health, and quality of life in old age: a structural equation model. Front. Psychol. **8**, 2003 (2017)

52. Fisher, R.A:. XV.—the correlation between relatives on the supposition of Mendelian inheritance. Earth Environ. Sci. Trans. Roy. Soc. Edinb. **52**(2), 399–433 (1919)

53. Kajdanowicz, T., Wozniak, M., Kazienko, P.: Multiple classifier method for structured output prediction based on error correcting output codes. In: Nguyen, N.T., Kim, C.-G., Janiak, A. (eds.) ACIIDS 2011. LNCS (LNAI), vol. 6592, pp. 333–342. Springer, Heidelberg (2011). https://doi.org/10.1007/978-3-642-20042-7_34

A Jigsaw-Based End-User Tool for the Development of Ontology-Based Knowledge Bases

Audrey Sanctorum[1][✉][iD], Jonathan Riggio[1][iD], Sara Sepehri[2][iD], Emma Arnesdotter[2][iD], Tamara Vanhaecke[2][iD], and Olga De Troyer[1][iD]

[1] WISE Lab, Vrije Universiteit Brussel, Brussels, Belgium
{Audrey.Sanctorum,jonathan.riggio,Olga.DeTroyer}@vub.be
[2] Research Group of In Vitro Toxicology and Dermato-Cosmetology (IVTD), Vrije Universiteit Brussel, Brussels, Belgium
{sara.sepehri,emma.arnesdotter,tamara.vanhaecke}@vub.be

Abstract. Knowledge bases are used to store and centralize information on certain topics in a domain. Using a well-structured and machine-readable format is a prerequisite for any AI-based processing or reasoning. The use of semantic technologies (e.g., RDF, OWL) has the advantage that it allows to define the semantics of the information and supports advanced querying. However, using such technologies is a challenging task for subject matter experts from a domain such as life science who are, in general, not trained for this. This means that they need to rely on semantic technology experts to create their knowledge bases. However, these experts are usually IT-experts and they are, in turn, not trained in the subject matter, while knowledge of the domain is essential for the construction of a high-quality knowledge base. In this paper, we present an end-user development (EUD) tool that supports subject matter experts in the construction of ontology–based knowledge bases. The tool is using the jigsaw metaphor for hiding the technicalities of the semantic technology, as well as to guide the users in the process of creating a knowledge base. The approach and the tool is demonstrated for building a knowledge base in the toxicology domain. The tool has been evaluated by means of a preliminary user study with nine subject matter experts from this domain. All participants state that with a little practice they could become productive with our tool and actually use it to represent and manage their knowledge. The results of the evaluation resulted in valuable suggestions for improving the tool and highlighted the importance of well adapting the terminology to the target audience.

Keywords: Knowledge representation · Domain ontology creation · Knowledge base · End-user tool · Jigsaw metaphor

Financially supported by Vrije Universiteit Brussel and Cosmetics Europe and the European Chemical Industry Council (CEFIC).

© Springer Nature Switzerland AG 2021
D. Fogli et al. (Eds.): IS-EUD 2021, LNCS 12724, pp. 169–184, 2021.
https://doi.org/10.1007/978-3-030-79840-6_11

1   Introduction

In many domains of life-science, there is a huge amount of data and information (publicly) available and research in these domains is not possible without considering previously collected knowledge. However, the information is often in the form of documents and reports with various formats and different levels of details, which requires manual processing of the data to unlock the information. This makes it hard and time-consuming to aggregate knowledge from these documents and reuse it in research. Therefore, and in order to allow intelligent data processing, there is an increased interest in the field of knowledge representation & reasoning.

In this paper, we will use the term *knowledge base* to refer to the storage of information on certain topics in a domain using a well-structured and machine-readable format and that enables AI-based processing or reasoning. Knowledge base creation can either be done manually or automatically. Although work exist in the context of automated knowledge base construction [1,10,12,28], this remains a true challenge, and the works are usually very domain specific or cover only a certain aspect of the knowledge base creation, e.g., the automatic identification of concepts with their hierarchy or populating a knowledge base from unstructured data. In this article we focus on the manual creation of the knowledge base which is still a widespread practice.

In some cases, subject matter experts use spreadsheets to collect and maintain the data (e.g., [20,37]). However, spreadsheets do not scale well, are not able to deal with variations in the data, and they do not support advanced querying and analysis [3]. The use of semantic technologies (e.g., RDF [13], OWL [2]) is more appropriate for the purpose of creating knowledge bases, as it allows to structure the information in richer and more flexible ways, supports reasoning and more advanced querying mechanisms. However, using such technologies to create a knowledge base is a challenging task for subject matter experts who are, in general, not trained for this. Note that when using semantic technologies for creating a knowledge base, usually the concept of an ontology is used, which is a formal representation of knowledge pertaining to a particular domain [29]. Current tools for creating ontologies (e.g. Protégé [30], OntoEdit [36]; see [35] for an overview) are rather technical. This means that subject matter experts need to rely on semantic technology experts, also called ontology engineers, to create the ontology/knowledge base. However, these are usually IT-experts and they are, in turn, not trained in the subject matter, while the manual construction of ontologies requires extensive knowledge of the domain. This lack of knowledge about each other's domain results in a vast knowledge gap between the two groups of experts. In addition, each group of experts uses its own vocabulary and has its own concerns. Bridging this gap is a difficult and laborious process.

In the literature, different authors have studied and analyzed the gaps and barriers in interdisciplinary research [9,27,34] and proposed various approaches for bridging the gap. For instance, in [27] the use of human translators or intermediaries who are trained in both disciplines, is suggested to solve the communication problem between collaborators from different disciplines. However, in the case of the development of an ontology-based knowledge base, this only moves the problem of mastering two completely different disciplines to the intermediaries. Kertcher [27] also mentions the use of technology to bridge collaboration barriers. This is the approach we want to follow. If we could provide the subject matter experts with tools that are easier to use than current semantic technology tools and that hide the technicalities, such tools could facilitate the creation of knowledge bases without being dependent on ontology engineers.

In this paper, we present an end-user development (EUD) tool for the creation of domain-specific ontology-based knowledge bases. The developed tool is an improvement and extension of an earlier version, discussed in [16]. While the previous version only allowed to compose and fill the knowledge base by means of predefined domain concepts, the new version also provides the possibility to define these concepts, that is, it also allows the creation of a domain ontology defining the required domain concepts. The solution we provide for the creation of an ontology-based knowledge base exploits the jigsaw metaphor [19] by making use of Blockly blocks[1]. These jigsaw-based blocks are used for two purposes. Firstly, blocks are used to define domain concepts. Secondly, the (automatically) generated blocks for these domain concepts are assembled to create new blocks that define the structure of the knowledge base, and the knowledge base is populated by filling in the fields in those blocks.

The paper is organized as follows: In Sect. 2, we explain the approach and principles used for an ontology-based knowledge base. Section 3 first presents the overall approach, followed by an explanation of the tool developed, i.e. DIY-KR-KIT (Do It Yourself Knowledge Representation Kit), as well as its implementation. Section 4 presents the results of a first user study. Related work is discussed in Sect. 5. The paper ends with conclusions and future work (Sect. 6).

2   Ontology-Based Knowledge Bases

A knowledge base can be compared to a database that organizes data according to a certain data schema, also called data model. In this way, the database is an instantiation of the data model. In the same way, a knowledge base can be considered as an instantiation of an ontology [11]. While a data model allows to define the structure of data in a domain, an ontology is much more powerful. Typically, an ontology describes concepts in a domain and their properties, as well as relationships between the concepts and domain rules that apply to them. Note that in some applications, the instances of the concepts and relationships (i.e., the real data) are also considered as part of the ontology, removing the strict separation between model and data. We follow the approach proposed by Chasseray et al. in [11], where the distinction between model and data is kept: a knowledge base is composed of a *domain ontology* and an *instantiated ontology*. The domain ontology is used to specify the organizational structure of the knowledge base, and as the name indicates, the instantiated ontology is an instantiation of the domain ontology containing the actual instances (data).

---

[1] https://developers.google.com/blockly.

Chasseray et al. combine ontologies with the OMG's Model-Driven Engineering (MDE) approach that defines four modelling levels: data level, model level, meta-model level, and meta-metamodel level. Following this MDE approach, the authors consider the domain ontology as an instantiation of an *upper ontology*, which defines the concepts and relationships needed to define domain ontologies and corresponds to the meta-model level from the MDE domain. This structure is shown in Fig. 1. Such an upper ontology contains general modeling concepts such as Concept, Relation, and Instance.

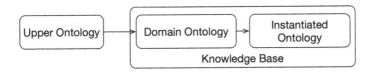

Fig. 1. Knowledge base structure with respect to MDE (adapted from [11])

We illustrate the structure of such an ontology-based knowledge base with a use case from the domain of toxicology. This use case will be used throughout the paper. In toxicology, Safety Evaluation Opinions issued by the Scientific Committee on Consumer Safety (SCCS), provide collections of information on safety testing of cosmetic ingredients. These Safety Evaluation Opinions are text documents[2]. In order to create a knowledge base containing all the information from these documents, and following the structure described above, the first step is to define a domain ontology describing the type of information that experts want to capture from these opinions, e.g., *test species used* and *test reliability*, and how this information should be structured. Next, this ontology needs to be populated by the actual information from the opinions, resulting into the instantiated ontology. The upper ontology should allow to define the domain ontology for the safety evaluation opinions, i.e., the concepts and relationships needed for capturing the information contained in the opinions.

3 Creating Ontology-Based Knowledge Bases with DIY-KR-KIT

In order to create an EUD tool that could help subject matter experts in building an ontology-based knowledge base, we decided to use the jigsaw metaphor [19], a metaphor that became popular with the programming language Scratch [32]. This metaphor is already used successfully in a number of domains (see Sect. 5). We start by explaining how the jigsaw metaphor is used to create a domain-specific ontology-based knowledge base (Sect. 3.1), next we discuss the tool and its implementation (Sect. 3.2).

---

[2] Example Safety Evaluation Opinion: https://ec.europa.eu/health/scientific_committees/consumer_safety/docs/sccs_o_199.pdf.

3.1   Using the Jigsaw Metaphor for Knowledge Base Construction

We first illustrate the principle of using the jigsaw metaphor for creating a knowledge base for the toxicological use case provided in the previous section. The concepts that typically appear in the Safety Evaluation Opinions are represented as jigsaw blocks (puzzle pieces), which contain placeholders for property values and connection points for composing concepts, see Fig. 2a for an example block. This example block represents the domain concept *Acute Toxicity*. Its main domain-specific property is *grading of lesion*. The two other properties, *additional information*, and *own comments* will be used to capture additional information provided in an opinion and comments that the subject matter experts wants to add. Its composing concepts are *Test endpoints acute toxicity*, *Test method of acute toxicity* and *Reliability of test acute toxicity*.

When a subject matter expert wants to store the information of an opinion into the knowledge base, (s)he composes a so-called *dossier* (representing the opinion) by connecting the relevant puzzle blocks and filling in the value fields in the blocks (see Fig. 2b for a (partial) example dossier). The jigsaw blocks can only be composed in a restricted way and validation for data fields is provided. The names of the blocks and fields correspond with the terminology used in the Safety Evaluation Opinions and the subject matter experts can fill the knowledge base while scanning the opinions. Based on the puzzle composition and its values, RDF is generated forming (a part of) the instantiated ontology.

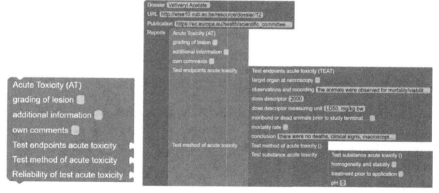

(a) Example jigsaw block for the domain concept Acute Toxicity

(b) Example jigsaw block for the dossier Vetiveryl Acetate

Fig. 2. Example blocks

However, not all Safety Evaluation Opinions contain the same type of data. This means that it would be necessary to extend or change the domain ontology whenever new opinions are considered which contain information about domain concepts not yet covered in the domain ontology, or when the structure of an existing domain concept (i.e., its properties and sub concepts) does not fit anymore with the one used in the new opinion. In addition, these adaptations to the domain ontology should be translated to the jigsaw blocks and their composition rules. In this way, the subject matter experts would still be dependent on the IT-experts each time changes or new jigsaw blocks are needed. Extending or adapting the domain ontology and adapting the jigsaw block tool accordingly is a time-consuming procedure.

A first solution to solve this issue is trying to anticipate all needed domain concepts and create all possible puzzle blocks beforehand. However, as the domain of toxicology is very broad, creating such a domain ontology would not only be a very large and time-consuming undertaking (and without any guarantee that the ontology is complete), it would also result in a very extensive domain ontology, which would probably not be manageable and usable by the subject matter experts. Although, the existence of such a domain ontology (even for a part of the domain) would be very useful and efforts to realize this are already undertaken (e.g., the Adverse Outcome Pathway Ontology[3], [7,22,24]), this should be a collaborative effort of different stakeholders from the domain.

We therefore opted for a different solution. We want to allow the subject matter experts to specify, adapt and/or extend their domain ontology by themselves, using the same principle as how we allow them to create, adapt and extend the instantiated ontology, i.e., using the jigsaw metaphor. By doing so, IT-experts are not required to create the domain ontology, adapt or extend it. The tool remains the same, however depending on the objective, i.e., creating the instantiated ontology, or creating the domain ontology, different jigsaw blocks are used. For creating the instantiated ontology, the jigsaw blocks are based on domain concepts (defined in the domain ontology), while for creating the domain ontology, the jigsaw blocks are based on general modeling concepts (defined in the upper ontology). This process is illustrated in Fig. 3. First, the subject matter experts will use general jigsaw blocks to create the domain ontology (Step 1 in Fig. 3), i.e., to define the concepts and their relationships of the specific domain. For each defined domain concept, a jigsaw block will be generated. These jigsaw blocks can then, in turn, be used by the subject matter experts to compose and fill the knowledge base (Step 2 in Fig. 3).

3.2 DIY-KR-KIT Tool

As mentioned before, the tool is an improvement and extension of an earlier version [16]. The previous version only allowed to compose and fill the knowledge base by means of predefined domain concepts. This new version also provides the possibility to define domain concepts, i.e., to create the domain ontology. While the previous version was implemented using the Apache Tapestry framework, the new version is using Spring Boot. Our tool is a web-based application, built on top of Apache Jena, which provides the triplestore and SPARQL endpoint. The jigsaw metaphor is implemented via the Google Blockly JavaScript library.

---

[3] https://github.com/DataSciBurgoon/aop-ontology.

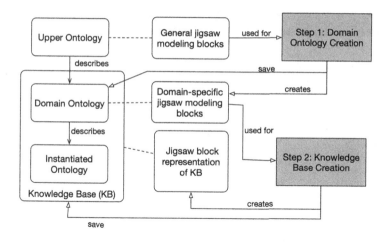

Fig. 3. Knowledge base construction process

The current DIY-KR-KIT tool is composed of two main parts, the *domain concept management* part, supporting step 1 of the knowledge base construction process, and the *dossier management* part, supporting step 2 of the knowledge base construction process. On the tool's home page the user can either choose to create (or modify) a dossier or add (or modify) a domain concept. Adding such an item is done by giving a name and optionally a link (url) referring to extra information about the item. For example, in case of a dossier, the url is a link to the corresponding Safety Evaluation Opinion. Once the item is created, its name will appear in the dossiers or domain concepts menu, respectively. Note that the current tool allows to perform step 1 and step 2 at the same time, allowing for more flexibility: domain concepts can be added or modified when needed. Further, the current tool has been customised to already provide the basis structure needed for defining a knowledge base for the Safety Evaluation Opinions. This means that the domain concepts *Dossier* and *Report* are predefined and shown as such in the user interface. This is done to give more guidance to the subject matter experts; in this way the knowledge base will always consist of dossiers, which are composed of reports. However, the subject matter expert still needs to define the different blocks needed to compose a report by defining the necessary domain concepts (if not yet available in the existing list of domain concepts).

The Manage Domain Concept page allows users to specify or adapt a domain-specific concept. Figure 4 shows the page for the domain concept *Test conditions acute toxicity*. On the left hand-side of the page, the top-level blue block "Domain Concept" allows to specify the structure of the domain concept. Pre-defined properties are: the name of the concept, an abbreviation, and a description, which the user can fill in. More properties can be added to a domain concept block by dragging and dropping the empty *Property* block from the *Custom Properties* tab in the menu at the left. Properties have a name, a value type and an optional default value. In the example, the first property of the domain

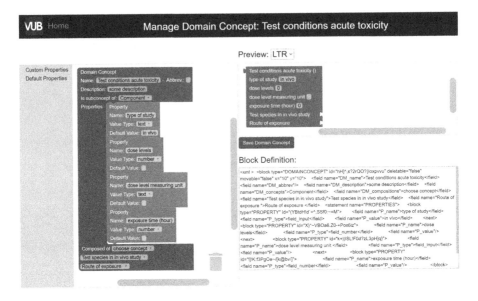

Fig. 4. Screenshot of the domain concept modification page

concept is given the name "type of study" with value type "text" and default value "in vivo". Note that in the left sidebar menu we also have the *Default Properties* tab, which provides recurring property blocks, such as the "year" property block. By using these default properties blocks, users can save time. A domain concept can be composed of other domain concepts. In Fig. 4, we see that the *Test conditions acute toxicity* concept is further composed of the *Test species in in vivo study* and the *Route of exposure* concept. This is shown in the blue Domain Concept block under the "Composed of" field. The "Composed of" dropdown allows to add other composing concepts.

On the right in Fig. 4, a preview of the generated jigsaw block for the domain concept defined at the left is given. In this case the block contains two puzzle connectors on the right side, one for each composing concept given. Any changes made on the left side is reflected in real time in the preview on the right.

Blockly defines blocks in XML format as shown in the bottom right of the figure (currently only shown for debugging purposes). However, when a domain concept is saved (using the "Save Domain Concept" button), this XML representation is transformed into RDF using an XSLT file so that it can be integrated into the domain ontology.

4   User Study

The tool has been evaluated with a preliminary user study. The purpose of this first user study was to investigate the usability of the tool for the target audience (subject matter experts), validate the use of the jigsaw metaphor, as well as the terminology and principles used. This user study did not evaluate whether the subject matters experts would be able to identify domain concepts without the help from ontology engineers. This will be evaluated in a next user study.

The study was done in the context of the example use case, i.e. the creation of a knowledge base for Safety Evaluation Opinions. The participants were 9 (7 female) subject matter experts, researchers and lab technicians of the IVTD (*In Vitro* Toxicology and Dermato-Cosmetology) team of our university. They were familiar with the terminology used in the Safety Evaluation Opinions, but they had no expertise in knowledge modeling or ontologies.

Each participant received a time slot to perform tasks related to the creation of the domain ontology, creating a dossier for an opinion, and entering data from this opinion. In the instruction document, it was explicitly mentioned that the goal of the user study was to evaluate the ease with which the tasks could be done with the provided tool by people without IT background. They were also informed that they would be asked to fill in an online questionnaire about the tool. The evaluation was done on an individual basis and at any point during the study they could contact the first author (via email or via a video call)[4] for more information or clarifications. The participants were asked to record their session and were encouraged to speak aloud while interacting with the tool.

The participant could start by watching a YouTube video that explained the tool using similar tasks but based on a different opinion than the opinion used for the actual tasks. The video could also be consulted during the tasks.

The participants had to perform two tasks. In the first task they had to create three new domain concept blocks for an existing domain ontology. Because it was not the purpose to evaluate their capability to identify domain concepts from an opinion, we already identified the required domain concepts and properties, and provided them in the form of a text hierarchy: the domain concepts and properties were given as a bullet list; indented bullet lists were used for sub-concepts. The value type for each property was given. In the second task, they had to use the available blocks (some created by performing the first task, some were already existing blocks) to create a dossier. Its structure was given in the form of a text hierarchy following the same conventions as in the first task. Participants were also asked to fill in values for properties, which were given and highlighted in yellow in the text hierarchy.

After finishing the tasks, the participants filled in the Post-Study System Usability Questionnaire (PSSUQ)[5], which consists of 16 questions with a 7 point likert scale (1 (strongly agree) to 7 (strongly disagree)) and an NA option. Participants could also leave comments. We also asked for their age and gender.

Results. The means per question (Q1 to Q16) and per category are summarised in Fig. 5. While the "Overall" score gives the average score of all 16 questions, PSSUQ also groups the questions into three categories, namely system

---

[4] Due to the COVID-19 restrictions it was not possible to be physically present while the participant was performing the tasks.

[5] https://uiuxtrend.com/pssuq-post-study-system-usability-questionnaire.

usefulness (SYSUSE), information quality (INFOQUAL), and interface quality (INTERQUAL). Note that, the lower the score the better the result.

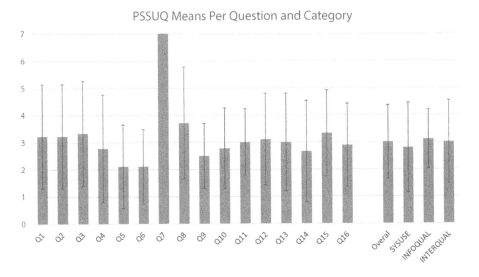

Fig. 5. Results of the post-study system usability questionnaire

All questions, except Q7, have a score better than the neutral score (4). Q7, related to whether the tool gave any error messages to fix problems, has been answered by only two participants who both rated it as "strongly disagree". These two participants encountered a bug which had to be fixed in order for them to continue with the user study, possibly explaining their low rating for this question. The questions with the best score are Q5 and Q6 related to how easy it was to learn the tool and quickly become productive using it. The score of Q8, scored by 7 of the 9 participants, is quite close to the neutral score (3.71). This question is related to Q7 and asked participants whether they could easily recover from a mistake using the system. This score was expected because our tool is at the prototyping stage and we did not yet focus on error handling and correction. Q3 and Q15 have the next highest score (3.33). The first one asked participants whether they were able to complete the tasks and scenarios quickly using the system. All participants spent approximately an hour on performing the tasks and watching the demo video. Compared to our own time when testing the scenario, i.e., 30 min, we believe that the participants who were using our tool for the first time still had a good time performance. However, the score could be an indication that some optimization in entering information could be necessary. Q15 asked whether the tool has all expected functionality. One participant mentioned that (s)he would like to be able to change the order of properties and sub-concepts which is not yet possible, as all properties are listed above all sub-concepts. This suggestion will be considered in the next version.

Note that certain questions, Q1 to Q4 and Q8, have a quite high standard deviation of ±2. The first questions are about whether the participant felt comfortable using the system. For this, the opinions were quite mixed: 3 participants responded rather negatively, while one person had a fairly neutral score and the remaining 5 participants were positive. Excluding Q7, the questions with the lowest standard deviation (1.2) are Q9 and Q11 asking participants whether the received information was clear and effective in helping them completing the tasks. This means that the participants agree on the fact that the explanation and demo video they received were useful to perform the tasks.

When comparing our results to the the norm defined by Sauro and Lewis [33] based on 21 studies and 210 participants, we see (Table 1) that the tool scored well on the system usefulness. The information quality is also well rated, but the interface quality should be improved: two participants had a really difficult time using the system and rated the interface as unpleasant to use.

Table 1. Preliminary study results compared to Sauro and Lewis' norm [33]

	Sauro and Lewis [33]	Preliminary study
Overall	2.82	3.01
SYSUSE	2.80	2.80
INFOQUAL	3.02	3.11
INTERQUAL	2.49	3.00

We also analysed the participants' interactions with our prototype:

- We noticed some confusion when moving blocks. When blocks are stacked on top of each other, Blockly considers this as a group of blocks that moves together. This means that whenever a user moves a block, all blocks underneath this block moves as well. While this was explained in our demo video, participants did not understand how to change the order of a block in the stack of blocks they created, causing some frustration.
- Certain participants had difficulties with converting the provided text hierarchy into a knowledge structure. They, for example, did not know when to create a property inside a concept (block) and when to create a new concept (block). This led to concepts with a single property, which did not make sense for the given case. A possible explanation could be that the text hierarchy did not provide enough information to decide when to model something as a property and when to model it as a domain concept. Given that this text hierarchy has been introduced uniquely for this study (to summarize information from an opinion), this problem might be gone when users use the opinion directly. However, another possible explanation could be that the difference between 'domain concept' and 'property' was not completely clear to these participants, which could be solved by providing a dedicated tutorial with criteria for deciding between modeling concepts and examples.

- A tutorial could also deal with the remarks received about the terminology used (i.e. reports, components, properties, ...), which some participants found a bit confusing at first. Although, we carefully avoid to use software specific terms, like sub-concepts and associations, we observed that using the right terminology is extremely important as it impacts the ease of learning. One participant mentioned: "I do however think that second use and thereafter would be much easier, since the system is not too complex to use once you get used to the terminology of things." Also the use of tool-tips giving additional information when hovering a modeling concept, could help. However, in addition, the terminology will be carefully revised in collaboration with the participants. It is possible that some terms used for structuring the knowledge, such a component, have a different meaning in their domain.
- Further, we observed the need for additional small adjustments to the user interface, such as adding an undo button, making the horizontal scroll-bars more visible and providing more space for composing the blocks.

Given that this was a first evaluation mainly intended to evaluate the principles used and to collect feedback to improve the tool, we are satisfied with the results. All participants state that with a little practice they could become productive with our tool and actually use it to represent and manage their knowledge. The use of the jigsaw metaphor was not criticized or questioned at all. None of the participants had any issue in understanding the metaphor and use it for representing knowledge, indicating that this was a good choice. However, we see room for improvement: improving the ease of use (e.g., the undo button); adding some extra functionality (e.g., changing the order of properties) and optimizing the input process; and improvements to further ease the learning, for example adding tool-tips, an online tutorial, and an improved terminology.

5   Related Work

In [8], it is proposed to derive ontologies from conceptual maps (Cmaps). Conceptual maps allow to express concepts and their relationships in the form of concept-relation-concept. Concepts are represented as boxes or circles and the relationships as lines, all labeled. The paper presents a set of heuristic rules to map a conceptual map into an OWL ontology. A distinction is made between classification relations, composition relations, bidirectional relations and other relations. A first implementation of the translation system was made using Prolog, but no evaluation with end users was reported. It remains an open question whether conceptual maps are easier to use for subject matter experts than for instance a graphical representation of RDF.

Some papers (e.g., [4]) propose to transform UML class diagam into OWL. However, we are not convinced that UML class diagrams are suitable for people without computer science background, as the ease to learn and understand them has already been questioned for computer analysts [17].

Another direction is the use of a natural language interface. For instance, GINO (Guided Input Natural language Ontology editor) [5] is using a natural language approach. However, to avoid the limitations of full natural language interfaces, the authors are using a guided and controlled language akin to English. To add a new construct to the ontology, the user should start by typing "there is" or "there exists" after which a popup shows possible constructs, such as "class". After having selected the appropriate construct, the user is prompted to give a label and ends the sentence with a full stop. Next the sentence, e.g., "there is a class Lake.", is translated into OWL triples and loaded into the ontology. Properties are also defined in this way where the datatype or object property, domain and range are specified by means of pop ups. GINO has been evaluated for usability by six users without experience in ontology building and with no computer science background. The participants performed a small task consisting of creating one class, one subclass, one datatype property, one object property, adding one instance with values for two properties, and changing the value of a property. An average SUS score of 70,83 was obtained. However, it must be noted that the task was very small. To define a large ontology in this way may be very time consuming as the interface is quite verbose. Other works that follow a similar approach are CLOnE (Controlled Language for Ontology Editing) [18] which allows multiple classes to be expressed in a single sentence and Rabbit [21] which language is also somewhat richer than GINO's.

The jigsaw metaphor has been used in the Semantic Web community for the creation of Linked Data mappings [26] and the formulation of SPARQL queries [6]. Junior et al. [25] report on an experiment that indicates that users achieved higher performance and had a lower perceived mental workload when creating Linked Data mappings using the jigsaw metaphor.

Recently, Öztürk and Özacar [31] propose a block-based approach, based on Blockly, for instantiating a recipe ontology. Their approach is similar to the second step in ours as they use the blocks to populate the ontology. The blocks are predefined, which has the disadvantage that the blocks need to be adapted when the ontology evolves, and for each new ontology, blocks need to be programmed. We overcome this problem by rendering the generation of blocks from the meta level in which the end user defines the necessary blocks. The system proposed in [31] was evaluated for usability with 14 participants (students), however more than half of them had a background in ontology engineering.

Next to the use of the jigsaw metaphor for the programming language Scratch, intended for children between the ages of 8 and 16, the metaphor has also been used to support end-user development in other domains, e.g., for the development of IoT [23]; for the development of mobile applications [15]; and for debugging IF-THEN rules in an IoT context [14].

6   Conclusion and Future Work

In order to support subject matter experts in the creation of ontology-based knowledge bases, we proposed an EUD tool based on the jigsaw metaphor, a metaphor that became popular with the programming language Scratch. The purpose of applying this metaphor is to hide the technicalities and terminology of the semantic technologies used for creating ontology-based knowledge bases.

The tool allows subject matter experts to create their own domain ontology, meaning that they can define the concepts and relationships used in their domain and needed to formally represent the available knowledge. In this way, the tool reduces the need to completely rely on an ontology engineer for creating the domain ontology. Next, the tool also allows the subject matter experts to actually set up the knowledge base and fill it with data. The approach, and the tool, is demonstrated and evaluated for building a knowledge base in the toxicology domain. The evaluation was a first preliminary evaluation done with nine subject matter experts from this domain, with the goal to use their feedback to improve the tool. All participants stated that with a little practice they could become productive with our tool and actually use it to represent and manage their knowledge. An important conclusion based on the received feedback is the need to pay due attention to the terminology used in the tool. The use of terminology that is not familiar to the subject matter experts or that has a different meaning in the subject domain might impact how comfortable users feel using the system.

As future work, the tool will first be improved and re-evaluated for overall usability. Next, a user study will be set up to investigate whether subject matter experts are able, after some training, to identify domain concepts, needed for structuring the knowledge base, without the help of an ontology engineer. Other future work includes the investigation for appropriate EUD methods and tools for knowledge base evolution, i.e., managing and propagating changes in the domain ontology to the knowledge base, for visualization of knowledge, for formulating advanced queries, and to provide reasoning capabilities.

References

1. Alobaidi, M., Malik, K.M., Hussain, M.: Automated ontology generation framework powered by linked biomedical ontologies for disease-drug domain. Comput. Methods Programs Biomed. **165**, 117–128 (2018). https://doi.org/10.1016/j.cmpb.2018.08.010
2. Antoniou, G., van Harmelen, F.: Web ontology language: OWL. In: Staab, S., Studer, R. (eds.) Handbook on Ontologies. International Handbooks on Information Systems, pp. 67–92. Springer, Heidelberg (2004). https://doi.org/10.1007/978-3-540-24750-0_4
3. Baškarada, S.: How spreadsheet applications affect information quality. J. Comput. Inf. Syst. **51**(3), 77–84 (2011)
4. Belghiat, A., Bourahla, M.: An approach based AToM3 for the generation of OWL ontologies from UML diagrams. Int. J. Comput. Appl. **41**(3), 41–48 (2012)
5. Bernstein, A., Kaufmann, E.: GINO – a guided input natural language ontology editor. In: Cruz, I., et al. (eds.) ISWC 2006. LNCS, vol. 4273, pp. 144–157. Springer, Heidelberg (2006). https://doi.org/10.1007/11926078_11
6. Bottoni, P., Ceriani, M.: SPARQL playground: a block programming tool to experiment with SPARQL. In: Proceedings of ISWC 2015, International Workshop on Visualizations and User Interfaces for Ontologies and Linked Data. Bethlehem, USA, October 2015
7. Boyles, R.R., Thessen, A.E., Waldrop, A., Haendel, M.A.: Ontology-based data integration for advancing toxicological knowledge. Curr. Opin. Toxicol. **16**, 67–74 (2019). https://doi.org/10.1016/j.cotox.2019.05.005

8. Brilhante, V.V.B.B., Macedo, G.T., Macedo, S.F.: Heuristic transformation of well-constructed conceptual maps into owl preliminary domain ontologies. In: Proceedings of IBERAMIA-SBIA-SBRN 2006, Workshop on Ontologies and Their Applications. Ribeirao Preto, Brazil, October 2006

9. Bruhn, J.G.: Beyond discipline: creating a culture for interdisciplinary research. Integr. Physiol. Behav. Sci. **30**(4), 331–341 (1995). https://doi.org/10.1007/BF02691605

10. Cahyani, D.E., Wasito, I.: Automatic ontology construction using text corpora and ontology design patterns (ODPs) in alzheimer's disease. Jurnal Ilmu Komputer dan Informasi **10**(2), 59–66 (2017). https://doi.org/10.21609/jiki.v10i2.374

11. Chasseray, Y., Barthe-Delanoë, A.M., Négny, S., Le Lann, J.M.: A generic meta-model for data extraction and generic ontology population. J. Inf. Sci. (2021). https://doi.org/10.1177/0165551521989641

12. Cimiano, P., Völker, J.: A framework for ontology learning and data-driven change discovery. In: Proceedings of NLDB 2005, International Conference on Applications of Natural Language to Information Systems, Alicante, Spain, June 2005. https://doi.org/10.1007/11428817_21

13. Consortium, W.W.W., et al.: Resource Description Framework (RDF) http://www.w3.org.RDF/. Accessed 4 June 2008

14. Corno, F., De. Russis, L., Monge Roffarello, A.: My IoT puzzle: debugging IF-THEN rules through the jigsaw metaphor. In: Malizia, A., Valtolina, S., Morch, A., Serrano, A., Stratton, A. (eds.) IS-EUD 2019. LNCS, vol. 11553, pp. 18–33. Springer, Cham (2019). https://doi.org/10.1007/978-3-030-24781-2_2

15. Danado, J., Paternò, F.: Puzzle: a mobile application development environment using a jigsaw metaphor. J. Vis. Lang. Comput. **25**(4), 297–315 (2014). https://doi.org/10.1016/j.jvlc.2014.03.005

16. Debruyne, C., Riggio, J., Gustafson, E., O'Sullivan, D., Vinken, M., Vanhaecke, T., De Troyer, O.: Facilitating data curation: a solution developed in the toxicology domain. In: Proceedings of ICSC 2020, International Conference on Semantic Computing, pp. 315–320, January 2020

17. Dobing, B., Parsons, J.: How UML is used. Commun. ACM **49**(5), 109–113 (2006)

18. Funk, A., Tablan, V., Bontcheva, K., Cunningham, H., Davis, B., Handschuh, S.: CLOnE: controlled language for ontology editing. In: Aberer, K., et al. (eds.) ASWC/ISWC -2007. LNCS, vol. 4825, pp. 142–155. Springer, Heidelberg (2007). https://doi.org/10.1007/978-3-540-76298-0_11

19. Gozzi, R.: The Jigsaw puzzle as a metaphor for knowledge. ETC Rev. Gen. Seman. **53**(4), 447–451 (1996)

20. Gustafson, E., Debruyne, C., De Troyer, O., Rogiers, V., Vinken, M., Vanhaecke, T.: Screening of repeated dose toxicity data in safety evaluation reports of cosmetic ingredients issued by the scientific committee on consumer safety between 2009 and 2019. Arch. Toxicol. **94**(11), 3723–3735 (2020)

21. Hart, G., Johnson, M., Dolbear, C.: Rabbit: developing a control natural language for authoring ontologies. In: Bechhofer, S., Hauswirth, M., Hoffmann, J., Koubarakis, M. (eds.) ESWC 2008. LNCS, vol. 5021, pp. 348–360. Springer, Heidelberg (2008). https://doi.org/10.1007/978-3-540-68234-9_27

22. Hessel, E.V., Staal, Y.C., Piersma, A.H.: Design and validation of an ontology-driven animal-free testing strategy for developmental neurotoxicity testing. Toxicol. Appl. Pharmacol. **354**, 136–152 (2018). https://doi.org/10.1016/j.taap.2018.03.013

23. Humble, J., et al.: "Playing with the bits" user-configuration of ubiquitous domestic environments. In: Dey, A.K., Schmidt, A., McCarthy, J.F. (eds.) UbiComp 2003. LNCS, vol. 2864, pp. 256–263. Springer, Heidelberg (2003). https://doi.org/10.1007/978-3-540-39653-6_20

24. Ives, C., Campia, I., Wang, R.L., Wittwehr, C., Edwards, S.: Creating a structured adverse outcome pathway knowledgebase via ontology-based annotations. Appl. Vitro Toxicol. **3**(4), 298–311 (2017). https://doi.org/10.1089/aivt.2017.0017

25. Junior, A.C., Debruyne, C., Longo, L., O'Sullivan, D.: On the mental workload assessment of uplift mapping representations in linked data. In: Longo, L., Leva, M.C. (eds.) H-WORKLOAD 2018. CCIS, vol. 1012, pp. 160–179. Springer, Cham (2019). https://doi.org/10.1007/978-3-030-14273-5_10

26. Junior, A.C., Debruyne, C., O'Sullivan, D.: Juma Uplift: Using a Block Metaphor for Representing Uplift Mappings, January - February 2018. https://doi.org/10.1109/ICSC.2018.00037

27. Kertcher, Z.: Gaps and bridges in interdisciplinary knowledge integration. In: Anandarajan, M., Anandarajan, M. (eds.) e-Research Collaboration, pp. 49–54. Springer, Heidelberg (2010). https://doi.org/10.1007/978-3-642-12257-6_4

28. Maynard, D., Funk, A., Peters, W.: Using Lexico-syntactic ontology design patterns for ontology creation and population. In: Proceedings of ISWC 2009, Workshop on Ontology Patterns, Washington, USA, October 2009

29. Noy, N.F., McGuinness, D.L.: Ontology Development 101: A Guide to Creating Your First Ontology. Technical report, Standford Knowldge Systems, AI Lab (2001). https://corais.org/sites/default/files/ontology_development_101_aguide_to_creating_your_first_ontology.pdf

30. Noy, N.F., et al.: Protégé-2000: an open-source ontology-development and knowledge-acquisition environment: AMIA 2003 Open Source Expo. In: Proceedings of AMIA 2003, Annual Symposium on American Medical Informatics. Washington, USA, November 2003

31. Öztürk, Ö., Özacar, T.: A case study for block-based linked data generation: recipes as jigsaw puzzles. J. Inf. Sci. **46**(3), 419–433 (2020). https://doi.org/10.1177/0165551519849518

32. Resnick, M., et al.: Scratch: programming for all. Commun. ACM **52**(11), 60–67 (2009). https://doi.org/10.1145/1592761.1592779

33. Sauro, J., Lewis, J.R.: Quantifying the User Experience: Practical Statistics for User Research, 2nd edn. Morgan Kaufmann, Cambridge (2016)

34. Siedlok, F., Hibbert, P.: The organization of interdisciplinary research: modes, drivers and barriers. Int. J. Manange. Rev. **16**(3), 194–210 (2014)

35. Slimani, T.: Ontology development: a comparing study on tools, languages and formalisms. Indian J. Sci. Technol. **8**(24), 1–12 (2015). https://doi.org/10.17485/ijst/2015/v8i1/54249

36. Sure, Y., Erdmann, M., Angele, J., Staab, S., Studer, R., Wenke, D.: OntoEdit: collaborative ontology development for the semantic web. In: Horrocks, I., Hendler, J. (eds.) ISWC 2002. LNCS, vol. 2342, pp. 221–235. Springer, Heidelberg (2002). https://doi.org/10.1007/3-540-48005-6_18

37. Vinken, M., Pauwels, M., Ates, G., Vivier, M., Vanhaecke, T., Rogiers, V.: Screening of repeated dose toxicity data present in SCC (NF) P/SCCS safety evaluations of cosmetic ingredients. Arch. Toxicol. **86**(3), 405–412 (2012). https://doi.org/10.1007/s00204-011-0769-z

Short Papers

'Expected Most of the Results, but Some Others...Surprised Me': Personality Inference in Image Tagging Services

Maria Kasinidou[1], Styliani Kleanthous[1,2(✉)], and Jahna Otterbacher[1,2]

[1] Cyprus Center for Algorithmic Transparency, Open University of Cyprus, Latsia, Cyprus
{maria.kasinidou,styliani.kleanthous,jahna.otterbacher}@ouc.ac.cy
[2] CYENS Centre of Excellence, Nicosia, Cyprus

Abstract. Image tagging APIs, offered as Cognitive Services in the movement to democratize AI, have become popular in applications that need to provide a personalized user experience. Developers can easily incorporate these services into their applications; however, little is known concerning their behavior under specific circumstances. We consider how two such services behave when predicting elements of the Big-Five personality traits from users' profile images. We found that personality traits are not equally represented in the APIs' output tags, with tags focusing mostly on Extraversion. The inaccurate personality prediction and the lack of vocabulary for the equal representation of all personality traits, could result in unreliable implicit user modeling, resulting in sub-optimal – or even undesirable – user experience in the application.

Keywords: Algorithmic bias · Cognitive services · Personality · Image analysis

1 Introduction

Image analysis algorithms, with their seamless functionalities, have been a boon to commercial technologies where modeling and applying user characteristics is vital. Tech giants (e.g., Google, Amazon, Microsoft) have all released "Cognitive Services" that are readily available for almost anyone to use through their websites, and for developers to incorporate into the software they are developing using their APIs. Users have indirect interaction with these tools, whether they are recognizing this or not, and they likely take their outputs for granted.

It is important to understand that image tagging APIs do not always treat people images in a fair and predictable way. Recent work [1,8,11] demonstrates that these services are anything but socially just, underscoring the need to be critical when using computer vision algorithms that shape human interactions. For instance, there are reports of gender misclassification, particularly for people

© Springer Nature Switzerland AG 2021
D. Fogli et al. (Eds.): IS-EUD 2021, LNCS 12724, pp. 187–195, 2021.
https://doi.org/10.1007/978-3-030-79840-6_12

with darker skin as compared to people with lighter skin, and women compared to men [2]. Black men were more likely to be tagged with negative emotions as compared to white men [11], when using Face++ and Microsoft's Face API.[1] Recent work [8] demonstrated that in neutral images, where only one person is depicted, most taggers had very low accuracy on using gender-related tags appropriately. Similarly, for emotion inferences [9], Clarifai uses emotion-related tags to describe two-thirds of the images, far more than Google or Imagga. Only Clarifai uses words that infer a person's traits, with images of men being described more often with trait tags, as compared to those of women and with Asians being described with the fewest trait-related tags.

Given that these are "black box" algorithms, understanding the source(s) of this behavior, is not straight forward. This becomes especially important when image tagging algorithms are used for implicitly modeling users' personalities in social applications and media (e.g., dating apps), a method that is much less intrusive than having the user to fill in a personality questionnaire. Previous work on personality analysis through images, focused mainly on visual and content features of social media images uploaded by users and suggest that these features are reliable enough for predicting personality [3]. However, there is a consensus that some traits are easier to predict than others through photos. Guntuku et al. [6] used Imagga for tagging a number of images posted and liked by Twitter users, to examine whether Big Five personality traits are related to this activity. Results indicate that only Openness and Neuroticism could be predicted.

Currently, we follow a human in the loop audit approach to examine the behaviors of two popular tagging services, Imagga and Clarifai, aiming to understand the extent to which they predict users' personalities, and if they do so accurately. The research questions we address are: RQ1 - Which traits of the Big Five are described in the APIs' tags? RQ2 - How accurate are the personality-related tags? RQ3 - How do users feel about the tags describing their photos?

2   Methodology

In order to answer the above questions we recruited 38 participants (20 women, 18 men), all being undergraduate university students. Participation was voluntary and all participants provided written, informed consent for their data (IPIP scores, photos and the APIs' outputs) to be used. To answer RQ1 - we asked participants to interact with two popular APIs (Imagga, Clarifai), collecting the output tags from each. For uniformity, participants were asked to take a picture (selfie) with a neutral facial expression, without a background. Participants were asked to upload the selfie to the two APIs and collect the generated tags along with their confidence scores. To answer RQ2 - participants were asked to complete the IPIP questionnaire, a 50-item questionnaire that assesses Goldberg's [5] Big Five factors. To answer RQ3 - participants responded in free text to the following three questions. *How did you feel when you saw the tags that described*

---

[1] https://azure.microsoft.com/en-us/services/cognitive-services/face/.

your photo? Which tags do you consider to be the most representative for you? Which tags do you consider to be the least representative for you?

Identifying Personality Related Tags. The most reliable methods for predicting measurable elements of personality are those based on traits. One of the most stable models is the five-factor solution based on adjectives. Such a model is based on the Big Five traits, for example, Goldberg's International Personality Items Pool (IPIP).[2] Norman's Taxonomy of traits was an initial attempt to create clusters of English language adjectives that could be used to characterize a person under the Big Five traits [10]. Norman published 1.431 trait adjectives under 75 categories representing each Big Five trait. Goldberg [5] expanded on Norman's Taxonomy of trait descriptive adjectives adding 479 synonym adjectives and developed the revised synonym clusters.

For this work, Princeton WordNet[3] was used to further extract synonyms of the trait adjectives based on Goldberg's revised trait synonyms.[4] For each term from Goldberg's sets, we conducted a search in WordNet, extracting the synonyms based on the meaning of the original word. We used this collection of trait adjectives and the synonyms extracted from WordNet to identify personality descriptive tags output by the two APIs. Imagga provided: 20 distinct tags for Extraversion (14 from the taxonomy and 6 from WordNet), 13 for Openness/Intellect (4 from the taxonomy and 9 from WordNet), 7 for Agreeableness (5 from the taxonomy, 2 from WordNet), 3 for Conscientiousness (from the taxonomy) and 2 for Neuroticism/Emotional Stability (from the taxonomy). Clarifai provided 6 distinct tags for Extraversion (4 from the taxonomy and 2 from WordNet), 4 for Openness/Intellect (1 from the taxonomy and 3 from WordNet), 1 tag for Agreeableness (from the taxonomy) and 1 tag for Conscientiousness (from the taxonomy) and no tags for Neuroticism/Emotional Stability.

3   Analysis and Results

A preliminary descriptive analysis showed that the mean across the 38 participants for each of the five traits, as revealed by the IPIP, was as follows: Extraversion - 30.61 ($SD = 6.57$), Agreeableness - 37.55 ($SD = 5.326$), Conscientiousness - 37.16 ($SD = 6.58$), Emotional Stability - 28.26 ($SD = 6.97$), Intellect - 35.74 ($SD = 4.46$). The scores on Extraversion, Conscientiousness and Emotional Stability were approximately normally distributed, while those of Intellect and Agreeableness were slightly skewed to the left.

Trait Representation in the Image Tagging APIs' Output (RQ1): We identified a total of 45 tags from Imagga and 12 from Clarifai, that are related

---

[2] https://ipip.ori.org/.

[3] https://wordnet.princeton.edu/.

[4] WordNet is the most widely used English lexical database which includes nouns, verbs, adjectives, and adverbs. The words are organized and linked based on their lexical concept (set of synonyms).

Table 1. Factor analysis models

Number of factors	χ^2 test statistic	p-value	Cumulative variance explained
7	463.1, 399	0.0146	0.655
8	414.15, 370	0.0563	0.678
9	371.11, 342	0.134	0.706

to personality.[5] Tags related to Extraversion (26) are more numerous than those relating to other traits, in both APIs. Extraversion is followed by Intellect (17) with more tags than the other three traits. Interestingly, for Emotional Stability (2), Clarifai did not have any related tags and Imagga had only two. Imagga has a richer vocabulary of personality-related tags compared to Clarifai, which had only one tag for Conscientiousness (4) and one for Agreeableness (8). Previous work reported that Extraversion was the easiest to predict from images on social media [12], however, to our best knowledge, there is no previous work on representing personality traits by Image Tagging APIs, to which to compare our results.

Personality Prediction Accuracy (RQ2): To this end, we analyze which traits are typically described by the taggers, and how their use correlates to our participants' scores on the IPIP personality questionnaire. First, we observed that while Imagga and Clarifai have several personality-related tags, many are used very sparingly. Therefore, we considered the tags which were used to describe at least five of the 38 selfies. The tags used less than five times were eliminated from the analysis. Thus, the final set analyzed comprised 36 tags. Furthermore, since many of our tags are conceptually similar (e.g., smile, laugh), we subjected the matrix of tag confidence scores, which for Imagga and Clarifai range from 0 to 100, to a factor analysis, to reduce the dimensions of the dataset and to create a new set of explanatory variables (i.e., tag scores) that are orthogonal to each other. This allows us to study the entire "profile" of the person inferred by the taggers, rather than considering the use of individual tags. It also captures the degree of certainty the tagger has about a particular trait adjective.

Factor Analysis. We first produced a scree-plot, a diagnostic tool for determining the optimal number of factors to account for the variance in the data [4]. The plot suggested a solution between five and nine factors. We used the factanal function in R,[6] which uses the maximum likelihood approach to fitting a common, orthogonal factor model, with varimax rotation. The function also outputs results from a chi square test, which evaluates the null hypothesis that the model fit is satisfactory. As shown in Table 1, the model with nine factors fits the data well (i.e., the null hypothesis cannot be rejected). The results of an orthogonal rotation of the 9-factor solution are shown in Table 2.

---

[5] It is important to remind the reader that these services are effectively "black boxes," thus, the complete list of their tags is not publicly available, not even to the developers who are incorporating them in the software they are developing.

[6] https://stat.ethz.ch/R-manual/R-devel/library/stats/html/factanal.html.

Table 2. Rotated factor loadings for the nine-factor solution

	F1	F2	F3	F4	F5	F6	F7	F8	F9
Casual	0.523		0.102	0.331	0.624	0.345	−.173	0.215	
Relaxed	0.282	−.194	0.254	0.834		0.101	−.279		−.122
Friendly	0.101	0.806	0.137			0.228			0.298
Good	0.581	−.584	0.120	0.464	0.222			−.142	
Nice	−.271	0.189		−.106		−.604			
Serious	0.194		0.233	0.270	0.186		−.142	0.494	
Mature	0.649	−.548	0.245	0.273	0.151		0.156	−.153	
Care	−.298	.298	.331		−.468	.661		−.144	0.133
Expression	0.230	−.452					0.284	0.560	0.123
Confident	0.499	0.271	0.640	0.276			0.161	0.274	
Happy	−.224	0.802	−.207		−.206	−.157	0.150	−.270	
Sexy	-.865			−.151	0.145	−.200			
Smiling	0.168	0.786	0.112		−.171		0.117	−.335	−.165
Smile		0.768		−.261	−.102	−.115	0.144	0.120	
Expressive	0.453	−.232	0.159	0.467			0.370		−.269
Cheerful		0.230	−.250					−.108	0.695
Happiness	0.101	0.343	−.830		−.222	0.107	0.185		−.189
Confidence	0.243	0.280	0.596	0.384	−.145	−.125	0.168		
Joy			−.566	−.119		−.209	0.205	−.174	0.172
Sensual	−.861		−.136		−.118	−.206	0.109		−.111
Sensuality	−.835			-.228	−.109				
Cool	0.420	−.386	0.239	0.534	0.220	0.247	−.164	0.107	
Smart	0.343	0.197	0.532	0.482	0.199				
Thoughtful	0.169	−.182	0.140				-.814		
Modern		−.156			0.554		−.169	0.252	0.239
Elegance	−.687		0.166	−.246		0.187		0.105	0.332
Elegant	−.588		0.237	−.175	0.210	−.275			0.117
Fashionable		−.143	0.129	0.133	0.683		0.158		
Trendy	0.242	−.150	0.106	0.798	0.189		0.118	0.213	0.150
Glamor	−.651		−.186		0.107	0.168		−.207	
Prop. Var.	0.183	0.122	0.093	0.092	0.059	0.046	0.040	0.039	0.033

Interpretation of Factors. The items heavily loaded onto Factor 1 indicate a casual, mature and good person with a lack of "flashy" characteristics such as sexy, elegant, etc. This factor was labelled, "Easy-going characteristics". Four items loaded onto the second factor, and related to individuals' positivity (e.g., happy, smiling). This factor was labelled, "Outward positivity". The three items

Table 3. Linear regression to predict the personality traits using the nine factors.

	E	C	ES	Log (I +1)	Log(A + 1)
(intercept)	30.61***	37.16***	28.26***	3.60***	3.64***
F1	−0.67	−1.14	0.52	0.03	−0.02
F2	−0.40	1.56	−0.33	−0.01	0.02
F3	0.56	0.49	2.03	−0.01	0.003
F4	−1.06	−0.58	0.35	0.02	−0.03
F5	−0.20	−0.95	1.31	0.02	0.03
F6	0.84	−0.88	0.70	0.03	−0.02
F7	1.45	−0.60	−0.21	0.03	−0.03
F8	−2.47*	−2.24	−0.09	0.001	−0.05*
F9	−.58	0.44	2.27	−0.002	0.005
R-squared	0.24	0.25	0.23	0.20	0.27

*** $p < 0.01$, ** $p < 0.05$, * $p < 0.1$

loaded onto Factor 3 identify the quality of being competent, such as the quality of having sufficient knowledge or confidence. However, such individuals are not characterized as happy/joyful, as evidenced by the negative loadings on these characteristics. Thus, Factor 3 was labelled, "Competence".

The five items that loaded onto Factor 4 relate to tags that describe a positive impression an individual has on others (e.g., cool, trendy). This factor was labelled, "Positive impression on others". Three items loaded onto Factor 5, which are related to physical characteristics that tend to have a positive impression on others (e.g., modern, fashionable, casual). This was labelled, "Positive impression on others, physical characteristics." Items with heavy loadings on Factor 6 are related to feeling concern or interest in something or someone. This factor was labelled, "Caring". Factor 7 has lots of negative weights, in particular "not thoughtful". This factor was labelled, "Less positive." Items for Factor 8 related to being serious and not happy. This factor was labelled, "Serious demeanor." Finally, Factor 9 had strong loadings on cheerful, elegant and stylish. This factor was labelled, "Cheerful".

To study the relationship between each of the nine factors - representing how the taggers perceived the depicted people - and the personality scores of the participants, we used linear regression. In particular, we regressed the scores that followed a normal distribution (Conscientiousness, Emotional Stability, Extraversion) onto the nine factors. We took the log transformation on Intellect and Agreeableness, which was approximately normal. Table 3 presents the regression model in which the nine factors are used to predict each personality trait.

Factor 8, which represents a serious expression, has a significant negative correlation to Extraversion and Agreeableness, which is quite sensible. However, for the other traits, none of the factors shows a significant correlation. It is interesting to note that the factors that are more important in explaining the

Table 4. Most (left) and least (right) representative tags by participants gender.

	Men	Women		Men	Women
Personality related (n = 34)	9	25	Personality related (n = 32)	16	16
Age related (n = 21)	7	14	Age related (n = 12)	8	4
Gender related (n = 35)	16	19	Gender related (n = 16)	6	10
Appearance related (n = 49)	21	28	Appearance related (n = 23)	8	15
Other (n = 17)	12	5	Other (n = 26)	8	18

variance in the way people are described (F1, F2), each of which explains more than 10% of the variance, do not appear correlated to personality traits.

Participants' View on Image Tagging APIs' Output (RQ3): Thematic analysis [7] applied, by two researchers, to participants' free text responses to uncover the key factors participants considered when they saw the tags assigned to their selfies by the APIs. Five categories, which were not mutually exclusive, have emerged. The number in the parentheses indicates the frequency with which participants' responses mentioned that concept.

Accuracy (19). The participant considered the tags as true or correct.

Weird (9). The participant "felt weird" about the tags.

Enthusiasm/Surprised/Impressed (13). Participants felt surprised because the tags were unexpected.

Expected/Unexpected (11). Whether or not the participant was expecting the output tags.

Subjectivity (1). subjective tags and based on real characteristics.

As observed, almost half of the participants discussed the tags' accuracy (either accurate or inaccurate). Nine responses mentioned that they felt weird about how an image tagging algorithm could recognize so many things from an image with no expression and no background or because they could not understand how the API chose specific tags. Interestingly, only one participant directly mentioned the subjectivity of the tags.

Participants were also asked to discuss the tags they deemed as the most/least representative ones. To reveal the key themes, we followed the same approach as above. Five themes emerged, Table 4 presents the number of responses in which participants mentioned each of the five categories as the most representative tags, broken out by participant gender. Both men and women mentioned that the appearance-related tags were the most representative for them (e.g., brunette, pretty). This resonates with previous findings on users' tendency to present themselves in a socially desirable way [3]. As observed, women expressed more often than men the feeling that personality-related tags were the most representative ones. Another interesting finding is that all personality-related tags mentioned were positive tags (e.g., happiness, friendly) or negative tags (e.g., anger, fear). Both men and women mentioned - although less often than other types - tags related to their age. Finally, men and women mentioned gender-related tags as the most representative with similar frequencies.

As can be seen, personality-related tags were often mentioned by both men an women. In particular, three respondents mentioned in their answers that all the tags related to emotions were the least representative (e.g. *"I think the tags related to the feelings were less representative of me."* - P1).

4   Concluding Remarks

Recent work has highlighted several concerns with respect to the use of image analysis algorithms in processing people images. In particular, previous studies demonstrated that computer vision algorithms are often producing less accurate results for some groups of depicted persons over others. The present work has echoed the concerns but from a different perspective. We found that while image tagging algorithms often output personality-related tags when processing a selfie, the tags do not correlate to the depicted person's actual personality.

This is clearly not an objective task especially when is used to implicitly build a user model. This finding was very much confirmed in the qualitative responses of participants, who overwhelmingly felt that tags related to their physical appearance were the most representative compared to personality related tags. In conclusion, developers should be aware of the behaviour of the image tagging algorithms when using them for implicitly modeling users' personalities.

Acknowledgments. This project is partially funded by the Cyprus Research and Innovation Foundation under grant EXCELLENCE/0918/0086 (DESCANT) and by the European Union's Horizon 2020 Research and Innovation Programme under agreements No. 739578 (RISE) and 810105 (CyCAT).

References

1. Barlas, P., Kleanthous, S., Kyriakou, K., Otterbacher, J.: Social b(eye)as in image tagging algorithms: Human and machine descriptions of people images. Proc. AAAI ICWSM **13**(01), 583–591 (2019)
2. Buolamwini, J., Gebru, T.: Gender shades: intersectional accuracy disparities in commercial gender classification. In: Conference on Fairness. Accountability and Transparency, pp. 77–91. PMLR, New York (2018)
3. Celli, F., Bruni, E., Lepri, B.: Automatic personality and interaction style recognition from Facebook profile pictures. In: Proceedings of the 22nd ACM International Conference on Multimedia, pp. 1101–1104. ACM, New York (2014)
4. Everitt, B., Hothorn, T.: An Introduction to Applied Multivariate Analysis with R (UseR!), January 2011. https://doi.org/10.1007/978-1-4419-9650-3
5. Goldberg, L.: An alternative "description of personality": the big-five factor structure. J. Pers. Soc. Psychol. **59**, 1216–29 (1991)
6. Guntuku, S.C., Lin, W., Carpenter, J., Ng, W.K., Ungar, L.H., Preoţiuc-Pietro, D.: Studying personality through the content of posted and liked images on twitter. In: Proceedings of the 2017 ACM on Web Science Conference, WebSci 2017, pp. 223–227 ACM, New York (2017). http://doi.acm.org/10.1145/3091478.3091522

7. Herring, S.C.: Web content analysis: expanding the paradigm. In: Hunsinger, J., Allen, M. (eds.) International Handbook of Internet Research, pp. 233–249. Springer, Dordrecht (2009). https://doi.org/10.1007/978-1-4020-9789-8_14

8. Kyriakou, K., Barlas, P., Kleanthous, S., Otterbacher, J.: Fairness in proprietary image tagging algorithms: a cross-platform audit on people images. In: Proceedings of AAAI ICWSM, vol. 13, pp. 313–322. AAAI, California (2019)

9. Kyriakou, K., Kleanthous, S., Otterbacher, J., Papadopoulos, G.A.: Emotion-based stereotypes in image analysis services. In: Adjunct Publication of the 28th ACM UMAP Conference, pp. 252–259 (2020)

10. Norman, W.T.: 2800 personality trait descriptors: normative operating characteristics for a university population. University of Michigan, Ann Arbor, Michigan (1967)

11. Rhue, L.: Racial influence on automated perceptions of emotions. SSRN **3281765** (2018)

12. Silveira Jacques Junior, J.C., et al.: First impressions: a survey on vision-based apparent personality trait analysis. IEEE Trans. Affect. Comput. 1 (2019)

Providing a Notifications System to Software Services with HomeSerBot

Fabio Cassano$^{(\boxtimes)}$ and Antonio Piccinno

Dipartimento di Informatica, Universitá di Bari Aldo Moro, Bari, Italy
{fabio.cassano1,antonio.piccinno}@uniba.it

Abstract. Nowadays voice assistants devices such as Amazon Alexa and Google Home, promise users to support the administration of their smart objects just by the usage of their voice, however, the adoption of this kind of interaction does not satisfy all users. This is particularly true for computer literate people, who can write their software components to interact with such devices. A common way users interact with their software is just by receiving notifications and send commands. In this paper we propose HomeSerBot, a notification system software that allows end users (in this case computer literate people) to customize and receive customized notifications from their services. It is composed of a Telegram bot that allows the user to get notifications and interact with the back-end part of the home service and an administration panel to handle the installation and management of the services available on the user's computer.

Keywords: Software service management · HomeSerBot · GO

1 Introduction

The last decade has witnessed the "explosion" of microservices architecture, allowing the development and the integration of multiple software services as one big piece of software. The growing adoption of this type of solution is pushing end users and developers to new horizons: on one hand, end users have very specific software services, on the other developers can build complex software solutions starting from Off-the-shelf components. For example, in the current user scenario, houses are becoming "smart" by the addition of devices that allows automation. However, each management is delegated either to a specific vendor app or by complex system software which needs to be deployed on an end-user computing device. So, users that want to keep track of a specific app behaviour through notifications (for example) must install and manage multiple apps on their PC or smartphone [1]. This leads to over-complicate simple tasks and confusion due to the decentralisation of the information source. A way to facilitate and automate the handling of such tasks is provided by event-condition-actions (ECA) software, e.g.: IFTTT and many others, but they require that the application must be strictly compliant with the Application Programming Interfaces

© Springer Nature Switzerland AG 2021
D. Fogli et al. (Eds.): IS-EUD 2021, LNCS 12724, pp. 196–203, 2021.
https://doi.org/10.1007/978-3-030-79840-6_13

(API) rules managed by the ECA provider [2]. This aspect might be acceptable and desirable for companies that need to provide apps and software to a wide plethora of people, giving them well known Graphical Users Interfaces to facilitate their usage. However, there is a niche of people, such as "computer literate" users, who are able to write software and that might need slightly different functionalities from those provided. For example, they might need to receive simple notifications on the status code of a single service, or the last piece of the log if it is failed, without the need to connect to the computer. Thus, the idea to build custom actions using third-party software is not the best solution to solve this problem, as the entire system relies on the availability of external services and standard-based API that must be considered as a black box.

We propose here HomeSerBot, a solution that allows users to define and manage software notifications on Telegram. The idea behind HomeSerBot is based on the following basics concepts:

1. We want the end user to take the control over the software he/she intend to deploy on a specific machine;
2. Such software (which might be installed as background service on a physical or remote host) needs to be monitored without the user interaction;
3. The user has the option to subscribe/unsubscribe to some specific notification(s) given by such software.

We have decided to implement the mentioned notification system on Telegram, which is a popular social messaging app, and has the option to let the users create some "bots", namely pieces of software with which the user can automatically interact. However, the Telegram Bot is just one of the two HomeSerBot front-end parts. It also provides a fully customisable dashboard, allowing the user to install the software as a service, and head over the control of what is going on in the system. The entire system is built on a database to store the notifications and the information provided to the user and related to the system services. This software ecosystem allows end users to get some specific notifications on their Telegram app, and the bot allows a secure interaction with the system, without obliging the user to be logged into their computer via Secure SHell (SSH).

The article is structured as follows. Section 2 propose some of the existing literature review on common services and user interaction with them. Section 3 describes HomeSerBot, and the technologies used to develop it. Lastly, Sect. 4 draws the conclusions and the future work.

2   Related Work

The first challenge we faced is related to the integration of HomeSerBot notifications with most of the smartphones available in such a way users do not have to download and install additional apps. Bots are considered one of the most effective means for automated notifications, thanks to their compatibility with all platforms or OS. They are widely used in fields, such as chatting, automating small procedures and so on, thanks to their simplicity of development [3]. Nowadays, it is common to find bots on all commercial websites, providing the first support to users who need simple functionalities that might not have been listed on the website [4]. Setiaji et al. proposes an insight on how bots should be created to quickly give information on a large group of users [5] and Sutikno et al. [6] make a nice comparison between three of the most important social network messaging tools: Viber, Whatsapp and Telegram highlighting the pros and cons of each app. Despite the existence of other well-known apps such as Instagram, Facebook etc., not all of them provide the same API access or functionalities and the possibility to create bots, so we have decided to adopt and develop a Telegram bot. Another reason to support our choice is the high level of security that Telegram offers to their users [7]. Furthermore, Telegram is widely used for bot services and notification, and many research of the last decade prove how effective this system is. For example, Wahyuni et al. use Telegram to monitor a sensor [8], while Saad et al. use the same approach to control remotely a pump [9]. Both these approaches follow the same idea proposed in our work, but their approach is limited to few static commands, and the Telegram bot is the only interface the user has to control the system. Besides, there is not a security layer between the application and the server; this allows unattended users to get into their system with ease. Lastly, the user does not have control over the commands sent through the channel, making the application limited to only a few functionalities

HomeSerBot is a solution that supports users to manage and control their software in any system environment. It provides End-User Development (EUD) functionalities, targeting computer literate users, facilitating their service notification management. In literature, there are many ways to support end users with their software customisation. For example, we have found that some research target different user types in a family context [10], while others propose the usage of a specific language in order to control IoT devices [11]. The idea to create a service/process manager tool builds its roots on the constant growth of services used by users without considering their level of computer knowledge. Many approaches have been proposed in literature defining different paradigms according to user target. For example, approaches like End-User Programming, End-User Programming and End-User Software Engineering define the specific role the user has in the creation of the software artefact [12,13]. In this work, the end user covers a different role: he/she is both administrator of services, and user, with the right skills to write his/her code. This would suggest that the user might become a target of two or more paradigms as suggested in [14].

3   HomeSerBot

HomeSerBot has been developed using GO, a recent and high-performance programming language [15]. We aimed at the possibility to develop a solution using a language that is efficient (fast and requires few hardware resources) and that can be easily maintained and extended by anybody. HomeSerBot consists of three components: the back-end, the front-end for the system administration (administration panel), and the telegram bot part for the user interaction through Telegram. The latest version of the entire system can be found and downloaded from Github at https://github.com/netphantom/homeSerBot and it can be installed by following the instructions on the README file or by performing the following steps. Supposing that the user is under a Debian environment, with GO, installed and the GOROOT correctly configured:

1. Download the package from Github using the "wget" or the "git clone" command;
2. Open the downloaded folder and compile HomeSerBot using the "go build main.go" command (alternatively, a pre-build package is available on the Github page, under the "Release" tab);
3. Run the compiled package providing the required parameters, such as the Telegram API key and the database connection details.

The program will start both the administration panel (which can be reached using the port 4000 of the host machine, typically "localhost") and the Telegram bot. The latter must be reached using the "search" option on Telegram, typing the exact name of the bot associated with the API key.

Figure 1 shows the service architecture of HomeSerBot. The registration of a new process is managed by the web dashboard that receives the processes list from the server operating system where HomeSerBot is deployed. From this list, the user can select which process wants to enable the notifications, doing so, the dashboard creates a symbolic connection to it into the database. At regular time intervals, the database polls the server to receive the status of all the registered processes and send the notification to both the home page of the dashboard and the Telegram bot.

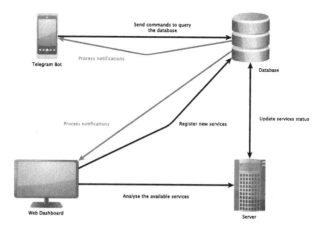

Fig. 1. The HomeSerBot architecture

3.1 Telegram Bot

The first aspect of HomeSerBot is why the user has to interact with the Telegram bot rather than other software. The first one is that from a user point of view, there is no need to install any additional application on the computer or the mobile phone, as Telegram is one of the most used social networks, and its users are constantly growing in number. Besides, Telegram offers the possibility to access its services through a web page, so there are multiple ways the user can interact without a bot. Furthermore, by providing a chat-like interface, users might find it easier to start using it rather than learning a new application. Telegram provides a simple interaction method based on common commands that are usually connected with the keyboard, so the user is presented into a "sandbox-like" environment, where the choices available are decided by the back-end of the bot, reducing the user error. Moreover, developing a Telegram bot allowed us to overcome almost all of the problems related to the communication channel, security, authorisation and user verification, because Telegram API take care of such routine stuff. To provide a reliable bot, we have used the Tucnak Telebot framework, which aim is to match the telegram API providing a standard GO interface.

It is important to mention that each Telegram bot is associated with a single API key provided by the user, thus the process of bot creation requires that for each system deployed, a personal API key must be requested to Telegram through the Botfather (which is the bot responsible for the association between the API key and the user). Once completed the registration, the API key must be passed to HomeSerBot as a flag. As Telegram bots can be published, searched and accessed by anyone, HomeSerBot implements an additional security layer that involves the user registration on the HomeSerBot system. So, each new user willing to use the HomeSerBot should be initially registered and authorised by the system administrator, which can be done by logging into the Telegram chat and send the system the "register" command. The bot will register the request and pass it to the admin dashboard, waiting to be accepted by the administrator. Once accepted, the user can perform the pre-loaded queries to the bot. At the moment of writing this article, queries are fixed and can be performed by using the typical Telegram "command" invocation:

- register: send to the admin dashboard the signup request. If the user is already found in the database, this command re-connect the chat with the back-end service (maybe the user has changed the phone or accidentally deleted the old chat);
- pidList: provides the user with the process list registered on the service. A unique ID number is associated to each process, thus the user can easily chose among the given list;
- subscribe "item": by appending the process ID from the previous command, the user receive notifications when those are available from the system;
- unsubscribe "item": in the same way, with this command the user can decide to stop receiving notifications from the given service;
- subscriptions: the user receives the list of all his/her process subscriptions.

3.2   Back-End and Data Management

Thanks to GO programming language and GORM (an Object-Relational Mapping or ORM), HomeSerbot can use any database engine among: MySQL, SQLite, PostgreSQL, SQLserver, to store all the information related to the user(s) and keep track of the most important system events. The database schema and its deployment on the machine is totally transparent to the user and is managed by GORM during the first HomeSerbot startup. Using the GORM database model, it is easy to filter deleted entries, or handle the last update on a given field, leaving the development of new functions easy and clean.

3.3   The Administration Panel

The administration panel empowers the end user with some functionalities to handle different situations that might occur during the management of the service installation and notification. After the login (which requires the user registration with his/her telegram ID), the user is prompted with the home page, providing all the unread notifications since the last login. Additionally, on the top of the page, it is shown a panel to allow the user to handle the different aspects of service management. The user can move through different panels and choose among: the edit of the profile information, the installation/uninstallation of new services and the management of the requests.

As mentioned, HomeSerBot is available for multiple users on the same machine. The "Notification" button provides information about pending requests from users on the Telegram side. By clicking on it, the administrator can see the user details and decide to approve or decline every single user that tried to access the Telegram bot.

Figure 2 shows an example of the process list shown by HomeSerbot in the "processes" section. On the top part of the figure, there is the navigation bar that the user must use to navigate the dashboard functionalities. On the centre of the page, the processes available for the user's notifications subscription are listed. The admin can populate this list by using the "add" button at the bottom of the page and then, by selecting the desired process from the system process list, prompted on a new page.

The Profile Overview. In the profile section, the user can handle all the information related to the login. After the initial login, the user is required to write the password for the first time, which is going to be encrypted and stored on the database; however, this can be changed anytime by clicking on the "change password" button. To access the web service, the user must insert his/her telegram ID.

The Services Management. In this panel of the dashboard, the user can add or delete new processes in the list that will be shown on the Telegram Bot side. Each service must be correctly enabled and started on the operating

HomeSerBot

Home   Profile   Processes   ○ Notifications   Quit

Process List

Here below are listed the processes that can be added from telegram

ID	4
Process Name	My home service 1
Description	Air monitor service
Management	Edit | Delete
ID	5
Process Name	Light garage sensor
Description	What is the light level of the garage?
Management	Edit | Delete
ID	6
Process Name	Bit Torrent alert service
Description	Alert when a torrent is finished
Management	Edit | Delete

Fig. 2. A process list example shows the processes that the user can select to receive notifications

system as HomeSerBot relies on the Linux Systemd daemon to check the user's service status. This allows the automatic connection between HomeSerBot and the system services in case of failure or reboot. The addition of new services to the telegram service list is performed by using the "Add" button at the bottom of the services page. Once clicked, the dashboard lists all the available services on the system and allows the user to add the desired one, just by adding the description. Once added, it will be available in the "pidList" command on the Telegram bot.

4   Conclusion and Future Works

The growing number of services that run in a home system environment requires more control by the end users. Despite all the solutions that provide easy access for automation and control of such services, computer literate users need a simple but powerful tool to get notification about their process status. In this article we presented HomeSerBot, a solution to support end users in service management and monitoring. Our system is composed of a Telegram bot that allows user to receive notifications on the smartphone, a web dashboard to handle the process installation on the system, and a back end that orchestrates the communication between the two parts. The so-created ecosystem supports users to develop their software service allowing them to have a quick handle to notifications on the mobile phone.

HomeSerBot is currently under development and additional functionalities are still under the hood, for example, the possibility to define and run new user commands. This would allow the user to quickly control the services and interact with them directly from the Telegram bot. Despite being of great interest, this aspect has some serious security implication as command cannot be launched with super-user privileges. Last but not least, a usability study must be performed, inviting some users to test the system.

References

1. Marengo, A., Pagano, A.: Innovative ways to assess soft-skills: the in-basket game online experience. In: European Conference on e-Learning, pp. 325-XVII. Academic Conferences International Limited (2020)
2. Caivano, D., Fogli, D., Lanzilotti, R., Piccinno, A., Cassano, F.: Supporting end users to control their smart home: design implications from a literature review and an empirical investigation. J. Syst. Softw. **144**, 295–313 (2018)
3. Shevat, A.: Designing Bots: Creating Conversational Experiences. O'Reilly Media, Inc. (2017)
4. Nuruzzaman, M., Hussain, O.K.: A survey on chatbot implementation in customer service industry through deep neural networks. In: 2018 IEEE 15th International Conference on e-Business Engineering (ICEBE), pp. 54–61. IEEE (2018)
5. Setiaji, H., Paputungan, I.V.: Design of telegram bots for campus information sharing. In: IOP Conference Series: Materials Science and Engineering, vol. 325, p. 012005. IOP Publishing (2018)
6. Sutikno, T., Handayani, L., Stiawan, D., Riyadi, M.A., Subroto, I.M.I.: Whatsapp, viber and telegram: which is the best for instant messaging? Int. J. Electr. Comput. Eng (2088–8708). **6**(3), 1–6 (2016)
7. Abu-Salma, R., et al.: The security blanket of the chat world: an analytic evaluation and a user study of telegram. Internet Society (2017)
8. Wahyuni, R., Rickyta, A., Rahmalisa, U., Irawan, Y.: Home security alarm using Wemos D1 and HC-SR501 sensor based telegram notification. J. Robot. Control (JRC) **2**(3), 200–204 (2021)
9. Saad, M.H.M., Shahad, R.A., Sarnon, M.Z., Shukri, M.F.M., Hussain, A.: Smart pump operation monitoring and notification (puma) via telegram social messaging application. JOIV: Int. J. Inf. Visual. **1**(3), 57–60 (2017)
10. Caivano, D., Cassano, F., Fogli, D., Lanzilotti, R., Piccinno, A.: We@Home: a gamified application for collaboratively managing a smart home. In: De Paz, J.F., Julián, V., Villarrubia, G., Marreiros, G., Novais, P. (eds.) ISAmI 2017. AISC, vol. 615, pp. 79–86. Springer, Cham (2017)
11. Buono, P., Cassano, F., Legretto, A., Piccinno, A.: Eudroid: a formal language specifying the behaviour of IoT devices. IET Softw. **12**(5), 425–429 (2018)
12. Lieberman, H., Paternò, F., Klann, M., Wulf, V.H.: End-user development: an emerging paradigm. In: End User Development. Human-Computer Interaction Series, vol. 9, pp. 1–8. Springer, Dordrecht (2006)
13. Burnett, M., Cook, C., Rothermel, G.: End-user software engineering. Commun. ACM **47**(9), 53–58 (2004)
14. Barricelli, B.R., Cassano, F., Fogli, D., Piccinno, A.: End-user development, end-user programming and end-user software engineering: a systematic mapping study. J. Syst. Softw. **149**, 101–137 (2019)
15. Donovan, A.A., Kernighan, B.W.: The Go Programming Language. Addison-Wesley Professional (2015)

Design Requirements
for Recommendations in End-User
User Interface Design

Audrey Sanctorum[1]([✉]), Luka Rukonic[2], and Beat Signer[1]

[1] Web and Information Systems Engineering Lab, Vrije Universiteit Brussel,
Brussels, Belgium
{asanctor,bsigner}@vub.be
[2] Institute for Language and Communication, Université catholique de Louvain,
Louvain-la-Neuve, Belgium
luka.rukonic@uclouvain.be

Abstract. User interface design has become increasingly difficult due
to the rise of new kinds of electronic devices and the emergence of the
Internet of Things (IoT). Further, user interface (UI) designers struggle
to adapt their UIs to evolving user needs and preferences. In order to
address these issues, we want to support end users in designing their
own user interfaces. However, end-user UI design represents a major
challenge, given that end users often lack the necessary design skills. We
investigated how design recommendations might be used to address the
research question on *how to help end users during the UI design process?*
A first step towards answering this question is the analysis of how end
users should best get recommendations about potential design improvements. We therefore conducted a survey on how end users would like
to get design recommendations, whether they trust user- or machine-
generated recommendations, and whether they agree that their interactions are tracked and shared in order to improve the recommendations.
Based on the results of our survey, we present a set of design requirements
for the integration of recommendations in end-user UI design tools.

Keywords: End-user development · UID guidelines · Design
recommendations · Artificial intelligence · Trust

1   Introduction and Related Work

Rapid technological advances make it increasingly difficult for designers and developers to create user interfaces that follow UI design trends, can adapt to different devices (e.g., tablets or smartwatches) and address evolving user needs
and preferences. Therefore, a number of methods and techniques to simplify the
UI design process for designers via dedicated authoring tools have been investigated. For instance, Meskens et al. [9] presented a design environment for managing UI consistency across multiple devices. Focusing on the interaction across

D. Fogli et al. (Eds.): IS-EUD 2021, LNCS 12724, pp. 204–212, 2021.
https://doi.org/10.1007/978-3-030-79840-6_14

devices, Nebeling et al. [10] introduced XDStudio to support the interactive development of cross-device web interfaces. Considering the UI distribution across devices, Park et al. [12] optimised the allocations of UI elements through a designer-in-the-loop tool. Further, Kubitza and Schmidt [7] proposed meSchup, a platform enabling programming by physical interaction with different devices and sensors in IoT settings. In addition to dealing with various devices and smart things, designers also need to cope with the widely varying and evolving user needs. Therefore, the end-user development (EUD) paradigm is paying attention to make systems *easy to develop* rather than only *easy to use* [1], and empowers end users to build their own solutions. Nevertheless, end-user UI design represents a major challenge given that end users are normally less skilled in developing their user interfaces than professional designers. An obvious question is therefore *"how to help end users during the UI design process in order to improve their UIs?"*

A rich body of work has been carried out to create *better* user interfaces complying to design guidelines for a given context. We focus on design tools helping users during the UI design process by either automatically generating parts of user interfaces or by suggesting design ideas. Lin and Landay [8] introduced Damask, a pattern-based design tool for early-stage design and prototyping of multi-device user interfaces. Damask includes a 'pattern sidebar' for browsing design patterns and applying them to specific designs. Following a rule-based approach, Henninger [5] presented the GUIDE methodology and tool for helping designers to create more usable interfaces.

More recently, Gajos et al. [4] introduced SUPPLE to automatically generate graphical UIs based on an optimisation algorithm. Quiroz et al. [13] use an interactive genetic algorithm combining UID style guideline metrics with subjective user input to evolve user interfaces. While these two approaches ask for little or no user input during the automated design process, other systems do not automate but rather assist designers during the design process. DesignScape [11] helps designers via interactive layout suggestions. *Refinement suggestions* help improve the current layout, while *brainstorming suggestions* propose major layout changes and different styles. A similar tool called Sketchplorer [16] uses different optimisation mechanisms to support interactive layouts and pays more attention to design aesthetics. Focusing on grid layouts, the GRIDS [2] wireframing tool allows designers to explore starting solutions, get suggestions for the completion of partial designs and search for alternatives. Paying attention to creativity Koch et al. [6] proposed an interactive design ideation tool that, based on machine learning, suggests visual inspirational materials.

Rather than helping designers and developers as in most existing work, Fernández-García et al. [3] introduced a recommendation system suggesting suitable components to end users in a sidebar. Approaches helping designers or users can also be found in commercial solutions such as Microsoft PowerPoint and its PowerPoint Designer, providing layout design ideas in an optional sidebar.

While many of the proposed solutions target developers and designers, parts of these solutions could also be applied in end-user UI development solutions. A major challenge is to find the best way to provide end users with the necessary recommendations and support them in creating their UIs. Given the different characteristics of the discussed systems, we conducted a survey to investigate what users find relevant with respect to recommendations in an EUD UID tool.

2   Design Recommendation Survey

We designed an online questionnaire[1] to collect end users' opinions on how they would like to receive design recommendations, examine their level of trust in user- or machine-generated recommendations and to determine whether they are willing to be tracked to improve their recommendations. We collected a total of 82 fully filled-in questionnaires (49 males, 31 females and 2 'other') and the participants' mean age was 30 years ($SD_{age} = 6.7$). About half of the participants (42) described themselves as computer scientists. In order to check for differences between the group of computer scientists (CS) and non-computer scientists (NCS) we conducted a t-test for each closed-ended question, but no significant differences were found at the p-level of 0.05. Further note that we used a 4-point Likert scale with an additional 'N/A' option for all rating questions.

2.1   Presentation of Design Recommendations

In a first question in this category we asked participants whether they would see design recommendations as something positive or negative. 78 participants indicated that they see recommendations as something 'positive' (56) or 'very positive' (22), while only 4 participants answered with 'negative' (2) or 'N/A' (2). The reasons why participants see recommendations as something positive are to get some inspiration and new creative ideas (21), to get help during the design process making it easier to create improved designs (27), to save some time (7) or to simply not having to think about making a good design themselves (8).

In order to find out about the preferred placement of design recommendations, we presented participants three possible options. A first option was the placement of recommendations in a sidebar, as done in PowerPoint and related work [2,3,6,8,11,16]. As a second option, we proposed recommendations given by a digital assistant, similar to virtual assistants on various existing websites. A third option consisted of showing recommendations as an overlay on top of the original UI design. Participants were asked to rate each of these three options separately. Recommendations provided in a sidebar was rated as best option, as illustrated in Fig. 1. Further, less than half of the participants (33) liked recommendations from a digital assistant and only 25 participants considered recommendations using an overlay as a good idea. Participants liked the sidebar due to its clear overview of different recommendations. Moreover, 14 participants mentioned that they were already used to a sidebar layout. Regarding the digital assistant, some participants (6) directly thought of Microsoft Clippy and disregarded the idea, and a few (6) just mentioned it would bother or annoy them. Overlays were in general seen as too confusing, crowded and invasive (26).

---

[1] The complete study material is available at https://doi.org/10.5281/zenodo.4721326.

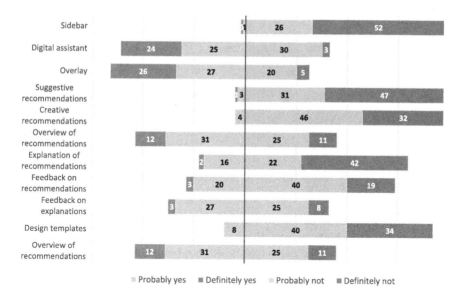

Fig. 1. Presentation of design recommendations

We also asked participants whether they would prefer recommendations in textual or graphical form. In related work recommendations are often given in a graphical way [2,4,6,11,13,16], but sometimes also in pure textual form [5] or a combination of both [8]. While many participants (59) expressed their interest in graphical recommendations, 19 participants selected the 'other' option and 17 out of these mentioned they would like a mix (e.g., text on hover). We further asked whether they would like to get suggestive recommendations to improve their design or creative recommendations. Figure 1 shows that the same number of participants (78) favoured suggestive or creative recommendations.

Koch et al.'s [6] ideation tool provides explanations why a certain recommendation has been given and we asked our participants whether they would like to have such explanations. As illustrated in Fig. 1, many participants (64) were in favour of getting such an explanation. 54 participants preferred on-demand explanations and 13 out of those mentioned that this way they would *"stay in control and be able to ignore it when not needed"*. Another 11 participants expressed that they *"did not want to be annoyed by the explanation or have repetitive information being displayed"*. 18 participants further wanted to *"avoid clutter, being distracted or being overwhelmed"*.

In Koch et al.'s [6] tool, feedback can be given about recommendations with the options 'more like this', 'not this one' or 'surprise me' and a feedback mechanism is also present in the GUIDE methodology [5]. A majority of our participants (59) were interested in giving feedback on recommendations. In contrast to the previous question related to the explanation of recommendations, many participants answered with 'probably yes' rather than 'definitely yes'. This might indicate that feedback would be considered as a plus rather than a must have. We further asked

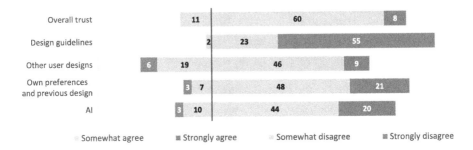

Fig. 2. Trust depending on recommendation source

the 64 participants interested in an explanation of recommendations whether they would also like to be able to give feedback on these explanations. The answers were mixed with almost half of the participants (30) not being interested in this feature. Further, as shown in Fig. 1, 74 participants were in favour of getting recommended design templates to start with.

Our final question in this category asked participants whether they would like an overview of all recommendations they received after finishing their UI design. This question was inspired by the timeline functionality in Sketchplore [16] and GRIDS [2], and the history panel of previous suggestions in [6]. The answers were mixed as 36 participants expressed interest in such overview, giving as reasons *"checking what has been selected from the recommendations"* (8) or for *"learning purposes"* (7) and *"traceability of why the UI design changed"* (3).

2.2   Trust in Design Recommendations

Since it is essential to know whether users would trust the recommendations of an end-user UID solution, we asked questions related to this subject. As shown in Fig. 2, 66 participants trust design recommendations and only 11 participants mentioned that they would 'probably not' trust them. Participants mentioned that their trust in recommendations depends on the quality of the recommendations (5), the corresponding explanations (5) and the assumption that recommendations would be made by experts based on common design practices (32).

We assumed that some recommendations could be considered more reliable depending on their source. From related work we learned that recommendations could be based on design guidelines [5,8,11,13,16], other users' designs (userbase) [3], a user's own preferences [4,13] and previous designs [3] as well as some AI components [3,6]. As shown in Fig. 2, almost all participants (78) believe that recommendations based on design guidelines are reliable, while 25 participants do not trust recommendations based on other users' designs. 69 participants would trust recommendations based on their own preferences and designs, and 64 would trust recommendations made by some AI.

2.3   Willingness to Share Personal Data

Given that design recommendations might be improved by tracking a user's interaction with the design environment, it is important to know whether users are willing to share such personal data. We asked participants whether they would accept their interactions to be tracked and shared. We offered participants three possible answers, including 'yes, but only for myself', 'yes, for everyone if my data is anonymised' and 'no'. Only 10 participants selected 'no', with half of them explaining that they do not like to be tracked as they are private persons. A majority (49) selected the second answer and the remaining 23 participants the first option. These results are promising as it means that an end-user UID tool might rely on this type of information to improve its recommendations.

3   Design Requirements

After identifying end users' needs through our analysis of the survey responses, we translated their opinions, attitudes and beliefs into a set of design requirements (DRs). Two authors independently analysed the answers, generated their set of design requirements and cross-checked these design requirements. While some design requirements such as DR1 and DR4 are rather evident, other requirements shed a new light on the design of UID recommendation systems.

DR1: Recommendations Should Best be Shown in a Sidebar. Given the large number of participants (78) favouring recommendations in a sidebar, we advise to do so in an end-user UID authoring tool. Participants' familiarity with sidebars in PowerPoint and other applications gives it precedence over other presentation types. As proposed by some participants, an optional overlay showing more detailed recommendations might be added on top of the UI design.

DR2: Recommendations Should be Shown Graphically. The majority of participants (59) expressed a preference for graphical recommendations. However, given that many (19) also suggested a combination of both textual and graphical recommendations, we advocate for a graphical representation of recommendations with a textual description of a recommendation on hover over.

DR3: Recommendations Should Cover Simple Improvements as well as Creative Aspects. Many participants (78) liked the idea of having simple and creative recommendations as realised by Donovan et al. [11]. While an end-user UID authoring tool should definitely provide recommendations for simple UI improvements, users will also appreciate receiving more creative recommendations, which is one of their motivations for using a design recommendation system.

DR4: The Visibility of Recommendations Should be Controllable. Given that 50 participants preferred to have on-demand recommendations and the fact that 15 participants mentioned (in comments) the need to control the visibility of recommendations, it is important that an end-user UID authoring tool provides a way to show or hide recommendations. This feature is present in commercial solutions but often not in related academic work.

DR5: Explanations Should be Provided on Demand Only. For a majority of participants (54), automatic explanations of recommendations would be considered annoying. However, explanations are seen as an opportunity for learning and they seem to increase the credibility of design recommendations. Given that a total of 64 participants were in favour of showing explanations, they should be provided on demand in order to not distract users during the UI design process.

DR6: Users Should be Able to Provide Ratings/Feedback on Recommendations. Giving feedback on recommendations is useful to improve the quality of the recommendations since poorly rated recommendations would less likely be shown. Further, feedback on recommendations might help in improving the recommendations in the long term [5] and a large number of participants (59) expressed interest in giving feedback on recommendations.

DR7: Users Should be Able to Provide Ratings/Feedback on Explanations. Explanations increase the trust and credibility of design recommendations. End users might consult explanations when they want to learn more about certain design guidelines or are simply curious about a design recommendation. Even though participants had mixed opinions about rating explanations, we believe that it can make low-quality explanations more understandable, useful and clear.

DR8: An Overview of Received Recommendations Should be Available. While participants had mixed opinions about an overview over the received recommendations, various reasons have been given by participants in favour of having such an overview. Therefore, an end-user UID authoring tool should preferably provide an optional overview of the recommendations users applied as well as the ones they did not apply.

DR9: Design Templates Should be Offered as Optional Starting Point. Given that 74 participants expressed interest in having design templates to start the design process, an end-user UID authoring tool should provide the choice between starting from a blank design or some pre-defined design templates. Providing such an option can save participants time which is one of their main motivations for using recommendations in the first place.

DR10: The Source of Recommendations Should be Selectable. Most participants (68) tend to trust recommendations. While almost all participants would trust recommendations based on design guidelines, this is not the case for recommendations based on other users' designs. Therefore, the recommendation system should allow users to define the source of recommendations, such as design guidelines, a user's previous designs, other user's designs or some AI component.

These ten design requirements and guidelines summarise the outcome of our survey and provide an answer to our main research question on "how to help end users during the UI design process?" Design recommendations are a good way to help end users during the design process as they are seen as something positive and trustworthy. By following the presented design requirements, a developer can create a UID recommendation system based on users' expectations and needs.

4 Conclusion

The findings of the presented survey serve as a foundation for helping end users during the UI design process. Overall, the results of our survey show that users would like to get design recommendations, that they are likely going to trust them and that they are willing to share some personal data about their interactions to improve these recommendations. We presented a number of design requirements summarising users' needs regarding a design recommendation system. The presented design requirements can be used by the research community to improve, extend or create new end-user UID authoring solutions with recommender systems that best fit their users and enable them to become better at designing their own user interfaces. Based on the presented design requirements, we are currently developing a design recommendation extension for the eSPACE end-user UID authoring tool [14, 15] and plan to evaluate the efficiency and effectiveness of the resulting design recommendations in an in-situ user study.

Acknowledgements. The research of Audrey Sanctorum has been funded by an FWO Postdoc Fellowship (1276721N) of the Research Foundation Flanders.

References

1. Lieberman, H., Paternó, F., Klann, M., Wulf, V.: End-user development: an emerging paradigm. In: Lieberman, H., Paternó, F., Wulf, V. (eds.) End User Development. Human-Computer Interaction Series, vol. 9. Springer, Dordrecht (2006). https://doi.org/10.1007/1-4020-5386-X_1
2. Dayama, N.R., et al.: GRIDS: interactive layout design with integer programming. In: Proceedings of CHI 2020, Honolulu, USA (2020). https://doi.org/10.1145/3313831.3376553
3. Fernández-García, A.J., et al.: A recommender system for component-based applications using machine learning techniques. Knowl. Based Syst. **164**, 68–84 (2019). https://doi.org/10.1016/j.knosys.2018.10.019
4. Gajos, K.Z., Weld, D.S., Wobbrock, J.O.: Automatically Generating Personalized User Interfaces with SUPPLE. Artif. Intell. **174**(12–13), 910–950 (2010). https://doi.org/10.1016/j.artint.2010.05.005
5. Henninger, S.: An organizational learning method for applying usability guidelines and patterns. In: Little, M.R., Nigay, L. (eds.) EHCI 2001. LNCS, vol. 2254, pp. 141–155. Springer, Heidelberg (2001). https://doi.org/10.1007/3-540-45348-2_15
6. Koch, J., Lucero, A., Hegemann, L., Oulasvirta, A.: May AI?: design ideation with cooperative contextual bandits. In: Proceedings of CHI 2019, Glasgow, UK (2019). https://doi.org/10.1145/3290605.3300863
7. Kubitza, T., Schmidt, A.: meSchup: a platform for programming interconnected smart things. IEEE Comput. **50**(11), 38–49 (2017). https://doi.org/10.1109/MC.2017.4041350
8. Lin, J., Landay, J.A.: Employing patterns and layers for early-stage design and prototyping of cross-device user interfaces. In: Proceedings of CHI 2008, Italy (2008). https://doi.org/10.1145/1357054.1357260
9. Meskens, J., Luyten, K., Coninx, K.: Jelly: a multi-device design environment for managing consistency across devices. In: Proceedings of AVI 2010, Rome, Italy (2010). https://doi.org/10.1145/1842993.1843044

10. Nebeling, M., Mintsi, T., Husmann, M., Norrie, M.C.: Interactive development of cross-device user interfaces. In: Proceedings of CHI 2014, Toronto, Canada (2014). https://doi.org/10.1145/2556288.2556980
11. O'Donovan, P., Agarwala, A., Hertzmann, A.: DesignScape: design with interactive layout suggestions. In: Proceedings of CHI 2015, Seoul, Republic of Korea (2015). https://doi.org/10.1145/2702123.2702149
12. Park, S., et al.: AdaM: adapting multi-user interfaces for collaborative environments in real-time. In: Proceedings of CHI 2018, Montreal, Canada (2018). https://doi.org/10.1145/3173574.3173758
13. Quiroz, J.C., Louis, S.J., Dascalu, S.M.: Interactive evolution of XUL user interfaces. In: Proceedings of GECCO 2007, London, UK (2007). https://doi.org/10.1145/1276958.1277373
14. Sanctorum, A.: Conceptual foundations for end-user authoring of cross-device and internet of things applications. Ph.D. thesis, Vrije Universiteit Brussel (2020)
15. Sanctorum, A., Signer, B.: A unifying reference framework and model for adaptive distributed hybrid user interfaces. In: Proceedings of RCIS 2019, Brussels (2019). https://doi.org/10.1109/RCIS.2019.8877048
16. Todi, K., Weir, D., Oulasvirta, A.: Sketchplore: sketch and explore with a layout optimiser. In: Proceedings of DIS 2016, Brisbane, Australia (2016). https://doi.org/10.1145/2901790.2901817

PAC-Bot: Writing Text Messages for Developing Point-and-Click Games

Luca Asunis, Vittoria Frau, Riccardo Macis, Chiara Pireddu,
and Lucio Davide Spano$^{(\boxtimes)}$ iD

Department of Mathematics and Computer Science, University of Cagliari,
Cagliari, Italy
{vittoria.frau,davide.spano}@unica.it

Abstract. In this paper, we investigate the effects of including a conversational intelligent agent for helping end user developers in defining the behaviour of point-and-click games through event-condition action rules. We discuss the rule support in a web-based authoring environment, together with the design and the implementation of the agent in the form of a chatbot. We compared the versions with and without the chatbot and the results show a decrease in the perceived cognitive load in complex tasks.

Keywords: End user development · Chatbot · Point-and-click · Natural language programming

1 Introduction

Rule-based approaches gained interest over the last years for enabling end users to define interactive applications [12,20]. The research in this field focused on the end user's ability in translating his/her intention into a rule language. This results in a cognitive effort for the end user in articulating the intention, which is a function of the language complexity. For keeping the complexity low, the EUD language designer usually limits its expressiveness, finding the right compromise between what end users can express and what they need [17]. In this paper, we try to attack the articulation problem using an intelligent chatbot, called PAC-Bot, which guides the user in translating the intention into rules. Similarly to other chatbots included in messaging or mobile applications, it allows executing commands resulting eventually in the definition of rules. We applied this approach to an existing editor for Point-and-Click games on the web, training a conversational agent. The user interacts with it through a text-based interface, using a messaging metaphor. The chatbot interprets the semantics of the user's request, modifying the definition of the game (e.g., adding objects or rules) or asking for further information for completing the required input list or for disambiguating the user's query. We assessed the support by comparing the effectiveness of the game editing interface with and without the chatbot. The results show a decrease in the perceived cognitive load in more complex tasks.

© Springer Nature Switzerland AG 2021
D. Fogli et al. (Eds.): IS-EUD 2021, LNCS 12724, pp. 213–221, 2021.
https://doi.org/10.1007/978-3-030-79840-6_15

2   Related Work

The evolution of web-based communication shows that people are media content consumers, but they also engage in creating content to share [16]. Among such media categories, we focus on the diffusion of video game technologies and their spread from spare time activities to other domains, including academia and cultural heritage promotion [3,4,8]. The interest in video games meant that even non-expert users engaged in creating customised contents, editing them through easy-to-use editors of existing games [7,13,21], but they are either limited or too complex. According to Ur et al. [19], a successful approach for involving end users is the Trigger-Action programming (TAP), which has been tested in different research work [9,15,18]. In this paper, we focus on a particular game genre, the point-and-click, whose relatively simple mechanics are a good starting point for exploring the EUD potential in this field [2,6].

We exploit the recent advances in natural language processing, which fostered the application of chat-based interfaces in EUD. For instance, Barricelli et al. [1] reviewed the available virtual assistants for the EUD of IoT applications. Stefanidi et al. [18] combine natural language and a chatbot into a rule-based model, again in the IoT domain. Unlike previous work, we use the natural language to obtain guidance in translating an intention into rules and not for defining the program itself.

3   The Intelligent Agent: PAC-Bot

In the PAC-PAC authoring environment, end users define the game behaviour through rules following the event-condition-action (ECA) pattern: a rule triggers when the specified event occurs in the game (e.g., the player clicks on an interactive object) and, if an optional condition is verified, the game executes one or more actions. Each rule is a meaningful sentence in natural language, but it is structured using the fixed pattern `when <Action> [if <Conditions>] then <Action>*`. The structure of the action contains three sub-parts: a "subject" describing who executes the action, the "verb" identifying the action type, and the "object" or "value" specifying the manipulated item or value. In the game authoring environment, a subject is either the player or one of the scene objects. Sample scene objects are the transition (an interactive area connecting two scenes), the switch (an interactive object flipping between the on and off state when the player clicks on it) and the key (a collectable object whose possession unlocks the interaction with other objects). The following are two rules for unlocking a transition towards a scene and activating a keypad object only if a key object is collected. More information on the PAC-PAC objects is available in [2,6].

```
when the player clicks the transition tr1
if the key battery1 is collected
then the player moves to the scene outdoor3

when the player collects the key battery1
then the keypad machinery1 changes to enabled
```

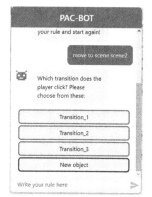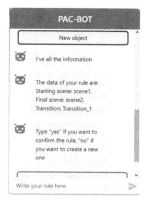

Fig. 1. The PAC-Bot user interface. The end user starts with entering her intention (left part), the bot will ask further questions (center), and the end user will specify the information either through new messages or using button shortcuts (right part).

We designed a conversational agent (called PAC-Bot) using Artificial Intelligence support to understand the end user's intention and help her in translating it into the rule language. We built it on top of Wit.ai (https://wit.ai), a common NPL engine for building chatbots. The interaction with the end user occurs through a "chat" interface, where she writes messages in natural language, depicted in Fig. 1. The user communicates with PAC-Bot using the input field at the bottom of the messaging interface, writing sentences in natural language. At the beginning of the conversation, the end user describes which behaviour she would like to model through the rules writing an initial request. Once received, the chatbot's final goal is understanding the end user's intention, which means mapping the request to a rule, including the specification of the triggering event and containing a least one action, including its subject, verb and object or value. The chatbot directs the conversation, asking specific questions for helping in specifying all the required pieces of information for building a rule (e.g., the action, the subject, the object or the value). Obviously, it is not always possible to complete the mapping process considering only the information contained in the first message. After interpreting the first request, we have three scenarios.

The first is the most common: the bot correctly interpreted the information contained in the first request, but it was not sufficient for creating the final rule. Therefore, the PAC-Bot asks some follow-up questions for supporting the user in specifying the missing pieces for building the rule. For identifying these pieces, the bot exploits the *a-priori* knowledge about the rule structure, identifying the parts requiring specification. Finally, when all the information is available, PAC-Bot responds with a confirmation message and creates the rule in the game, which appears in the rule editor part of the authoring environment.

The second and the third are the positive and negative extreme cases. The positive one happens when the first request contains all the required information, and PAC-Bot can correctly interpret it. The bot immediately creates the rule, and the result is equivalent to the previous one. The most negative case is a complete failure in understanding the end user's sentence. In this case, the bot asks further questions providing examples of requests it can manage. As we will discuss better while describing the actual implementation, this will trigger the storage of the end user's input and open a request for human labelling to let the intelligent support learn how to manage it.

To understand what the chatbot interaction looks like, we provide an example. Suppose that the end user writes the following message "go to scene2". The intelligent support understands that the end user's intent is moving from a scene to another. Also, the destination scene should be the one called scene2. We suppose that it already exists in the environment. What is missing for completing the task is how the player will actually trigger the navigation. So, the chatbot asks which transition she would like to use, providing a list of candidates, which reduces the possibility of error significantly. Alternatively, the end user may want to create a new transition, and this is listed as the last option to choose. In both cases, after having selected the transition, the chatbot has all the elements for creating the rule for moving the player when the selected transition is clicked, and the rule will appear in the interface.

3.1   Technical Implementation

For processing the end user's natural language sentences, we exploited the Wit.ai NPL service by Facebook. The recognition requires some labelled training samples, and the service augments them through the existing knowledge on the considered language (e.g., synonyms, sentence structures etc.) to cover many alternative formulations of the same utterance. Two basic pieces of information describe the utterance: the *"intent"*, representing what the user wants to perform with the application, and the *"entities"*, which are the different parts of the sentence that contains the meaningful pieces of information, such as the name of the scene objects, actions to be performed on them or values to set in their state. We trained the library to recognize intents corresponding to the available scene objects, using a limited number of examples. Besides, we provided the labelling for the entities, including the recognition of statically defined names in the rule language (e.g., the scene object types, such as transition, key, switch, or the verb in the actions they support) and the references that vary considering the current game under development (e.g. the names of scenes or objects).

Figure 2 shows the sequence diagram for the chatbot interaction. The process starts with the user that writes a message. If it is not a help request, the first step is to send a request to Wit.ai to analyse the user's message. The response contains the intent and the entities recognised in the player's sentence encoded in a JSON format. The bot analyses it and three different scenarios may occur. The first (and worst) is that Wit.ai does not recognise the intent, and it returns an error response. In this case, PAC-Bot warns the user it could not understand the sentence, asking the end user to reformulate the request. Wit.ai stores the unrecognised utterance for manual labelling, and we will receive a notification as

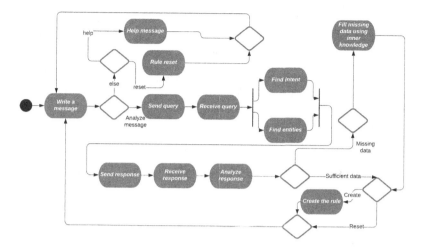

Fig. 2. Sequence diagram for the interaction with PAC-Bot.

to the chatbot developers. In this way, it is possible to reinforce the bot training and further develop its understanding capabilities.

The second scenario is the best one: Wit.ai recognises the intent and entities, and the information is enough to generate the rule. Then, the chatbot will provide the end user with a brief recap of the rule that is going to create and, if the end user gives her confirmation, it will ask for any condition or more actions to add. Finally, the bot adds the rule to the scene, and the authoring environment displays it in the rule panel.

The third and more frequent scenario consists in a correct recognition of intent and entities, but the collected information is not enough for creating the rule. In this case, PAC-Bot asks for more information without further calls to Wit.ai. It computes the possible options, asking the end user to pick the desired one(s) in a button list. Such a process is repeated for each missing piece of information. It is worth pointing out that sometimes, during this rule completion step, the end user may need to create new scene objects. This is possible using the button included as the last option, which activates a wizard asking for the new object name and selecting the interactive area in the scene background.

4   Assessing the Chatbot Effect on the Rule-Authoring

This section details the results of a user study assessing the intelligent conversational agent's impact on the EUD of point and click interactions.

Procedure. Each participant was assigned to one of the authoring environment versions (between-subject design): the *chatbot*, including the intelligent support described in Sect. 3.1, and the *form* version, supporting the interaction through a standard graphical user interface [2]. Participants in the chatbot condition were asked to use it for completing the tasks. After reading the introductory material to the study, including information on the objectives, the tasks and the management of personal data, participants had to complete the following tasks, identified as recurrent in many point-and-click games [2]:

T0 A training task for familiarizing with the authoring environment. It requested to create a new game, load some assets and use them for creating two scenes.

T1 Introduce the navigation between the scenes created in the previous task, exploiting a transition object.

T2 Allow the navigation between two scenes only if an elevator is turned on. The solution required using switch object.

T3 Add a scene containing a jetpack in the background, which the player can use only if he previously collected a fuel tank. If so, the jetpack starts and the player flies (playing a video shot using a drone). The solution required using a key object.

The authoring environment provided all participants with a list of tutorial videos describing how to use each object type in the environment. They were free to watch them at any time during the test to simulate the real application usage. For each task, except the T0, we tracked the completion time and the number of interaction errors. After each task, we asked the participants to fill the NASA-TLX questionnaire [10] measuring the cognitive task load.

At the end of the study, we asked the participants to fill the SUS questionnaire [5] measuring the overall usability of the authoring environment, and the AttrakDiff^{TM} measuring the pragmatic and the hedonic quality of the support, together with the attractiveness of the overall interaction experience. Finally, we asked the participants to list three positive and three negative points in the application, and we provided them with an optional field for suggestions.

Participants. We recruited 30 participants for this study. Considering the Covid-19 limitations, we met them using MS Teams, enabling the screen sharing and control on our development sandbox. In this way, we observed their interaction, and we were able to guide them during the study. After reading the study description containing information on the tasks, the study purposes and the collected data, they signed informed consent to continue the procedure. The participant group included 12 females and 18 males. Their age spans between 19 and 58 years old ($\bar{x} = 25.57$, $sd = 6.74$). They had different education level degrees: 1 middle school, 16 high school, 6 bachelor and 7 master. They self-rated their level on using standard office applications as good ($\bar{x} = 4.8$, $sd = 1.3$), but almost half of them scarcely use Excel and PowerPoint, the other half used it daily or weekly. They rated as poor their programming knowledge $\bar{x} = 2.0$, $sd = 1.5$. They frequently used all main computer and mobile applications.

Results. Figure 3 summarises the results for the post-task metrics we collected. All participants completed all the tasks. We did not registered significant differences in the task completion time for the different conditions. However, we registered a practical significance in favour of the form version in T1 ($\bar{x}_c = 126$, $sd_c = 77$, $\bar{x}_f = 84$, $sd_f = 40$, $t(21.216) = 1.84$, $p = .08$), which saves about a third of the time (42 s).

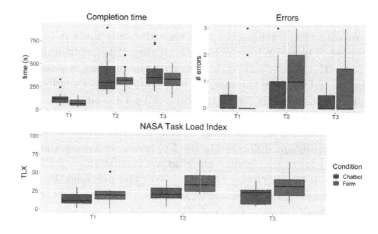

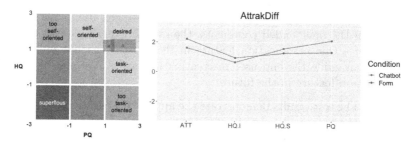

Fig. 3. Summary of the post-task metrics and questionnaires.

Fig. 4. Summary of AttrakDiff^{TM} [11] post-test questionnaire.

We did not register any significant difference in the number of errors during the task. However, the number of errors seems steady among the different tasks in the chatbot version, while it increases in T2 and T3 in the form version.

Such a conclusion is confirmed by the NASA-TLX [10] results. We registered a significant difference for T2 ($\bar{x}_c = 23.3$, $sd_c = 10.2$, $\bar{x}_f = 37.9$, $sd_f = 14.8$, $t(24.8) = -3.14$, $p = .004$) and T3 ($\bar{x}_c = 22.1$, $sd_c = 11.5$, $\bar{x}_f = 34.7$, $sd_f = 17.7$, $t(24.0) = -2.31$, $p = .03$). The relative decrease caused by chatbot interface on the task load is respectively 0.38 and 0.36, marking a good impact on the end user's support. In particular, we noticed in both cases a significant impact on the physical demand. This may be explained considering that the form interface requires more exploration for finding the appropriate interactive elements. Also, we registered a practical significance on both the mental demand and the effort dimensions, which are connected to the intent formulation and articulation.

Considering the post-test evaluation, we did not find any significant difference in the SUS score [5]. The registered values are good for both versions of the authoring tool ($\bar{x}_c = 78.8$, $sd_c = 12.9$, $\bar{x}_f = 80.8$, $sd_f = 9.7$), setting the tool in the 85th and the 90th percentile of the score distribution [14]. Figure 4 results of the AttrakDiff^{TM} [11] questionnaire. It evaluates three scales. The first is the pragmatic quality (PQ), related to how easy the user finds it to manipulate the environment. The second is the hedonic quality (HQ), split in identification (HQ-I related with the user's identification with the product in a social context) and stimulation (HQ-S, how the product encourages the personal growth of the user). Finally, the last scale is the attraction (ATT), i.e. a summary of the overall experience. We registered comparable values on the HQ scale, with the chatbot slightly more stimulating and the form version fostering more identification.

We found a significant difference in the PQ scale, indicating that the participants consider easier to manipulate the chatbot version ($\bar{x}_c = 2.12$, $sd_c = 1.29$, $\bar{x}_f = 1.32$, $sd_f = 0.76$, $t(22.6) = 2.06$, $p = .05$). The portfolio diagram (Fig. 4, left part) shows that both versions are located into the upper-right square, reaching a desired balance between PQ and HQ. In addition, we found a significant difference in the ATT scale, but this time the form version was better evaluated ($\bar{x}_c = 1.63$, $sd_c = 0.90$, $\bar{x}_f = 2.22$, $sd_f = 0.67$, $t(25.8) = -2.03$, $p = .05$). This suggests that, even if the manipulation was easier in the chatbot version, the overall experience was more satisfying for the form version users. We found an explanation in the open-ended comments: the overall experience was degraded by the lack of a rule modification feature in the current chatbot implementation, but it can guide the end user in creating new rules. We plan to add the rule-modification feature in the future.

Discussion. The test results demonstrate the approach's effectiveness: the chatbot decreases the perceived difficulty of the tasks requiring a more complex logic. This confirms our hypothesis in designing the support: the intelligent agent eases the translation of the end user's intention into the rule language, as highlighted in the AttrakDiff results on the pragmatic quality. Furthermore, we did not register an increase in the time spent creating the rules in complex tasks, so its time efficiency seems comparable to the form version. However, the current implementation has also limitations. The main one is the support for modifying existing rules, which would require additional training for the agent. Such a limitation degraded the participants' overall user experience, and it needs fixing in the next version of the conversational support.

5   Conclusion and Future Work

In this paper, we described the design and the implementation of a chatbot for supporting end user developers in translating their intentions into rules. We took as a case study the development of point-and-click games in a web environment. We assessed the support by comparing two versions of the same authoring environment: one with one without the chatbot. The results show that the chatbot decreases the perceived task load for the more complex tasks while maintaining efficiency. Future work will include developing support for modifying existing rules through the chatbot interface, which was identified as the main limitation of the current implementation.

References

1. Barricelli, B.R., Casiraghi, E., Valtolina, S.: Virtual assistants for end-user development in the Internet of Things. In: Malizia, A., Valtolina, S., Morch, A., Serrano, A., Stratton, A. (eds.) IS-EUD 2019. LNCS, vol. 11553, pp. 209–216. Springer, Cham (2019). https://doi.org/10.1007/978-3-030-24781-2_17
2. Blecic, I., et al.: First-person cinematographic videogames: Game model, authoring environment, and potential for creating affection for places. J. Comput. Cult. Herit. **14**(2) (2021). https://doi.org/10.1145/3446977
3. Bock, B.C., et al.: Exercise videogames, physical activity, and health: Wii heart fitness: a randomized clinical trial. Am. J. Prev. Med. **56**(4), 501–511 (2019)
4. Bracq, M.S., et al.: Learning procedural skills with a virtual reality simulator: an acceptability study. Nurse Educ. Today **79**, 153–160 (2019)
5. Brooke, J.: SUS: a quick and dirty usability scale. In: Usability Evaluation in Industry, vol. 189 (1996)
6. Fanni, F.A., et al.: PAC-PAC: end user development of immersive point and click games. In: Malizia, A., Valtolina, S., Morch, A., Serrano, A., Stratton, A. (eds.) IS-EUD 2019. LNCS, vol. 11553, pp. 225–229. Springer, Cham (2019). https://doi.org/10.1007/978-3-030-24781-2_20
7. Fungus Games: Fungus. https://fungusgames.com
8. García, G., et al.: Agile development of quiz-based multiplatform educational games using a domain-specific language. Universal Access in the Information Society (2019)
9. Ghiani, G., Manca, M., Paternò, F., Santoro, C.: Personalization of context-dependent applications through trigger-action rules. ACM Trans. Comput. Hum. Interact. **24**(2), 1–33 (2017)
10. Hart, S.G., Staveland, L.E.: Development of NASA-TLX (task load index): results of empirical and theoretical research. Adv. Psychol. **52**, 139–183 (1988)
11. Hassenzahl, M.: The effect of perceived hedonic quality on product appealingness. Int. J. Hum. Comput. Interact. **13**(4), 481–499 (2001)
12. Huang, J., Cakmak, M.: Supporting mental model accuracy in trigger-action programming. In: Proceedings of UbiComp 2015, pp. 215–225. ACM (2015)
13. ICEBOX Studios: Adventure creator for unity. https://www.adventurecreator.org
14. Lewis, J.R., Sauro, J.: Item benchmarks for the system usability scale. J. Usability Stud. **13**(3), 158–167 (2018)
15. Mi, X., Qian, F., Zhang, Y., Wang, X.: An empirical characterization of IFTTT: ecosystem, usage, and performance. In: Proceedings of the 2017 Internet Measurement Conference, pp. 398–404 (2017)
16. Paternò, F.: End user development: survey of an emerging field for empowering people. ISRN Softw. Eng. (2013)
17. Repenning, A., Ioannidou, A.: What makes end-user development tick? 13 design guidelines. In: Lieberman, H., Paternó, F., Wulf, V. (eds.) End User Development. Human-Computer Interaction Series, vol. 9. Springer, Dordrecht (2006). https://doi.org/10.1007/1-4020-5386-X_4
18. Stefanidi, E., et al.: ParlAmI: a multimodal approach for programming intelligent environments. Technologies **7**, 11 (2019)
19. Ur, B., et al.: Trigger-action programming in the wild: an analysis of 200,000 IFTTT recipes, pp. 3227–3231 (2016)
20. Ur, B., McManus, E., Pak Yong Ho, M., Littman, M.L.: Practical trigger-action programming in the smart home. In: Proceedings of the CHI 2014, pp. 803–812. ACM (2014)
21. YoYo Games: Gamemaker studio. http://www.yoyogames.com/gamemaker

Work-in-Progress Papers

Supporting Museums and Robot Theatre Using Quando - an Event First, Visual Block Toolset

Andrew Stratton[1][✉], David Cameron[2], Dorothy Ker[3], Terry O'Connor[4], Balraj Johal[1], and Andrei Clopotel[1]

[1] Department of Computer Science, The University of Sheffield, Sheffield, UK
a.stratton@sheffield.ac.uk
[2] Information School, The University of Sheffield, Sheffield, UK
d.s.cameron@sheffield.ac.uk
[3] Department of Music, The University of Sheffield, Sheffield, UK
d.ker@sheffield.ac.uk
[4] Forced Entertainment, Sheffield, UK
fe@forcedentertainment.com

Abstract. This paper describes the concepts that have emerged within Quando, an end user toolset, used for creating digital interactives through browser based code generation for museums and theatre. End user focused concepts and recommendations have been identified with Research through Design, including the ability to create new visual blocks as part of the toolset.

Keywords: Visual programming · End user development · Robotics

1 Background

Visual Block languages, including Scratch, Maloney et al. (2010) and Blockly, Fraser (2015) and Pasternak et al. (2017), are often used for teaching introductory programming skills, with success reported for *'greater learning gains'* and *'interest in the topic'*, Weintrop and Wilensky (2017), and *'focus'* and *'more tasks performed in less time'* reported by Price and Barnes (2015).

Blockly and Scratch seek to help novice programmers by reducing the need to know the underlying language syntax. Both promote fundamental programming concepts, as identified by Strachey (2000), including assignment, expressions, named variables, conditional execution, functions, types, lists/arrays.

Event programming for GUIs/interactivity is typically by language extensions, or APIs/libraries, where events 'call back' code.

This work follows a Research through Design approach to creating Quando, a visual 'event first' toolset for non-programmers, including Cultural Heritage Professionals creating Museum interactives, see Stratton et al. (2017) and the creation of two performances with robots, by visual and audio performance experts in theatre and music, including real time 'puppet' control of multiple Nao robots, see Fig. 1.

D. Fogli et al. (Eds.): IS-EUD 2021, LNCS 12724, pp. 225–230, 2021.
https://doi.org/10.1007/978-3-030-79840-6_16

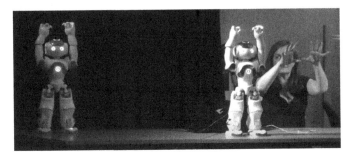

Fig. 1. Nao live theatre performance

2 Quando Block Concepts

Quando uses browser based Html elements to contain visual blocks within a drag and drop editor, with blocks laid out in a top to bottom order, with some blocks 'containing' other blocks, as shown in Fig. 2.

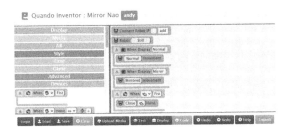

Fig. 2. Quando editor

2.1 Visual Elements

Two types of blocks are used to describe digital interactions:

1. **Action** blocks, which are used to perform/execute changes, e.g. displaying an image.
2. **Container** blocks, which contain other (typically action) blocks which are then called according to the container logic, e.g. when a mouse button is pressed.

Action blocks are usually one row (but may have more), styled according to their type, and show Unicode text, inputs (string or number), and toggle/radio buttons or menus. Examples are shown in Fig. 3.

The parameters for blocks are selected using toggles, menus, string/number inputs, or custom selections such as a picked file (name), colour selection, etc.

Container Blocks can hold other blocks, where the 'logic' of the container block is specific to the meaning. The examples in Fig. 4 include blocks that respond to touching a Nao robot on the back of the head and web cam image detection of a train.

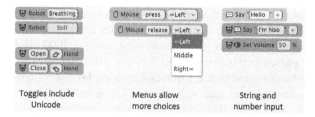

Toggles include
Unicode

Menus allow
more choices

String and
number input

Fig. 3. Example action blocks showing input/parameter choices

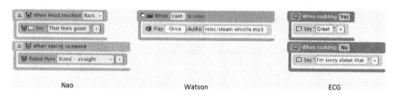

Nao   Watson   ECG

Fig. 4. Example container (and action) blocks

These examples show 'call back' to contained actions; containment may have different meanings, such as repeated execution and randomly picking between a list of blocks.

2.2 Less Used Parameter Hiding

Most blocks hide less used parameters within 'extra' rows, where the visibility is flipped with a toggle between '+' and '-' as shown in Fig. 5, leaving one row as typically visible, with other rows shown when needed.

Fig. 5. Hiding and revealing 'extra' parameters

2.3 Run Time Varying Values Within a Numeric Range

A key feature of Quando is to avoid naming of variables. Named variables can introduce perceived complexity for non programmers. Data Types also introduces more complexity with mapping between types then being needed. Therefore, one 'run time varying value' is accommodated[1] by using a single variable, always called 'val', in the generated JavaScript, which then applies within the contained scope.

The 'val' parameter is represented within blocks using a 'lightning bolt' unicode icon, as shown in Fig. 6 and shown within this text as ⚡.

---

[1] Currently only one other variable exists - 'txt' that represents strings.

The ⚡ parameter is held as a floating point value between 0 and 1 inclusive, with a default value of 0.5. The ⚡ value is mapped for all run time linear and angular values to a standard range. e.g. consider mouse movement across a 1000 pixel screen, where pixel 0 would be passed as 0.0, pixel 249 as 0.25 and pixel 999 as 1.0.

In Fig. 6, the blocks show mouse ⚡ values across the browser window, leap motion right hand grip 'strength', leap motion X axis movement and ECG headset yaw.

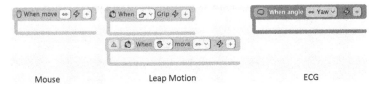

Mouse   Leap Motion   ECG

Fig. 6. Example blocks passing 'val' producing events

With all of the above blocks, an event is only raised when ⚡ changes. There are also rules for handling changes beyond the minimum or maximum and handling rotational changes, e.g. when passing anticlockwise through −180° to +180°.

In Fig. 7, the examples show blocks and generated code[2]. In this example, movement of the right hand over a Leap motion from left to right, is translated into ⚡, which then turns the Nao's right shoulder to the left/right. The second pair of blocks do the same for up-down hand position translating to shoulder rotation up/down. Both handlers effectively run at the same time.

Fig. 7. Mapping ⚡ to different actions

The generated code also shows an anonymous function generated from the contained blocks, which shows ⚡ passed in to the event call back as 'val'.

3 Developing End User Visual Blocks

Quando blocks are held as Html with specific Quando data attributes, that are then used to generate (mostly) JavaScript API calls. The selected parameters are passed in at generation time; the ⚡ is run time varying. Contained blocks are (usually) generated into a callback function.

---

[2] This code has been reduced for clarity by manually removing less used parameters.

For example, Fig. 8 shows an Action block that can be used to switch a Nao between two autonomous life states, being *solitary*, where the Nao moves slightly to give the appearance of being 'alive', and *safeguard*, where the default movement of the Nao is to remain perfectly still.

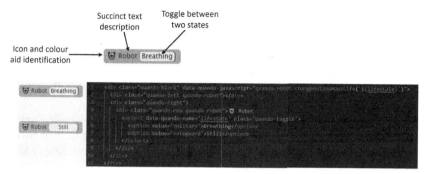

Fig. 8. Action block for Nao 'Autonomous Life'

The visual interface shows one of two toggle states, between the two options of 'Breathing' and 'Still'; these terms were co-created with theatre experts.

3.1 Inventor Blocks

Creating/editing Quando blocks is mostly through using Inventor blocks from within the Quando editor. e.g. the block in Fig. 8 can be created using the Inventor blocks in Fig. 9. This example also shows how a 'toggle' can be created that sets an API parameter on code generation.

Fig. 9. Inventing new Quando blocks from within Quando

Inventor Blocks have also been to create new inventor blocks, i.e. the creation of blocks that themselves generate the Html of inventor blocks, which subsequently generate executable JavaScript code.

Container blocks are similar, though they also allow (up to three) named container 'boxes' for action blocks which can then generate API call backs.

4 Discussion and Conclusion

Quando has allowed very rapid interaction experimentation, where developers and domain experts can quickly try, and discard, ideas that needed to be seen to be understood. One of the developers noted that Quando '...*let us really quickly explore (those) ideas as soon as we came up with them...*'.

An end user focused approach is needed to discover/design the language and concepts appropriate for domain experts. This typically takes three, or more, iterations to create new designs. The first iteration is often biased towards the technical requirement, but seems to be necessary to discover a more end user focused design. The second design is usually much more suitable with the third design being typically a smaller improvement/adjustment to the second.

The ⚡ parameter, combined with separate event handling, offers a simple, but effective, solution to passing around complex data structures and having to map between many data types and range of values. Any event that can produces a ⚡ can simply initiate any runtime varying action that consumes a ⚡.

Being able to rapidly prototype new visual blocks using Inventor blocks is very effective in reducing visual block coding errors and turnaround time.

In conclusion, the Quando toolset can describe interactions using event based visual blocks by combining different device blocks. The ⚡ parameter allows simple and fast 'mapping' of interactions between events and actions, once the underlying API and visual blocks have been designed.

References

Fraser, N.: Ten things we've learned from Blockly. In: 2015 IEEE Blocks and Beyond Workshop (Blocks and Beyond), pp. 49–50. IEEE (2015)

Maloney, J., Resnick, M., Rusk, N., Silverman, B., Eastmond, E.: The scratch programming language and environment. ACM Trans. Comput. Educ. (TOCE) 10(4), 1–15 (2010)

Pasternak, E., Fenichel, R., Marshall, A.N.: Tips for creating a block language with Blockly. In: 2017 IEEE Blocks and Beyond Workshop (B&B), pp. 21–24. IEEE (2017)

Price, T.W., Barnes, T.: Comparing textual and block interfaces in a novice programming environment. In: Proceedings of the Eleventh Annual International Conference on International Computing Education Research, pp. 91–99 (2015)

Strachey, C.: Fundamental concepts in programming languages. High. Order Symb. Comput. 13(1), 11–49 (2000)

Stratton, A., Bates, C., Dearden, A.: Quando: enabling museum and art gallery practitioners to develop interactive digital exhibits. In: Barbosa, S., Markopoulos, P., Paternò, F., Stumpf, S., Valtolina, S. (eds.) IS-EUD 2017. LNCS, vol. 10303, pp. 100–107. Springer, Cham (2017). https://doi.org/10.1007/978-3-319-58735-6_7

Weintrop, D., Wilensky, U.: Comparing block-based and text-based programming in high school computer science classrooms. ACM Trans. Comput. Educ. (TOCE) 18(1), 1–25 (2017)

Doctoral Consortium

Supporting End User Development in Extended Reality Through Natural Language Rules

Vittoria Frau[✉]

Department of Mathematics and Computer Science, University of Cagliari,
Cagliari, Italy
`vittoria.frau@unica.it`

Abstract. This paper presents the early stages of my PhD work, which consists of a solution for supporting end users in configuring eXtended Reality (XR) environments, exploiting templates created by experts. The proposed approach is based on an EUD [8] methodology for solving this problem, employing Event-Condition-Action (ECA) rule-language defining the environment behaviour and the design of an immersive authoring interface.

Keywords: End-user-development · User interface programming · Virtual reality · Mixed reality · Natural language · Rule system · eXtended reality

1 Introduction

Nowadays, the hardware and software for enjoying eXtended Reality (XR) - including virtual, augmented and mixed reality - is available for consumers at a reasonable cost. In addition to this increased availability, technologies for reconstructing objects or locations in virtual experiences and the embedded devices for creating digitally-augmented experiences in the real world are quite mature and affordable. However, to become actually adopted, we are positive that end users should be involved in the content creation process, as happened in web-based communication [11]. Involving more people in the content creation process can boost the adoption of such a medium by new market segments and create new business opportunities, especially in reaction to the Covid-19 pandemic. That is one of the most difficult challenges for spreading XR.

Nevertheless, shifting the entire building process towards end users is not entirely feasible because it requires different skills and usually involves various skills, e.g., 3D modelling, code development, design etc. Existing software development life cycles require only technical people and are too slow to respond to the evolving needs of variegated users' categories. Thus, a viable way to make XR

© Springer Nature Switzerland AG 2021
D. Fogli et al. (Eds.): IS-EUD 2021, LNCS 12724, pp. 233–239, 2021.
https://doi.org/10.1007/978-3-030-79840-6_17

applications better comply with users' expectations is to have users more active in the process, making them capable of "programming" the intended behaviour.

This is basically the goal of the PhD research discussed in this paper: the identification of an appropriate metaphor and technological support for creating - and customizing - extended reality environments designed for people not having programming experience or technical skills.

In the next sections, we will describe the overall method we are applying, starting from the challenges that emerge from the art state.

2   Related Work

In this section, we briefly identify the relevant work for the proposed research and the open questions in the field.

Most literature targeting EUD for VR contents is limited to static scenes or multimedia content overlay. Fanni et al. [2] propose an authoring tool for designing point and click games, defining the behaviour through rules. PAC-PAC shares the behaviour definition technique with our project: using a rule-based mechanism that substitutes the usual scripting system. However, despite the VR mode, the authoring environment is limited to first-person point-and-click games, and the objects that the user can control are limited to solving riddles and puzzles, so they are not expressive enough for representing general XR environments. Besides, the immersive experience is limited to 360° photos and videos.

Fungus [5] is an open-source visual storytelling tool designed as a Unity 3D extension. It allows creating visual novels through flowcharts, but the visualization is demanding in terms of screen space, limiting the end user's comprehension [7].

Ottifox [10] is a WebVR creation tool that works similarly to Unity's editor but exports A-Frame code for building generic VR environments. The tool supports an entirely visual development of the VR environment, and it exploits a simplified version of rules for the animation system. In this mechanism, the rules contain the when part for specifying the interaction event, while the then part is limited to the animation. Note that it has no support for the conditions and works only with animations.

Regarding Augmented and Mixed Reality, most EUD tools are just visual [1,12], providing abstract representations disconnected from the real world, so requiring cognitive effort to associate digital representations of objects with real counterparts. Although AR/MR holds the promise of supporting more direct, situated links between physical and virtual worlds, this potentiality has remained mostly unexplored in this area.

HoloHome [9] provides an MR environment on HoloLens, supporting home inhabitants to control real devices. However, it was used only in basic AAL[1] scenarios (e.g., turn on/off light), so its possibilities to program the behaviour of different devices seems limited.

A very interesting parallel EUD approach is called *Meta-design*, where both professional designers and users are considered as designers. The design phase is not limited at the typical *project time*, but also *at use time*, which means that every use situation is a potential design situation. Fischer and Scharff [4] and Fisher and Giaccardi [3] well described this concept in their works.

3   Current Status of the Research

In the previous section we have discussed about the current state of the art from the perspective of the Virtual, Augmented and Mixed Reality. All the proposed solutions lack of the union of the following elements: the creation of XR experiences tailored to the user needs, the active involvement during the process, an Event-Condition-Action rule-language with compact syntax. The methodology discussed in this paper is a step toward developing powerful and flexible environments intended to foster the creation of XR content by a more extensive set of users.

To actively involve end users in the development process, we have been inspired by the world of the web, inspecting the usual workflow of people that need to create and customize his/her web site. Many web builders and content management systems support such development (e.g., Wordpress, WIX, web.com, etc.). In general, they do not ask the end user to start from scratch, but they provide some templates to customize according to different use cases (e.g., creating personal blogs, portfolios, e-commerce websites, etc.). Similarly, in the process we propose, end users modify the behaviour of existing XR (*templates*), which are general-purpose environments set-up by skilled users, which they will configure and adapt to their needs. Many templates will be available for the end users, representing homes, virtual shops, museums etc.

We identify three different roles in this process: *Template Builders* for building the environments, *End User Developers* (EUDevs) and the *Users*. The EUDevs category represent users without skills in 3D modelling and game programming but having an average familiarity with computer use. They cannot build an entire environment on their own but may require creating contents. Finally, the Users will be the final consumers of the contents (e.g., the customers of a virtual shop). Template Builders will provide highly customizable elements representing real or virtual objects in their environment, which provide high-level actions understandable by end users (e.g., walk, open, turn on/off etc.). The roles mentioned above are strongly connected in the same way as designers and users are in Meta-design approach.

---

[1] Ambient Assisted Living.

For customizing the environment behaviour, an approach that had particular success in EUD is the trigger-action rule programming [6, 12]. The rules we aim to define will have a structured definition (following a precise syntax scheme), but a EUDev will read them as natural language (English) sentences for grasping their meaning. We will enforce this syntax scheme through the authoring UI, which will guide the user in selecting only among syntactically correct options.

The proposed rule-based mechanism has been validated in an important project our research group led in the past: PAC-PAC [2][2]. PAC-PAC project stands for Gamification and interactive storytelling for the promotion of environmental and cultural heritage (Sardinia regional government, 2018–2020). The project's goal was to create an authoring tool for point-and-click games designed for end users without programming skills. The games are based on 2D and 360° images or videos and exploit event-condition-action rules for defining the behaviour.

In order to build a support for a general XR environment, we are defining the following building blocks:

- A compact, simplified yet complete taxonomy of the objects that one can manipulate inside an XR environment. For each object category, we define a set of high-level actions they support.
- A way for specifying the interaction among these objects, resulting in the definition of the XR environment behaviour. We propose to support it through rules, readable and understandable as natural language sentences
- Finally, we will provide a user interface for entering the rules while immersed in the environment.

In addition, we are planning a validation phase that includes all the actions for evaluating the effectiveness and the usability testing of the EUD interfaces. The validation will be defined in detail according to the design and implementation of the different parts of the solution. They will include formative evaluation for guiding the design choices and summative evaluations for validating the scientific results with users. We will measure standard quantitative usability dimensions such as efficiency, satisfaction, errors and collect qualitative data for gaining hints for improvement. The validation will involve a representative sample of the EUDev population the research addresses.

In summary, the major steps and pillars of the research are listed in the image 1.

---

[2] https://cg3hci.dmi.unica.it/pacpac-project/.

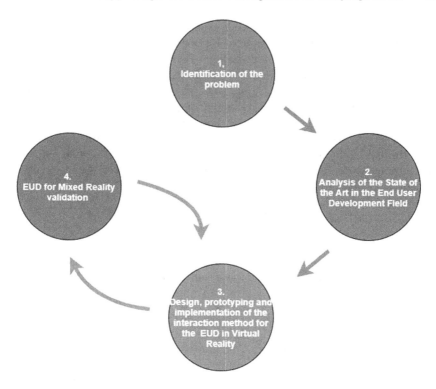

Fig. 1. Research phases.

4   Conclusions

To conclude, this paper presents a feasible solution to some of the open problems in the EUD field related to XR building environments. The methodology consists of the definition of templates by skilled users and customization by another category of end user (EUDevs), applying Event-Condition-Action (ECA) rule-language. The research we described will be supported by visiting leading research groups abroad during the PhD, and it will also involve stakeholders in the tourism promotion field in the municipality of Belvì (Italy).

5   University Doctoral Program and Context

The PhD project is carried by Vittoria Frau, a first-year PhD student in Computer Science in the Department of Mathematics and Computer Science of the University of Cagliari (Italy). She has a master degree in computer science at the University of Cagliari in 2020, with a thesis based on a Mixed Reality interface for medical records. She wrote two papers on that project. Her main research interests fall under the Human-Computer-Interaction field, especially with End-User Development and eXtended Reality programming.

She works in the CG3HCI research group (Computer Graphics, Computational Geometry & Human Computer Interaction), funded by prof. Riccardo Scateni, which works on Computer Graphics (led by prof. Riccardo Scateni) and Human-Computer Interaction (led by prof. Lucio Davide Spano).

The PhD supervisor is prof. Lucio Davide Spano, an Associate Professor at the Department of Mathematics and Computer Science of the University of Cagliari, Italy. He got his PhD at the University of Pisa, Italy, in 2013. He previously worked in the HIIS lab at ISTI-CNR. His main research interest is Human-Computer Interaction (HCI), and he wrote several papers on novel interaction techniques and visualisations, gestural interaction, virtual and augmented reality applied on cultural heritage, mobile museum guides and end-user development.

Acknowledgements. This work is supported by the Italian Ministry and University and Research (MIUR) under the PON program: The National Operational Program "Research and Innovation" 2014–2020 (PONRI). We also gratefully acknowledge the main parent project 'PAC-PAC', that was a source of inspiration for this research.

References

1. Desolda, G., Ardito, C., Matera, M.: Empowering end users to customize their smart environments: model, composition paradigms, and domain-specific tools. ACM Trans. Comput. Hum. Interact. (TOCHI) 24(2), 1–52 (2017)
2. Fanni, F.A., et al.: PAC-PAC: end user development of immersive point and click games. In: Malizia, A., Valtolina, S., Morch, A., Serrano, A., Stratton, A. (eds.) IS-EUD 2019. LNCS, vol. 11553, pp. 225–229. Springer, Cham (2019). https://doi.org/10.1007/978-3-030-24781-2_20
3. Fischer, G., Giaccardi, E.: Meta-design: a framework for the future of end-user development. In: Lieberman, H., Paternó, F., Wulf, V. (eds.) End User Development. Human-Computer Interaction Series, vol. 9. Springer, Dordrecht (2006). https://doi.org/10.1007/1-4020-5386-X_19
4. Fischer, G., Scharff, E.: Meta-design: design for designers, pp. 396–405 (January 2000). https://doi.org/10.1145/347642.347798
5. Fungus Games: Fungus. https://fungusgames.com
6. Ghiani, G., Manca, M., Paternò, F., Santoro, C.: Personalization of context-dependent applications through trigger-action rules. ACM Trans. Comput. Hum. Interact. 24(2) (2017). https://doi.org/10.1145/3057861
7. Green, T.R.G., Petre, M.: Usability analysis of visual programming environments: a 'cognitive dimensions' framework. J. Vis. Lang. Comput. 7(2), 131–174 (1996)
8. Lieberman, H., Paternó, F., Klann, M., Wulf, V.: End-user development: an emerging paradigm. In: Lieberman, H., Paternó, F., Wulf, V. (eds.) End User Development. Human-Computer Interaction Series, vol. 9. Springer, Dordrecht (2006). https://doi.org/10.1007/1-4020-5386-X_1
9. Mahroo, A., Greci, L., Sacco, M.: HoloHome: an augmented reality framework to manage the smart home. In: De Paolis, L.T., Bourdot, P. (eds.) AVR 2019. LNCS, vol. 11614, pp. 137–145. Springer, Cham (2019). https://doi.org/10.1007/978-3-030-25999-0_12
10. Ottifox: Ottifox. https://ottifox.com/index.html

11. Paternò, F.: End user development: survey of an emerging field for empowering people. ISRN Softw. Eng. **2013** (2013)
12. Ur, B., et al.: Trigger-action programming in the wild: an analysis of 200,000 IFTTT recipes. In: Proceedings of the 2016 CHI Conference on Human Factors in Computing Systems, pp. 3227–3231 (2016)

Author Index

.

Printed in the United States
by Baker & Taylor Publisher Services